Contents

SCHOOLS COUNCIL CURRICULUM BULLETIN No. 1

MATHEMATICS IN PRIMARY SCHOOLS

FOURTH EDITION

LONDON: HER MAJESTY'S STATIONERY OFFICE 1972

Also in this series of Curriculum Bulletins

2 A SCHOOL APPROACH TO TECHNOLOGY (HMSO, 1967)

3 CHANGES IN SCHOOL SCIENCE TEACHING (Evans/Methuen Educational, 1970)

4 HOME ECONOMICS TEACHING (Evans/Methuen Educational, 1971)

First published 1965
Reprinted (*twice*) 1965
Reprinted 1966
Second edition 1966
Reprinted (*twice*) 1967
Third edition 1969
Reprinted 1969
Fourth edition 1972

SBN 11 880019 1

Foreword

This first edition of this curriculum bulletin was published in May 1965. It was prepared for the Schools Council by Miss E. E. Biggs, HMI, and draws extensively on contributions from other sources and on the author's wide knowledge of the work of teachers in the primary schools. The Council wishes to thank Miss Biggs, and all who worked with her, for making their ideas and experience available for the use of all teachers, and is once again indebted to her for the work involved in revising material for this new edition.

The Curriculum Bulletins make no claim to cover their subject comprehensively or to give the last word. Their purpose is simply to put forward some suggestions, which teachers may use as they wish. The Council will be best pleased if their main influence is to set in train a new cycle of professional discussion, research and development, leading to new Bulletins recording successive changes in the continuous growth of ideas and practice within the schools.

The Council wishes to emphasise again that its sole object in publishing these Bulletins is to assist individual teachers to reach their own decisions about changes and developments in the curriculum. Comments and criticisms will be welcome, and will be taken into account in further work sponsored by the Council.

SCHOOLS COUNCIL
May 1972

APPENDICES

Introduction

The publication of the Mathematical Association's *The Teaching of Mathematics in Primary Schools* in 1955 evoked an unprecedented interest in the teaching of mathematics from teachers in schools of all types, and a second pamphlet has been published. The Association of Teachers of Mathematics published *Notes on the Teaching of Mathematics in Primary Schools* in 1967. During the past ten years there have been conferences, courses and study groups run by the Department of Education and Science, by Teachers' Associations, by both Mathematical Associations, by Local Education Authorities and by Institutes of Education in every county and county borough. Much has been written, new text books and topic books are being published, commercial structural apparatus in increasing variety is appearing on the market. Sound radio and television (both B.B.C. and I.T.A.) have included mathematics in their programmes not only for children but for teachers and for parents as well.

The Bulletin itself and the Schools Council/Nuffield Foundation's Development Projects in mathematics (five to thirteen) and in primary science (which the Bulletin preceded) have focussed teachers' interest on current changes in teaching methods. Over 130 Local Education Authorities are concerned with the projects. Two most important outcomes have been the establishment of Teachers' Centres and the close partnership which these ensure among infant, junior and secondary teachers who are able to meet regularly, in small groups, in and out of school hours to experiment and discuss. Teachers' Centres have now become part of the fabric of in-service training in the majority of areas and leader teachers are running successful courses for their colleagues. Here teachers exchange ideas and methods, and nothing but good can come of the increasing knowledge gained in this way of problems at varying stages of children's education. In many areas lecturers from colleges of education give their expert help and meet teachers in an informal way at the centres. The use of these centres has extended not only to many schools outside project areas but also to many other aspects of the curriculum.

The contacts between infant, junior and secondary teachers have focussed attention on the continuous development of children's learning and, more specifically, on children's learning of mathematics. At the secondary stage, too, there has been considerable experiment not only with content but, more recently, in method of presentation. In some secondary schools as well as in the majority of primary schools every effort is being made to give pupils opportunities for individual or small group investigation whenever a new topic is introduced.

There have been major changes, too, in the type of mathematics courses provided for teachers (see Appendices of this Bulletin). From the outset, infant, junior and secondary teachers work in small groups, discovering mathematical relationships at their own level, using selected environmental materials. They also prepare topics for the pupils they teach, paying careful attention to progression over the age range five to sixteen. There is free interchange of ideas between groups and much discussion of the development of increasing mathematical abstraction in the work they produce.

Arithmetic also receives detailed consideration so that, on the one hand children may be enabled to devise their own methods and helped to refine these, while on the other hand they are given sufficient practice to achieve efficiency. Perhaps progression in arithmetic is one of the most difficult problems for us all.

Many professional bodies as well as Local Education Authorities are giving consideration to the changeover to metric measures by industrial and commercial firms, and the implication of this for schools. As a result of the suggestion made by the Department of Education and Science to the Schools Council, practical advice to teachers has been published in the booklets, *Change for a Pound: a Teaching Guide for the Introduction of Decimal Currency and the Adoption of Metric Measures* (HMSO, 1968) and *Measure for Measure: a Guide to Metrication for Workshop Crafts and Technical Studies* (Evans/

Methuen Educational, 1970). (See also publications by the Consultative Committee on the Curriculum sponsored by the Scottish Education Department: *Going Metric: Implications for the Primary School*, and *Implications for Secondary Schools*, HMSO, 1968). The Royal Society has convened meetings of educationists most concerned and as a result has published pamphlets for primary and secondary teachers.

The education sector of the Metrication Board has (1) collaborated with the Schools Council in the preparation of a booklet to help primary teachers to introduce metric measures—*Metres, Litres and Grams: Introducing Metrication in the Primary School* has now been published for the Schools Council (Evans/Methuen Educational, 1971); (2) sponsored a videotape showing groups of children learning to measure and using metric units; and (3) set up a small committee of teachers and manufacturers of educational equipment to recommend to the British Standards Institution appropriate standards of accuracy for metric measuring equipment. Equipment conforming to these standards will bear a kite mark.

There is a consensus of opinion about one factor in the many issues raised: that children should be introduced to metric measures as soon as appropriate material is available and that during this period there should be no conversion at all. It is most important that as soon as practicable the youngest children should use metric measures as their first standard measures so that they 'think metric'. Teachers may well find the changeover more difficult than children and, for some time, the Department's Learning Mathematics courses have provided opportunities for teachers to use and become accustomed to metric measures.

Since this Bulletin contains actual examples done by children using discovery methods during the years 1958 to 1964, no attempt has been made to change from imperial measures to metric measures in anecdotal sections. The Bulletin does not attempt to cover all those aspects of mathematics which young children are capable of learning nor to give answers to all questions which teachers ask.

I hope that the combined experience of teachers (head and assistant), college of education lecturers, organisers and inspectors will encourage many teachers to think afresh.

I thank all those colleagues and teachers who have contributed in one way or another and the many children whose discoveries we have been privileged to enjoy and who have unconsciously taught us all so much.

E. E. Biggs
May 1972

Note to fourth edition

Chapters 3 and 4 have been substantially revised for this edition. An attempt has also been made to establish the minimum number knowledge that a child needs to have before he can profit from practice in written calculations (in isolation from experience).

In the Appendices, the booklist has again been revised and updated. Appendix 3 now includes revised notes for guidance of leaders of mathematics courses. Appendix 4 'Sorting, Classification and Sets' has been revised and Appendix 7 'Development of Representation, including Graphs' is new.

A NOTE ON CONTENTS

The scope of this Bulletin is wide. It aims not only at presenting the philosophy of the changes to which reference has been made but at providing material help for teachers in their classrooms and particularly for the teachers with large classes in small classrooms.

Two factors described in Chapters 1 and 2 lend overwhelming support to the views expressed in the introduction. First, the changes now affecting mathematics are part of a wider movement enveloping the whole pattern of education. Secondly, the research undertaken during the past twenty years into the psychology of learning provides unchallengeable evidence that sound and lasting learning can be achieved only through active participation. This is no new philosophy or theory of education. But methods founded on such theory have only recently been put to the test with large groups of pupils of widely differing ages and abilities.

Subsequent chapters are concerned with two main themes: children's learning of mathematics, and the problems facing teachers in the classroom. Young children are shown discovering a variety of mathematical relationships for themselves and subsequently communicating these in symbolic form. But children can make discoveries only if their teachers contrive the real situations which will give rise to the discoveries. This implies that teachers must themselves be aware of the mathematical ideas children should learn.

Chapters 3, 4, 5 and 6 comprise the mathematics which teachers have found to be within the capabilities of primary school children of widely differing abilities. Chapters 3 and 4 contain a reappraisal of the traditional arithmetic of the primary school and a description of the underlying mathematical structure. Examples are given of children discovering all the concepts included—even the written computational processes. But although discovery methods take longer in the initial stages (between the ages of five and eight or nine years) far less practice is required to attain and maintain efficiency in computation when children have been enabled to make their own discoveries. There is an increasing volume of evidence to show that where selection tests (in mechanical arithmetic) are still in use, the proportion of children obtaining grammar school places has shown a steady increase in those schools where a different approach to mathematics has been introduced. The amount of mechanical practice given in these schools varies from one to two forty-minute periods a week.

When less time is given to computational practice more time is available for children to explore and discover exciting mathematical relationships in the spaces and shapes about them. Chapter 5 describes the geometrical relationships which have been found to be within the potentialities of young children, and Chapter 6 describes the graphical representation of these and other discoveries. Children from five years old have represented their mathematical discoveries in graphical form—sometimes unconsciously—and have subsequently interpreted their discoveries by means of their graphs. This is particularly true of slow children for whom numbers may not hitherto have had much significance.

Chapters 7 to 9 are directly concerned with teachers' problems. Chapter 7 covers the practical problems of the classroom: ways and means of making a start, of making a syllabus, of assessing and recording children's progress and of allaying the anxieties of parents.

Chapter 8, concerned as it is with the training of teachers, introduces a new and important problem. If teachers are to be convinced that children can learn mathematics through their own discoveries, they must first experience discovery of mathematical concepts for themselves. This experience has been provided, in the first place, by means of courses in mathematics. Many teachers subsequently express a need to learn more mathematics. Suggestions to meet this need are made in this chapter. The chapter concludes with a reference to the change in professional courses in training colleges for intending teachers of primary schools. In Chapter 9 teachers of infants and juniors, head teachers and training college lecturers describe their personal experiences of the changes they have made in the teaching of mathematics in their schools and colleges.

The science of pure mathematics, in its modern developments, may claim to be the most original creation of the human spirit.

A. N. WHITEHEAD Lovell Lecture, 1925

1 The changing pattern of primary school education

One of the most interesting features of our educational system is that reforms have usually come from within the schools themselves and have not, primarily, been made in response to external pressures. Developments in primary schools are no exception to this, despite the difficulties caused by large classes, by changes in staff and by cramped conditions which have affected so many of these schools at one time or another. The changes which have taken place could have occurred only at the present time when strenuous efforts are being made to give full educational opportunities to all.

One hundred years ago, at the time of the first Education Act, the scope of education was restricted to instruction in the three Rs, and factual knowledge and skills were all-important. There was insufficient concern for children as they are, for their interests, or for the way they learn. On the contrary, the aim was to turn a child into a wage-earner as quickly as possible. The developments which we have seen, particularly during the past two decades, are the outcome of an entirely different attitude to children, foreshadowed by the Hadow report of 1931.[1] In 1944 the Education Act drew attention to the importance of the environment, and schools were empowered to provide an environment in which children could grow imaginatively as well as intellectually. Consideration was to be given to the provision of an environment in which learning could best take place. At about the same time Piaget published his early work on the way in which children develop concepts. In this he revealed the importance of the child's own activity in his learning, and suggested ways and means of providing opportunities for active learning.

[1] Report of the Consultative Committee on the Primary School (HMSO, 1931).

What are the characteristics of the changing pattern in primary education? A. N. Whitehead made the cardinal point in his essay, *Aims of Education*, when he wrote: 'Every child should experience the joy of discovery', and all educational research since that time has supported Professor Whitehead's contention. What does this mean in terms of environment? Attention has been focussed first on the materials available in the classroom and then on the learning situations themselves. But there is an even more important element without which the changes could not have been effected at all. When children explore for themselves they make discoveries which they want to communicate to their teacher and to other children, and this results in frequent discussion. It is this changed classroom relationship which is the most important development of all. From the teacher's point of view it has meant an ever-increasing understanding of individual children, of their problems and of the way they learn. The children, for their part, have become increasingly confident in their own abilities.

The planning of the learning situations themselves and the right choice of tools can best be discussed in relation to various aspects of the primary school curriculum. It is, perhaps, not surprising that the first signs of change appeared in the visual arts, one of the channels through which the senses, as well as the emotions, are educated. In the 1920s Marion Richardson proved that, if children were stimulated visually and emotionally, they would create their own images of the world around them in their paintings without first being taught techniques. They were encouraged to explore a range of colours and textures and shapes and subsequently to evolve their own techniques in each of the chosen media. The materials with which they were provided were the fabric of the world around them, neither poor substitutes nor expensive commercial materials: clay, sand, stones, wood, water, paper, woven materials in wide variety, and paint, thick and opaque. The children were given suitable tools that they might gain increasing mastery over the materials they used. They were not taught techniques but they were encouraged to use the tools in the right way.

But materials and tools are not in themselves sufficient. As teachers we must contrive learning situations and quicken children's imaginations. For this we have a rich cultural heritage to draw on: myths, folk tales, the best poetry, the true stories of history and exploration, the interesting ways in which people live in other countries, the best painting and music, and, not least, the natural forms and shapes in our environment. Now if we have to arouse children's imaginations, we must be excited ourselves, and this means that we ourselves must have a real appreciation and knowledge of literature, poetry, drama, painting, sculpture and music. What are our own resources for this appreciation and knowledge? Some teachers can draw on first-hand experience from their travels at home and abroad: for others there are excellent photographs, pictures and reproductions; and, most important of all, there are books. Perhaps the most valuable contribution a teacher can make is to give children an enjoyment of books, of good stories, good poems and good books of reference, and to encourage them to use such books not for second-hand reproduction (of pictures or printed material) but to put their own stamp on the information they discover and to express this in their own way.

In concerning ourselves with children's learning at this stage we have inevitably strayed over 'subject' boundaries, for children's recordings in art and craft and in words frequently develop simultaneously. Most of the work the children do, whether in painting or modelling, or in words, should be their own record of what they see or know, expressed in their own way and at their own level. But the vocabulary they use will reflect not only their own reading but their teacher's own sensitivity to words. Practice in punctuation and spelling will arise from the children's mistakes in their own recordings.

How have the other aspects of primary school education developed during this transitional period? We have seen radical changes in physical education during the past two decades. The following excerpts from *Planning the Programme*[1] illustrate the similarities between the development in this subject and that in art. The primary school age is described as, 'A time when children explore tirelessly both their own powers and all that is of interest in their environment.' The teacher's part in providing the learning situations and materials is described as follows: 'If the teacher provides the general framework and then allows the children to make their own discoveries in their own time, he not only opens up for them a different sort of opportunity but makes a different demand on them.' Again, the teacher's understanding of individual children and their needs is essential: 'The teacher's knowledge both of the progress of each child and of the way in which mastery of movement is developed is in constant demand, and the timing of help so that progress is neither forced, nor checked, requires much skill.'

Two important aspects of the primary school curriculum remained virtually unchanged until about ten years ago: science and mathematics. Each, in its own field, has often suffered from rigidity of approach, from being divorced from the happenings of every-day life and consequently from lack of vitality. Yet here are two closely related subjects which are not only intimately concerned with our daily lives and with our survival but which have had long and exciting histories. Young children display a natural curiosity about their environment which provokes them to explore and to ask questions. The world they live in is unrestricted by subject barriers and the questions they ask concern nature study or science in its widest sense. Now science is not only a systematised body of knowledge but also a way of learning. It is this second aspect of science which makes it particularly appropriate for exploration by young children, since the keynote of the changes we have been considering is discovery by the children themselves. A question is asked (by the children or by the teacher), an experiment is devised, preferably by the children themselves, to find an answer to a problem that has arisen.

[1] HMSO, 1953.

The children observe and record the results for themselves and repeat the experiment as many times as they need in order to convince themselves, or for pure enjoyment. The pamphlet, *Science in Primary Schools*[1] concludes, 'We are concerned not so much that children should arrive at the same result as highly trained experimenters have obtained, as to see that they draw fair conclusions from their own information'. In other words, science learnt in this way is a potent stimulus to recording, and a training in integrity. The recording, be it a collection, a diagram, a design, or written work, reflects the children's desire to communicate their discovery.

What is the right environment and what are the materials necessary to excite children's interest in science? The environment is the world in which they live, so the best advice a teacher can be given is: 'Go out and see what is there'. Materials for exploration are often the living plants and creatures in the children's environment. As for the experiments, the homelier the apparatus the better. Young children are always ready to utilise the objects about them both in play and in their more serious investigations. But if children do not ask questions about the natural happenings in their environment, the teacher must stimulate and provoke them to do so. In the first instance she may need to ask the questions which later, she hopes, will come from the children.

This brings us to the last subject to be affected by the far-reaching changes of the last thirty years: mathematics. As G. H. Hardy[2] wrote, 'It is a study which did not begin with Pythagoras and will not end with Einstein, but it is the oldest and the youngest of them all'. We have seen that the essential elements of the changes in learning are exploration, discussion, and recording by the children themselves. How do these apply to mathematics? Here are the questions we must answer. What is the right environment for the learning of mathematics? What kind of discoveries ought the children to make, and what mathematics ought the children to learn? How can we contrive situations in which children can make their own discoveries? It is surely reasonable to apply to mathematics the principles of learning which have already affected all other aspects of the curriculum; Professor Whitehead was himself a mathematician and was convinced that mathematics could be learnt in this way.

But there is another movement which must be taken into account in the field of mathematics. Much has been written internationally as well as nationally about the changing pattern of mathematics. One of the most convincing reasons for this is the changing relationship between mathematics and science. It is said that scientists no longer need a bag of tools from the mathematician; computers can perform, at lightning speed, all the calculations they require. The overriding need is for mathematicians who can think for themselves and who can conceive problems as well as solve them.

There is, at present, a public demand for the following branches of mathematics to be included at the secondary school stage:

1 The study of general algebraic structure (sets, relations, logic). This is important because, for example, in making the programme for a computer to solve a particular problem, the conditions must first be expressed in algebraic form.
2 Probability and statistics. Industrialists want to know exactly how reliable are the predictions made by a mathematician from a given set of conditions
3 The field of mathematical models. A mathematical model is constructed to represent a real life problem (often in the social or biological sciences) from which an approximate solution can be obtained and hence a prediction can be made.

What concerns us here is the effect that the major changes which are being initiated at the secondary stage should have on the work in primary schools. It is clear that the major requirement of scientists (they want mathematicians who are able to think for themselves) is a requirement which might well be made of children of any age learning mathematics. Moreover, the underlying emphasis on structure is making teachers aware, often by first-hand discovery, of the meaning of some of the arithmetical processes and of the possibilities of their discovery by children themselves.

[1] HMSO, 1961.
[2] *A Mathematician's Apology*, C.U.P., 1940, 1967.

Subsequent chapters show that all three important branches of mathematics now being introduced into secondary schools have their roots in the work of the primary schools.

It has been shown by a number of teachers, here in this country and abroad, that children can learn the vocabulary of sets and can derive some pleasure from this. It seems probable that mathematics as a formal language leading to logic will become mainly the province of the secondary stage. However, there seems to be no reason why younger children should not be introduced to its vocabulary, and to some of its ideas, in preparation for this next stage, provided the teacher is interested, enthusiastic and willing to do this.

A number of illustrations will be found in the ensuing chapters of young children employing elementary statistical methods, of their own accord, to answer the simple questions they asked. Some of the graphical representations children make are of the statistical data they have collected for themselves.

Children's construction of mathematical models of real situations soon becomes a familiar aspect of mathematics. The construction represents their attempt to abstract the mathematics from the real problems they have to solve. The materials they use to construct their 'models' include commercial structural materials such as rods, and 'counters' such as pebbles, shells and other objects they have collected.

The foundations of these three topics of modern mathematics are therefore already being laid in primary schools. We shall be concerned, in the chapters which follow, with the gradual development of these topics. How far should we go in topics which are new to primary schools? Before we answer this and other vital questions posed in this chapter we shall review some of the findings of the research of the past twenty years concerning the way in which children learn mathematics.

2 Research into children's method of learning

'True or living learning originates from the *child* and indeed directly from some of his stronger interests and drives'.

NATHAN ISAACS, *Psychology, Piaget and Practice*

In this chapter we shall review the work of Piaget and others concerning the learning of mathematical concepts by young children. We shall then attempt to decide what influence their findings ought to have on our teaching of the early stages of mathematics.

Let us first turn to D. O. Hebb, of McGill University, for an unequivocal statement about the requirements of intellectual growth. 'There are two determinants of intellectual growth: a completely necessary innate potential and a completely necessary stimulating environment'.[1] If we accept this statement (and it is supported by the weight of prolonged research), our attention as teachers is directed once more to the importance of the environment. As we shall see, Piaget in his experimental methods sets us a pattern for use in planning our learning situations. In his preface to *The Child's Conception of Number* he writes, 'Conversation with the child is more reliable and more fruitful when it is related to experience with adequate material, and when the child, instead of thinking in the void, is talking about actions he has just performed'.[2]

Piaget set himself the task of finding out, as accurately as possible, how the principles of conservation and of reversibility, as applied to numbers and to spatial thinking, develop in the minds of young children. These two principles are fundamental to all mathematical (and logical) thinking. For example, in the field of numbers, conservation means that the number of objects in a group remains the same however the objects are arranged (in a heap, in a long line, etc.). Or if we are considering quantities, a quantity of lemonade remains the same if it is poured, for example, from a shallow dish into a tall, narrow glass. The understanding of reversibility involves a realisation that reversing an action would result in a return to the original state of affairs.[3] Piaget devised a variety of tests and tried these out on children of pre-school and primary school age.

Although the ages are always quoted in the records, it is the stages of learning to which Piaget draws attention. He was the first to discover that the formation of a concept takes far longer than had been supposed. His findings, and the stages of learning he postulates, are most easily understood in reference to one of his well known simple experiments.

This experiment was the third of a series concerned with one-to-one correspondence. In the test, the child was shown a set of seven egg cups in a row and also a group of eggs (containing more than seven eggs). He was asked to take just enough eggs for the egg-cups. In Stage I (normally between the ages of four and five) one child made a row of the same length but containing too many eggs. He was then asked to put the eggs into the egg-cups to check his answer and was surprised to find there were too many eggs! The extra eggs were removed and the child agreed that now there were the same number of eggs and of egg-cups. But when the seven eggs were taken out and put in a heap in front of the egg cups the child said that there were more egg-cups than eggs. It was clear from the similar responses of many children that, at this stage, children are not capable, by themselves, of making the one-to-one correspondence and that

[1] *The Organisation of Behaviour*, Wiley, New York, p. 302

[2] *The Child's Conception of Number*, 1952. *La Genèse du Nombre chez l'Enfant*, Geneva, 1941.

[3] Not all operations are immediately reversible. When we let a bath of water drain away we cannot get the same water back again.

they would not have discovered it if the relations between the egg and its cup had not forced them to do so. As for the equivalence of the two sets (eggs and egg-cups), the child's answers were based entirely on a visual (perceptual) comparison of the length of the rows, even when one-to-one correspondence had been established by the nature of the materials.

In Stage II (normally between the ages of five and six) the child, of his own volition, took seven eggs to correspond to seven egg-cups and put the eggs in the cups. When the eggs were removed and spaced further apart, the child said there were more eggs than egg-cups. When asked if there would be the right number of eggs to put one egg back in each cup he did not know. Here the child created one-to-one correspondence for himself, but he no longer recognised the equivalence of the two sets once the configuration was changed.

In Stage III (normally between the ages of five-and-a-half and six-and-a-half) the child achieves 'operational correspondence and lasting equivalence'. Even when the eggs were spread out the child maintained that the number of eggs and egg-cups were the same, 'because they all go into the egg-cups'. It is only at this stage that reversibility is understood; that is, the child can reverse the thinking process and put the eggs back into the egg-cups in imagination. So the child has achieved full operational control of the concept.

Piaget has thus drawn attention to the fact that there are variations in kinds of thinking according to chronological or mental age. Of these kinds of thinking, Dr. E. A. Lunzer in *The Work of Piaget and its Relevance for the Teacher*[1] writes: 'The ability to carry out actions in our heads, actions of ordering and reordering, and of appreciating equivalences .... is what Piaget calls operational reasoning. Such reasoning always involves systematic equivalences; for example, doing something (like adding) and then doing the opposite (like subtracting the same number) brings us back where we began'.

The forerunner to 'operational reasoning' is what Piaget calls 'intuitive reasoning' or reasoning guided by perception and imagery. Of this type of reasoning Dr. Lunzer writes:

'I like the term "metamorphoses" to highlight the results of such reasoning. The world is full of strange and inexplicable, but perfectly foreseeable, events, as far as the little child is concerned. Turning a switch enables him to see and hear the Queen on Christmas Day; hanging up a stocking ensures that a fat old man will somehow come down a hot chimney and fill it, the very same fat man (or is it?) whom he saw both at Lewis's and the Co-op. What is there to be surprised about if re-arranging a row of eggs makes them less than they were? Or if adding an egg to the compact row restores the balance, but spreading them out again upsets it again?

'Number is only one of the instruments whereby we carry out this ordering and systematisation of our experience. But it is certainly one of the first. English and Swiss children may be expected to have no difficulty with this first experiment by the age of at any rate six-and-a-half on the average. Many will be there a whole year sooner, although some may not reach it until a year later or more if educationally subnormal'.

Dr. J. Biggs[2] describes the operational thinking stage in these terms:

'The ability to make simultaneous judgments and to solve classifactory problems appears at the next stage which commences at an approximate mental age of six to seven years . . . where the reversibility and conservation principles make their appearance . . . Simultaneous judgments become possible, so that in the lemonade and glass experiment, the child makes allowance for the fact that the new glass is both taller and narrower whereas previously he concentrated either on narrowness or tallness, usually the latter. While conceptual thought as such now becomes possible, it must remain concrete and directly related to the child's own experience. His thinking is limited to the world he knows, sees and touches'.

The importance Piaget placed on the use of the spoken word in his experience with children raises the issue of the place of language in children's learning. In a carefully controlled piece of research work with a limited number of English children between the ages of 5·3 and 5·9

[1] Unpublished manuscript, Manchester University.
[2] *Anxiety, Motivation and Primary School Mathematics*. N.F.E.R., 1962.

Mrs. J. Tough[1] investigated the contributions made by relevant experience and language to the formation of a number concept by five-year-old children.

Of the four groups considered, the group with whom the appropriate language was introduced at the same time as the experience made significant progress in the learning of the concept under consideration. Half the children in the group having experience without appropriate language had made some progress but in two control groups very little progress had been made. In Mrs. Tough's own words: 'Of the three situations explored, the basic concept is more efficiently formed when language and concrete experience appear together. For the schools this means the provision of good concrete experience together with active teacher-participation and the stimulation of discussion'. Although this experiment involved a relatively small number of children the results are decisive and merit much further research. We are therefore left with the following three questions. Are we sufficiently aware of the concepts basic to later mathematical understanding? Do we provide the right kind of concrete experience during the early years? Do we provide at the same time language which helps efficient organisation of the experience?

This investigation shows the significance which one aspect of Piaget's work can have for teachers. What significance has Piaget's work in general for us as teachers? Once more let us turn to the experts in this field for more specific guidance. Dr. Lunzer[2] writes: 'The principal field for the application of Piaget's methods and results in educational practice is that of curriculum and method'. Of children's understanding of number he writes that such understanding cannot be taught nor does it come by itself, independently of experience. It is the fact that number is an integral part of our daily lives which ensures that children do come to this understanding. 'This does not mean that there is nothing the teacher can do except wait for the dawn of understanding'. He can provide the kind of experience which will assist the child to move from intuitive to operational thinking. 'This (operational thinking) means activity, but activity in the sense of mental activity'. Not only must the experience provided be of the right sort; it must occur in a context in which the child is interested in the result. From this we can conclude (1) that we can promote understanding of mathematical concepts by providing experience of the right kind, (2) that the experience or activity provided is not an end in itself although it is planned to arouse interest; it is devised with the declared purpose of stimulating spontaneous discovery by the child.

Now if we want to plan the right kind of experience we must know (1) the mathematical concepts we want the children to learn, and (2) how children learn.

We shall turn our attention to the first problem in subsequent chapters. Piaget's methods help us with the second for he based his conclusions on his observation of young children. It is almost impossible for us as adults either to remember how we learnt mathematical concepts or to imagine ourselves ignorant of them (imperfect though our knowledge may be). Therefore it is essential, if we want to discover how children learn, to plan learning situations for them and to observe what they do. It was by observing their actions, and by questioning them and listening to their answers, that Piaget discovered how the children were thinking and reasoning and learning.

Now let us see what a research worker in a different field has to say about Piaget's work. Dr. Z. P. Dienes relates Piaget's three stages of forming concepts to different types of learning situations. He calls the first the preliminary or play stage and writes: 'In order to make play possible, freedom to experiment is necessary.'[3] This stage is marked by an undirected and seemingly purposeless activity. The second stage is more directed and purposeful but there is no clear realisation of what is being sought. At this stage a certain degree of structured activity is desirable but, because children think in different ways, Dr. Dienes recommends the provision of a number of experiences of varying structure, all leading to the same concept. The third stage must provide the practice necessary

[1] A study of the contributions made by relevant experience and language to the formation of a number concept of five-year-old children, unpublished thesis, 1963.
[2] op. cit.
[3] Z. P. Dienes, *Building up Mathematics*, Hutchinson, 1960, p. 39.

for fixing the concept. He therefore refers to:

(*a*) *preliminary games*
(*b*) *structural games*
(*c*) *practice games*

but adds, 'Clearly a practice game for one concept can act as a preliminary game for a later concept. It is important, however, not to use practice games as preliminary games for the same concept, a common error in infants' schools'.

In the light of this advice, that we ought as teachers to contrive learning situations of different kinds for each mathematical concept, let us examine the kind of learning we frequently find at present in primary schools. Is it fair that this should be called 'rote learning' or 'mechanical' learning? Have we not, in all sincerity, used all our teaching skill and experience to teach number bonds, the multiplication tables, the weights and measures, and the processes, to our large classes? And have we not done our utmost to see that the children understood a process (at least on the first occasion that we demonstrated this on the blackboard)? Of course we have included practical work, to give children experience of weights and measures, and even of money. At the end of six years in the primary school do we not often say, 'The children can do mechanical arithmetic, and like it, but they cannot do problems'?

What do those outside the school say about the present state of mathematics teaching? Professor Lauwerys, commenting on the Ministry of Education pamphlet, *The Teaching of Mathematics in Secondary Schools*, said 'No subject arouses so much distaste in boys and girls as mathematics'. Dr. J. Biggs,[1] at the conclusion of an article on number anxiety, attributes this distaste to the teaching. 'The most common reasons for negative attitudes are based upon a lack of proper understanding of the subject, which in many cases is due to mechanical teaching, and upon plain boredom, a product of uninteresting teaching'. Are these fair criticisms? May there not be something in the nature of mathematics which makes it inherently difficult to learn? Is it too abstract? A. N. Whitehead wrote, in 1898, 'The whole of mathematics consists in the organisation of a series of aids to the imagination in the process of reasoning'. Mathematics has also been described as a purely mental activity, so that the practical situation—even paper and pencil—is a means to an end: the learning of mathematics, itself an abstract subject.

Dr. Biggs suggests an answer to the question posed in the previous paragraph in his summary of the implications of research into the varying achievements in arithmetic of boys and girls at different ages. The results are also relevant to the learning of mathematical concepts. Recent research shows that, at the ages of seven and of ten, the performance of girls in mechanical arithmetic is substantially better than that of boys, whereas in problem arithmetic girls are only slightly better than boys. In an attempt to discover whether differences at ten were inherent or not, a coaching experiment was carried out with boys of this age. It was found that under really strong motivation boys will readily equal or surpass girls at this stage. This would indicate that differences at the end of the primary stage may well be due to differences of temperament, such as girls' desire to please.

When the results at fourteen years of age are studied it is found that, although the performance of boys and girls in mechanical arithmetic is about the same, the boys are far superior to the girls at problem arithmetic. But a closer examination of these results reveals that, in the sample of girls tested, only those from secondary modern schools are inferior to boys in problem arithmetic. This leads Dr. Biggs, in a careful assessment of the evidence, to conclude that the changes which occur in the secondary school are partly due to social pressures (girls accepting inferiority in mathematics as part and parcel of their role as women) and partly to the fact that women find analytical thinking more difficult than men do. His concluding question has an important implication for teachers in primary schools: 'This leads us to ask the fundamental question: ought sex differences in mathematical ability to disappear if abstractive[2] teaching methods were used, particularly in the primary stages where they are most appropriate?' This question suggests that, if discovery methods

[1] op. cit.

[2] i.e. methods by which children are led to discover—and so to abstract—mathematical concepts.

PLATE I

Infants: "See how it fills and flows".

PLATE II

In model making infants estimate, match and measure.

PLATE III
Infants: Making a train.

PLATE IV

Infants: Building and beginning of the appreciation of mathematical shapes.

were applied throughout a girl's mathematical education, she might subsequently hold her own with boys in mathematics. It also suggests, by implication, that abstract mathematics might not present difficulties if the right learning methods (as opposed to teaching methods) are employed.

With discovery methods in mind and encouraged by Piaget's experiments, let us create a dynamic definition for the learning of mathematics. To be brief we might content ourselves with: 'Mathematics is a discovery of relationships'. But if we (or the children we teach) have discovered such a relationship for ourselves we want to communicate the exciting discovery to others. We may first describe the discovery in words to a friend or teacher. Subsequently we may find a more effective way of expressing the relationship; for example, in numbers (as in arithmetic), in letters (as in algebra), by a diagram (as in geometry) or by a graph. Therefore a more comprehensive definition would be, 'Mathematics is a discovery of relationships and the expression of the relationship in symbolic (or abstract) form'. This is no static definition but implies action on the part of the learner, of whatever age and whatever ability. It is the fact that mathematical relationships can be discovered and communicated in such a variety of ways that puts mathematics within reach of children and adults of all abilities. In the following chapters we shall show how young children can learn mathematics by their own efforts and how we can plan the learning situations which will effect this. For this purpose we may summarise the conclusions derived from the research to which reference has been made in this chapter as follows:

(1) Children learn mathematical concepts more slowly than we realised. They learn by their own activities.

(2) Although children think and reason in different ways, they all pass through certain stages depending on their chronological and mental ages and their experience.

(3) We can accelerate their learning by providing suitable experiences, particularly if we introduce the appropriate language simultaneously.

(4) Practice is necessary to fix a concept once it has been understood, therefore practice should follow, and not precede, discovery.

3 Early experiences in mathematics (arithmetic)

No one nowadays will question the desirability of including mathematics in the primary school curriculum. Any doubts should be dispelled by the following excerpt from *Primary Education.*

'Mathematical thought is part, and a great part, of the heritage of the race . . . . By its aid man has measured the distances to the stars, forecast eclipses, navigated the seas and the air, made maps of the earth, built cathedrals and bridges, split atoms and designed machines from the simple lever to the most complicated space satellite or electronic computer; all the elaborate business transactions between men, between groups of men, and between nations are founded on a knowledge of mathematics. And the subject is growing; the need to know more about the structure of the atom led to the development of new algebras and geometries . . . . The elegance, the order, the pattern and the generality which are inherent in even the most elementary work can be appreciated by all children. Clearly the teacher must be aware of these qualities himself and appreciate them'.[1]

In this, and in subsequent chapters, we shall be concerned with the content of mathematics courses for primary school children. We shall examine the structure of the mathematical ideas children can learn between the ages of five and eleven years. Bearing in mind the changing trends in education to which reference has already been made, we shall discuss ways of planning the work so that children are enabled to make their own discoveries. Dr. Z. P. Dienes described the classroom situation we want to create when he wrote: 'It is suggested that we shift the emphasis from teaching to learning mathematics, from our experiences to the children's, in fact from our world to their world. We shall then be already well on the way to a solution of our difficulties.'[2] Dr. J. Biggs is no less definite when he writes: 'There are two major aspects to mathematical ability: an ability to rote-learn facts and connections and an ability to deal with the structure; these abilities correspond to arithmetical techniques and concepts respectively.'[3]

Perhaps the classroom situation we want to create will be further clarified by a statement of our aims in the teaching of mathematics. We shall limit these to three. The first is to make children think for themselves. The second is to give children a knowledge and appreciation of mathematics as a creative subject; of its order and pattern (in number as well as in geometrical form); of its vital presence in everyday life and in the environment, not only in man-made things but in natural forms as well. Children who learn to appreciate mathematics in this way, as a subject in which they make their own exciting discoveries and which holds fun and fascination for them, have full confidence in their own abilities. The third aim is to give children a facility with number and quantity relationships or, more briefly, to give them skill in computation.

Sir T. P. Nunn, in *The Teaching of Algebra*, wrote, of mathematics: 'Mathematical truths always have two sides or aspects. With the one they face and have contact with the world of outer realities lying in time and space. With the other they face and have relationships with one another'.[4] To gain an appreciation of mathematics, children must have experience and knowledge of both these aspects of the subject. We shall draw on the first, mathematics in the environment, as a basis for the discoveries of the abstract mathematical relationships implied by the second.

Children come to school at five years old with very varied mathematical backgrounds based on situations which have arisen naturally in their day-to-day experience inside and outside the

[1] HMSO, 1959.
[2] *Building up Mathematics*, 1960.
[3] *Anxiety and Motivation and Primary School Mathematics*, London, 1962.
[4] London, 1931.

home. In fact they have already begun accumulating 'that knowledge of number, quantity and space which adults take for granted'.[1] In most infant schools, at least in the first term or so, this experience is continued. Teachers of reception classes make the most of opportunities which arise for introducing mathematical ideas and, more important still, for associating the correct mathematical language with the situations which arise. Thus for example, numbers are not met in isolation from language or experience as the following records show: Alan, aged five years, was very interested in telling the time. He made a clock book and kept adding to it. He learned to recognise the symbols up to 12 by this means. He used the cookery pinger clock and became familiar with five-minute intervals. 'Ten minutes until eleven o'clock. Five minutes more and it is coffee time', he said. When using the water measures he said: 'I want the biggest one . . a gallon of water in it for my car'. Alan made such rapid progress as a result of these varied experiences that, when the boy who was counting the number of children requiring milk asked him how to write twenty-three, Alan replied: 'You will find 23 in the calendar, Paul'.

In another infant school the children had recorded their answers in writing to the question: 'What can you weigh?' These included:

My shoe weighs 10 oz.
50 small dog biscuits make $\frac{1}{4}$ lb.
The largest brick weighs 2 lb.
The middle-sized brick weighs 10 oz.
The smallest brick weighs 4 oz.
1 stone balances 14 lb.
46 lemonade tops to balance $\frac{1}{4}$ lb.
The lightest thing in our room is a feather.
The heaviest thing in our room is a radiator.

'Our Zoo Number Book' at yet another infant school contained the following passage:

Uncle Jack took me to the Zoo today. It was 9d. for Uncle Jack and 6d. for me. How much did he pay for the tickets. 1/3d. I had a bag of 12 buns. I threw 5 of them to the bears. How many buns had I left. 7. First we went to see the monkeys. There were 9 big monkeys and 4 baby ones. How many monkeys did we see. 13. It was lovely to see the kangaroos. There were 5. How many legs had they all. 20. Elephant is big and heavy. Mouse is little and light. Tortoise goes very slowly. Giraffe is very tall. We went in at 10 o'clock. We left at 4 o'clock. We stayed 6 hours.

But such mathematical opportunities as arise naturally in the classroom, though excellent in themselves as a continuation or extension of earlier experience, are rarely sufficient and broad enough even at this stage. We, as teachers, shall need to provide the right kind of experience to serve as a basis for more systematic learning. In order to do this we must examine the mathematical concepts which it is possible for most children to learn by the age of seven to eight years. (Some children will, of course, learn considerably more and others far less, according to their abilities.)

Here is a summary of these concepts, processes and facts:

i. Sorting and classifying objects into sets. Comparing sizes of two sets (the number of objects in each set) by matching or one-to-one correspondence; learning the language, and later the symbols, of inequality; is greater than $>$, is less than $<$.

ii. Counting the number of objects in a set (cardinal number). This, in effect, involves putting each object into one-to-one correspondence with one in the series of number names. Conservation of number. Composition of numbers up to 10 known without counting on or counting back. Addition of 10 to numbers 1 to 10. Addition of 9 (from 10) to numbers 1 to 10. Knowledge of doubling, up to (and beyond) 2×20. Knowledge of the 'near' doubles, e.g. $6 + 7$, in two ways: $2 \times 6 + 1$ and $2 \times 7 - 1$. Knowledge of reversibility of addition, using this, e.g. $2 + 9 = 9 + 2$ (after children have learnt to add 2 to any number).

iii. The number line. Numbers in sequence or in order up to 100 (ordinal numbers). 'Nodding acquaintance' with numbers beyond 20 but, except for a few children, no written manipulation of these numbers in isolation from experience. Growing awareness of place-value in the number notation.

[1] *The Teaching of Mathematics in the Primary School*, Mathematical Association, London, 1955.

iv. Measurement and money. Conservation of measures. Knowledge of the relationships between one unit and another (the common units of weights and measures which normally come within the experience of young children.)
v. Simple fractions: halves, quarters, three-quarters.
vi. Varied aspects of the operations of addition, subtraction, multiplication and division as these arise in the real situations of the classroom.
vii. Shape and size (proportion).

Before each of these aspects is considered in more detail the part which oral discussion and written recording can play in the work should be assessed. Reference was made in the last chapter to the importance of associating the appropriate language with the experience. This oral discussion, between a teacher and a group of children, or between children, serves many purposes. The suggestion has already been made that the learning of concepts is accelerated by discussion. Children frequently learn by their attempts to put into words what they are doing, and what they have discovered. 'How do I know what I think till I see what I say?' is an adult version of this aspect of learning. By talking to the children teachers can find out the stage the children have reached in learning a concept. A child can work through an assignment card and answer every question correctly and yet still fail to grasp important aspects of the concept. Such a failure is usually revealed only in discussion between teacher and child.

An example of this, which occurs quite frequently, is of children who were given oral practice, as a class, in adding 10 to different numbers less than 10. By the time the teacher had selected a child to answer $10 + 6$, for example, most children had had time to count on from 10 to 16 and had the answer ready. The children were then given a written exercise on this and nearly all of them obtained full marks. But subsequent questioning revealed that one child only, of a group of 24, had discovered the pattern $10 + 3 = 13$ (or $3 + 10 = 13$), $10 + 4 = 14$, etc. and so did not need to count on in ones to find the answers. A few minutes' discussion with small groups of children at less frequent intervals is always far more effective than oral class work of this kind.

It sometimes happens, too, that a child, using structural apparatus, may give the impression that he understands a concept when, in fact, he may be enjoying the visual pattern without appreciating the mathematical significance at all. For example, a six year old, using structural rods, was asked to find all the pairs of rods which together were of the same length as a given (black) rod. The boy soon discovered that when he had found one pair of rods together equal in length to the black rod he could then reverse the order of the rods and so obtain a second pair. With evident pleasure he matched up, in a similar way, all the pairs of rods (and reversed pairs) which were equivalent to the black rod. Although the boy was able to assign numbers to the rods he was quite unaware that he was on the brink of an important mathematical discovery: that in addition the order of adding two numbers does not matter (e.g. $3 + 4 = 4 + 3$, the commutative law). The teacher talked to the boy, focussing his attention on each pair and reversed pair in turn and asked him, as she did so, to name the number pair. After each pair of two rods she asked the boy if he noticed anything interesting. At first, he looked puzzled but, at the third pair, the boy's face lit up and he said: '6 and 1 and 1 and 6 are the same', and then proceeded to name all the other pairs. It was quite clear that if the teacher had not discussed the number patterns with the boy, and questioned him, he would not have made the discovery at all.

Since language has such a fundamental part to play in the learning of mathematics, it follows that children working as suggested are learning English and mathematics simultaneously. (It is important to remember this when the question of time allocation is raised!). If vocabulary is restricted, the experience provided for learning mathematics can also be used as one means of learning to read. One headmistress has stated that the children in her school learn to read at least six months earlier now that reading and recording have such an important place in the learning of mathematics. A five-year-old in his second term was trying to read a card which said, 'Which is heavier, a cup of peas or a cup of rice? Guess first'. The boy found the words 'heavier' and 'lighter' on a pair of scales. He matched the words 'peas' and 'rice' with the labels on the jars containing these objects. He then asked an older boy what the word 'guess' was. He said aloud, 'I guess peas because they are bigger'. He was astonished to find that the cup of rice was heavier. He repeated the experiment three times and was still puzzled. He discussed the result with his brother, an eight-year-old, who, apparently, had done this experiment the day before. This boy's explanation was: 'Rice grains are littler but you get more in t'cup'.

At a later stage, when children are writing their findings entirely in their own words, very good opportunities are provided for written recording, Some children who find other forms of expression difficult excel at this kind of direct recording based on their own experiments.

No mention has been made of 'Sums'. In the early stages discussion should take the place of written recording until the children are able to copy from a card and fill in their own results or record their results entirely in their own words. This kind of spontaneous recording should play a large part at the infant stage. The signs $+$ $-$ $\times$ $\div$ should be introduced fairly gradually, as a shorthand, and not until the children have had a very wide and varied experience of situations requiring these operations. Children will certainly require to perform them to answer the questions they (or their teacher) ask but the operations should not be isolated from experience. Very few children are ready, at this stage, for mechanical practice. In particular, rarely will more than a small minority of an age group be ready for practice with tens and units at the infant stage.

We do not mean that children between the ages of five and seven years will not come across and use numbers greater than 10. On the contrary, young children frequently meet such numbers before, or soon after, they first come to school as the following example shows. A teacher of a reception class who had decided to base mathematics on the children's natural conversation about numbers, quantities and shapes, kept an accurate record of the children's sayings. One boy said: 'My daddy only goes at 70 on the Motorway. His clock goes 10, 20, 30, 40, 50, 60, 70, 80, but my daddy only goes at 70'. The boy could not write the numbers of course, but he could recognise them when he saw them and already had some idea of the sequence in tens.

What is meant by 'tens and units' is the following, all too frequently found in 'sum' books of the six-year olds.

TU	TU	TU	TU
37	52	46	$3\overline{)54}$
+28	−34	×2	
___	___	___	
___	___	___	

It is this kind of experience, introduced too soon, and practised too often, which leads boys and girls in the first year of the secondary school to say: 'We always knew the kind of sums we were going to do in arithmetic. They were always the same. The only thing we did not know was the answers'. No wonder a speaker on a B.B.C. programme chose as the title for his talk: 'Down with Arithmetic!' We shall try to show what we consider to be the right time for systematic practice; a readiness test for such practice will be mentioned in the next chapter.

How is the knowledge included in our summary to be achieved? What kind of experience should be planned? How can we use ordinary classroom situations to the best mathematical advantage? We shall try to answer these questions as we consider each aspect of the summary in turn, using as illustrations the work of young children of varying abilities in primary schools in many different parts of the country.

I. Pre-counting experiences

Probably the earliest mathematical experiences of young school children are those concerned with sets of objects. Children select the sets of objects they need for their immediate purpose from such miscellaneous sources as the shop, the home corner, or the box of scrap materials. Sometimes the objects they select fall into one class, such as cotton reels or matchboxes from the scrap box. At other times they may select a set of different things such as an orange, a pear, a banana from the greengrocer's shop. Frequently children are unconsciously matching the objects in one set with the objects in another set. For example, when they are preparing the table for a meal at school or at home they may be asked: 'Are there enough plates for everyone?' Or 'Is there a cup for each saucer?' 'A knife for each fork?'

Children usually find the answers to these questions by the process of matching. They reply in many ways, learning to use the language appropriate to the situation; 'not as many as', 'too many', 'too few', 'not enough', 'the same as', 'is equal to', are but a few of these. It is important to remember that, in real experience, it is much more usual to come across numerically unequal sets than equal sets so that 'greater than' and 'less than' and other terms denoting inequality are quite as important as 'equal to'. This experience of matching or of one-to-one correspondence precedes counting, as Piaget has shown in the experiment with the eggs and egg-cups to which reference was made in Chapter 2. Such experience is an essential forerunner of counting, as the history of men's progress in mathematics shows. Long ago, before men had a system of spoken number-names or had invented written symbols they numbered their flocks of sheep (or their armies) by making one notch in a piece of wood or adding one pebble to a pile for each sheep (or man). As a result of their experience of matching sets, children learn to place sets of objects in order according to the number of objects in the set before they can count. For example, if children are given, in any order, sets containing 1, 2, 3, 4, 5 objects they will discover that these can be arranged in order beginning with the smallest and that each successive set contains one more object than its predecessor. The first example considered in the next section illustrates the stages which succeed this early matching and ordering of sets of objects.

II. Counting, conservation of number, composition of number

It is easy enough to provide abundant and varied early experience of counting. There is a stage when the youngest children can count out a few objects, matching each object to the next number name, but do not recognise the written number symbols for all the sets they are able to count. To help children over this stage, and to give them experience of counting out successive sets of objects, a young teacher devised the following simple material.

In a large reception class, instead of the usual number charts on the wall, with their pictures or dots, the teacher had provided the children with a different kind of counting experience. Each of twenty boxes bore a large numeral (1 to 20). These boxes were filled at the beginning of the day with as many objects as were indicated by the numeral, the objects being chosen by the two children responsible. The children dealt with all the numbers familiar to them, and set the boxes out in sequence. One day the boxes contained one apple, two pencils, three sweets, four conkers, five pennies and so on. The next day the boxes contained different objects according to another child's choice. Now the counting experience these children were having was particularly valuable in this instance because the counting was not associated with a static pattern as with dots or pictures of objects. For example, one day the '5' box would contain five pencils, another day five books, five pennies, and so on. From such wide experience children eventually abstract the property common to all sets of the same numerical size, in this instance of five, the number name of the last object to be counted in the set.

Material of this kind can also be used for the learning of conservation of number, as the following example will show. This example also serves to illustrate how two children subjected to the same experience for the same length of time can be at very different stages of mathematical development. The teacher had provided similar experience to that of the other reception class: twelve trays, each bearing a numeral from 1 to 12 and a dozen of each of twelve attractive objects so that the children could make their own choice when setting out the trays in order. Later in the day these trays were used by the youngest children to make problems. For example, one boy in his second term was sitting with a tray containing eight toy cows. He was asked: 'If you took out six cows, how many would be left?' Without touching the cows he gave the answer immediately. He was then asked a complete range of similar questions; each time he gave the correct answer immediately and without touching the cows. Later this boy recorded his results in words and numerals.

A second boy, sitting next to the first, was using a tray containing seven trolley buses. He had started school on the same day as the first boy, yet his response to a similar question was entirely different. He was asked: 'If you take five buses out of the tray how many will be left?' He removed five buses, counting them as he did so. Then he counted the buses left in the tray and gave the answer. When he had returned all the buses to the tray he was asked how many buses were now in the tray. In order to answer, he counted the buses in the tray again. From further examples it seemed that the first boy realised that whatever he did to the cows, whether they were crowded together or spread out, the number remained the same when they were all returned to the tray. He also seemed to know all the pairs of numbers which made eight. When asked how he knew these, his reply was: 'I just think and it comes'. But the other boy had not yet achieved conservation of number and always resorted to counting to find the answers to the questions he was asked.

An interesting and unexpected sequel illustrated that the first boy had not yet completely mastered the composition of eight. Some hours later, when he no longer had access to the trays, he was again asked one of the questions to which he had given an immediate answer earlier in the day. This time he hesitated, shut his eyes and counted out, in imagination, six cows; he also counted the two cows remaining in the tray to give the required answer. It was clear that, at this stage for this boy, availability of the material was essential since he was not yet able to manipulate abstract numbers.

A different kind of experience used by a teacher to give children practice in counting was found in a set of assignments involving the use of balancing scale pans. These read:

> How many acorns balance 5 conkers?
> How many screws balance 5 nails?

Many similar examples can be devised to give children the varied experience they require.

We have now come to what teachers often regard as the most difficult for children to learn: composition of numbers up to 20. By this is meant a knowledge of number trios, such as 5, 8 and 13, or 9, 7 and 16, which result from the combination or separation of two of the constituent sets. A knowledge of these number trios is most important for young children. It is essential that these number facts should eventually become so well known that they can be recalled quickly without counting on or counting back in ones. But such readily available knowledge must be based on considerable and varied experience of appropriate situations.

How can this be achieved? Attention needs to be focussed on different numbers in turn. Many teachers start with a target of 5 or 6, then 10, then 12, gradually raising the ceiling until 20 is reached. The following devices have all been used by teachers for this purpose.

(1) The number trays already described. This material was used by older five-year-olds to record simple problems in addition and subtraction. For example, one child wrote: 'There were 8 horses in my tray. I took 5 out. There were 3 left'. He recorded his result in symbols too:

$$8 - 5 = 3$$

'I put 5 horses back in the tray. Altogether there were 8'.

$$3 + 5 = 8$$

In fact these children were gaining valuable experience of addition and subtraction, of subtraction as the inverse of addition, and of the number trio 3, 5, 8, in its four-fold relationship:

$$5 + 3 = 8$$
$$3 + 5 = 8$$
$$8 - 5 = 3$$
$$8 - 3 = 5$$

Once the children have discovered that in the addition of two or more sets of objects it does not matter whether they add the smaller set to the larger, or the larger set to the smaller, the number of facts to be learned is almost halved. Indeed this discovery can be used profitably at this stage since children usually know 5 + 2 before they know 2 + 5 and the teacher can then encourage the children to draw on their knowledge and to add the smaller set to the larger and so avoid counting on in ones.

Although each number trio represents a four-fold relationship there are many different ways of asking questions which will lead to these relationships. This is particularly true of the last two (subtraction). It is therefore most important that children should meet these relationships in many different situations so that they become familiar with the varied language which defines these relationships.

(2) In another school some six-year-olds were given concentrated experience of combinations of various numbers through their shop. It was a cake shop. For example, one day the pair using the shop were told first to set out the stock, putting out 9 of each. They then affixed price tickets ranging from 1d. to 9d. After this they opened the shop and sold the cakes to the young shoppers. When the shop was shut again they had not only to count the money taken but also to count the remaining stock, and enter this in a stock book. In the second column in this book they had to enter the number of cakes required to bring the stock of each kind up to 9 again. When they had finished the teacher asked them some questions about their work, bringing in the combinations of 9 to see what progress they had made.

(3) In another infants school a stock book was kept in the home corner and used to account for deficiencies. The stock—cups, saucers, plates, knives and forks—was checked before the house was used.

(4) The use of measuring. Measuring of all kinds can afford abundant opportunities for the addition and subtraction of numbers. At this stage, however, the instruments of measurement should be of simple type with units not broken into fractions, e.g., marked in centimetres not millimetres as on a tape measure. In Appendix 2 there is a list of measures which teachers have found useful in infants schools.

One school had a weighing corner in which various parcels had been made by the teacher. The children were asked: 'How heavy are these parcels? Guess first. How near was your guess?' For each parcel the children had to do a subtraction in order to find out how near their guess was. This same method can be applied to measures of any kind: length, capacity, area and time.

One boy guessed the weight of a parcel to be 8 oz. and found, on weighing it, that it was 11 oz. He wrote: 'I guessed 8 oz. The parcel was 3 oz. heavier than my guess.

$$8 + 3 = 11$$'

The teacher seized the opportunity to ask how heavy a parcel 3 oz. less than the one weighed would be. The boy replied correctly and wrote:

$$11 - 3 = 8$$

The use of money, too, can provide frequent and varied experience, and later practice, in the number trios. Once the children recognise the coins and their equivalents (they cannot discover these for themselves), real coins can be used to give practice in counting and in the discovery of the number trios. In a reception class a number of 'purses' were set out with the invitation: 'Check the money in each of these purses. How much would each need to make it up to 1s. 0d.?' The money was real money and the teacher affirmed that the children learnt far more quickly with real money and that, since one child counted the money at the end of each day, none had been lost.

Many further examples will be discussed later in this chapter in the section specifically devoted to measurement.

(5) It is at this stage, when children are beginning to consolidate their experience of the addition and subtraction of numbers up to 20, that they require help in abstracting. Some teachers find it useful to introduce commercial structural apparatus, so that children can discover number relationships (particularly in addition and subtraction) divorced from the varied situations which give rise to them. Such apparatus can be valuable, not only in giving children visual experience, but in weaning them from 'counting on or counting back' when adding and subtracting. By the use of such apparatus children can both extend and summarise the number relationships they are learning. For example, they can write 'The Story of Seven'[1] and record this subsequently in symbols. But there are many more teachers who, knowing what they want the children to learn, prefer to arrange their own structural experience for them. In either case, the *only* means we, as teachers, have of knowing whether

---

[1] See the example on p.12. When a child learns to record the equivalents he has found for the 7 unit rod he writes, for example,

$$\begin{gathered}6 + 1 = 7\\ 1 + 6 = 7\\ 4 + 3 = 7\\ 1 + 1 + 5 = 7 \text{ etc.}\end{gathered}$$

a child knows his number relationships immediately, without resorting to counting, is frequent discussion and oral questioning of individuals or of small groups.

Nevertheless, all teachers would benefit from a personal knowledge of the potentialities and limitations of the various sets of structural apparatus on the market. The soundest way to obtain first-hand experience is to experiment with the material oneself. Investigations can be made of the potentialities of the material for the discovery of simple number relationships; as a means of giving insight into (a) the simple operations of addition, subtraction, multiplication and division (b) place-value (c) fractions. The official books accompanying each type of structural apparatus should be read critically. Some of these books contain a coherent and logical account of our number system as well as some useful ideas which teachers will want to try with the children they teach. It cannot be over-emphasised, however, that these books were not devised for any individual child and that children learn in different ways. There will by many individual variations for which teachers must be prepared if the material is to be used to the best effect.

In the first instance, teachers will want to introduce the material chosen to a small group of children, watching them use it and questioning them to discover the way each child is learning and the stage each child has reached. This is important because money can be wasted on the purchase of expensive material if its full potentialities, as well as its limitations, are not first understood. Indeed some teachers, aware of the commercial pressures to which they are subject when making enquiries about structural apparatus, find it difficult to make a fair assessment.[1]

There follows a summary of the points which should be kept in mind by those using, or intending to use, commercial structural apparatus:

(i) Structural apparatus is designed to give opportunities for discovering certain mathematical relationships (in particular, basic number relationships) in isolation from their application in the environment (e.g. $5 + 3 = 8$ not associated with measures, weight, money, etc.).

(ii) Experience with structural apparatus should therefore form only a part of mathematical learning, and opportunities for discovery of relationships, using the children's environment and weights, measures and money should also be provided. It is particularly important that children's first experiences with numbers, counting and the number sequence, should be with real things in the environment, including the weights and measures of everyday life, adapted for use by young children. This should precede discovery of number relationships from structural apparatus.

(iii) Structural apparatus gives the child valuable opportunities:
- (a) to discover and organise number relationships up to 20.
- (b) to extend this knowledge, by discovery of numbers up to 100. (For some children this stage will come at about seven).

(iv) Teachers need to spend some hours using the apparatus themselves, discovering its possibilities (at first without the book) before deciding to introduce it to their children.

(v) This apparatus is essentially for individual or group and not class activity. In the first instance, it might well be introduced as an experiment to a small group of children.

III. Numbers in sequence: place-value

Experience of the number line (numbers in sequence, or ordinal numbers) was also provided by the teacher who gave her reception class 20 boxes, numbered 1 to 20, to fill and to

[1] A comprehensive description of the different types of structural apparatus and an evaluation will be found in the following articles:
J. D. Williams, Teaching Arithmetic by Concrete Analogy
I 'Miming Devices'; *Educational Research*, Vol. III. Nos. 2, 3.
II 'Structural Systems'; *Educational Research*, Vol. IV. No. 3.
III 'Issues and Arguments'; *Educational Research*, Vol. V. No. 2.
and in *Mathematics Teaching*, No. 16. 1961, et seq.

set out in order of the size of the sets of objects contained. The children set out the boxes in order: the first, the second, third and so on, as they filled each with the right number of objects. They met 11 in its position in the number line, coming after 10 and before 12, long before they understood the significance of the written symbol 11 (or 10 and 12); in other words, long before they realised the significance and economy of our number notation (dependent as it is on the position of the numerals). They came to realise that each successive number is one more than the number which precedes it.

Another infant teacher encouraged each child in her six-year-old class to make match-box houses for 'Coronation Street'. At first the houses, as they were finished, were given a number and placed in order, as though on one side of the road. But soon the children suggested that the houses should be arranged as in their own roads, starting at 1 on one side and counting on in twos, and starting at 2 on the other side of the road and counting on in twos. They soon came to recognise these as the 'odd numbers' and the 'even numbers'. At their post office, they addressed letters to houses in Coronation Street and they took it in turn to be postman to deliver these. They soon came to recognise numbers which were '2 more than' or '2 less than' the numbers in Coronation Street (which finally contained houses up to 40).

In another class of older six-year-olds, the children decided to make chairs for the audience for their puppet theatre. They numbered the chairs up to 50 and then set them out in rows of 10. They discovered, in doing so, that for example: 2, 12, 22, 32, 42 came one behind the other in the five rows. They asked why and found that out each was 10 more than the one in front.

By means of experiences similar to those just described, children gradually become aware of the significance of the individual figures (or digits) in numbers greater than 9. A class of six-year-old infants kept a visual record of the number of girls and the number of boys present each day. They decided to use poppet beads, a blue one for each girl and a white one for each boy. Each day a boy and a girl were responsible for giving out the beads of the appropriate colour, one to each boy and girl, and for collecting the beads and fastening these together in two strings, one of white beads, the other of blue beads. But it was sometimes difficult to tell from a glance at the two strings how many boys and how many girls there were. So, after discussion with the teacher, the children decided that they would make the beads into strings of ten and then they would be able to see quite easily how many beads there were. There were altogether 45 children in the class, 24 boys and 21 girls. When the headmistress came in she always asked how many children there were altogether. To find this total they decided to put all the strings of 10 beads together and the short lengths together and gave the answer: 'Four tens and five'. At first they wrote 40 under the strings of tens and 5 under the short string but they soon found that this could be written 45.

One day, when there was an epidemic in the school, there were only 15 boys and 17 girls in the class. The children solved the problem of finding the total for themselves by making the girls' short string up to ten with white beads from the boys' short string; they filled in the record, 32.

The next stage in the gradual insight into place-value is given by the example which follows. Some six-year-olds were asked to count some acorns they had collected. They tried to count the acorns as they took them from the bowl which contained them, but they lost count. To help them the teacher told them the story of how Alexander counted his army. Each soldier, as he passed the check-point, dropped a pebble into a small pot. As soon as the pot contained ten stones it was emptied and the 'counter' placed a larger stone in the second pot to record the ten pebbles. When this pot became full a piece of rock was placed in a third pot to represent the ten stones (equivalent to 100 pebbles).

The children decided to use a conker for every 10 acorns collected. They chose a boy to be the 'counter' and each child in the group filed past the bowl, removing an acorn as he did so, and placed the acorn on a saucer. As soon as the saucer contained 10 acorns the 'counter' emptied it and placed a conker on a plate. When the bowl was empty it was found that there were 8 conkers and 6 acorns. The children said at once that there must have been 8 tens and 6 acorns and recorded this as 86. (Later, when the collection grew and was counted again, the children used an orange for 10 conkers and so were able to complete the count of 142 acorns).

Such experiences as those described here are not difficult to contrive, and they give children some understanding not only of place value in our number system but also of the endless sequence of natural (or counting) numbers. At this stage, except for the few very able children (probably never more than twenty per cent), a systematic knowledge of and written computation with these numbers over 20 should not be expected. If written practice is given in tens and units before children are ready for this, they will use and often perpetuate inefficient methods, counting on in ones to do this computation.

Various forms of abacus are also used by teachers to give children visual and kinaesthetic experience of place value at this stage. The simplest form consists of two upright pegs each of which will take 9 rings (of uniform size) and no more so that, when a child has 10 rings, he puts one ring (often of another colour) on the 'tens' peg to record: 10 units (or 1 ten). A model in which the rings move on two looped wires which pass over the top of a stand can be used for subtraction also. (Fig. 3.1). In this model 18 rings are needed on each wire, some in front and some behind the stand.

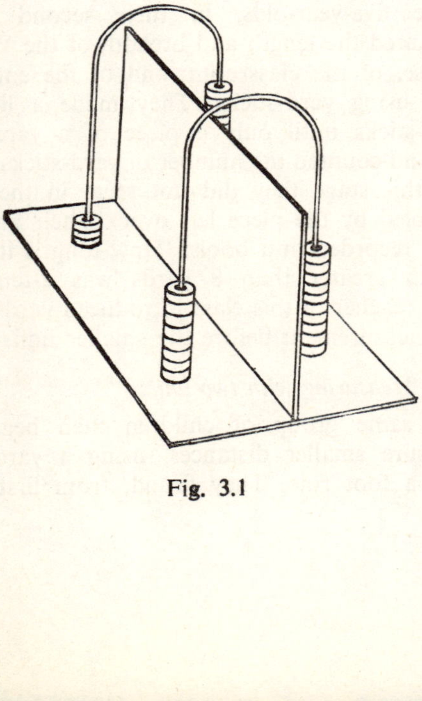

Fig. 3.1

An essential feature of every classroom should be the number line. (In structural material this appears as the 'number track', one hundred units long. This can be extended gradually as the children's knowledge extends. In its simplest form it can be a strip of 2 cm graph paper, 4 cm wide, covered with Sellotape (2 metres long when it achieves its full length) numbered 1 to 100, at two centimetre intervals, with the 10, 20, etc., graduations in red. It can be stuck to the wall horizontally, where it occupies little room. Strips of 2 cm paper one unit to ten units long, stiffened with cardboard and covered with sellotape, are also required. The number line and the strips can be used together to find the answers to such combinations as $8 - 3$, $3 + 5$, etc. or how far is it from 22 to 37?

IV. Measures and money

Experiences which involve measurement probably provide the most varied mathematical opportunities for young children. Children's development of understanding in measurement is slow and must be based on very full experience. A knowledge of the history of measurement will help teachers to appreciate the stages of development. At the infant stage, and subsequently, children need wide experience with money and with every kind of measurement: length, weight, capacity, time, speed, area and volume. Only frequent experience gives them the confidence illustrated in the following example. A five-year-old, in his second term, was asked: 'How do you know that your yard-stick (which was unmarked) is 3 ft. long?' He replied: 'Because I've measured and measured and measured', and added, as an afterthought: '*And* it is 36 inches long.'

Because measurement occupies such a major part of the experience of young children, a sequence of actual incidents is given. The incidents do not, of course, relate to the same children. Similar sequences can be collected for weight, for capacity, money, and time, by any teacher in contact with young children. This helps the teacher in planning the work and in preparing simple questions. An excellent sequence for weight will be found in the Mathematical Association's *The Teaching of Mathematics in the Primary School* (Bell, 1956).

Measuring: Length

(a) Conservation of length

This concept is usually, but not always, mastered by the age of six. For example, a boy of eight who showed quite clearly that he had mastered the concept of conservation of area was confused when this idea was applied to length. He was given two identical new pencils of the same colour and, when these were placed side by side, he readily agreed that they were the same length. As soon as the position of one of the pencils was changed so that they were no longer side by side, the boy said that the upright pencil was the longer. When the position of the pencils was changed again, he always pointed to the pencil nearest to the upright position as being the longer.

A group of eight-year-olds was shown a framework of four equal rods. Initially this was held in the position of a square; then it was pushed out of shape. (Fig. 3.2).

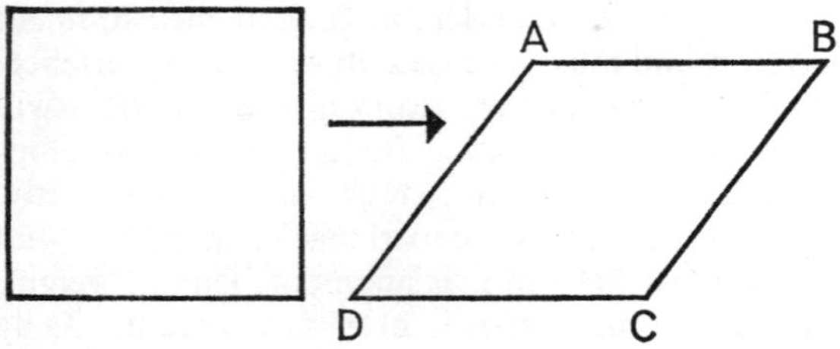

Fig. 3.2

The children at once volunteered that the 'slanting' rods (AD and BC) had become shorter. They spent a long time experimenting with the framework in different positions and measured the sides in each position before they were convinced that the lengths of the rods did not change when they were moved.

Clearly, young children from the age of five onwards need to be given varied experiences which will lead them to master the concept of conservation of length, and also to be given opportunities for appropriate discussion.

(b) Incidental measurement. Measuring for a purpose

Many of the normal activities of the infant class-room involve measurement. For example, the infants at one school always covered the models they made with newspaper which they pasted on before they painted the models. Their first efforts were usually guesses. Later on they measured the models before cutting the news-paper. Doll-making and dressing show the same progression: first attempts are guesses; later the doll is measured and patterns are made 'to measure' before cutting material.

(c) Measuring without a standard unit

Some young five-year-olds were interested in sizes of feet. Each drew round one foot of another child and cut out the pattern. The sizes were compared until the largest and the smallest patterns were found. The patterns, with the names of their owners written on them, were made into a frieze with the smallest at one end and the largest at the other. Then the children decided to collect the patterns of their fathers' feet to find out whose was the largest. The boy whose father was a policeman was delighted to find that his father had the largest feet!

The children next began to count the number of footsteps they each took as they walked, heel to toe, across the room. They compared the number taken by the girl with the smallest foot with that taken by the boy with the biggest foot. At this juncture the teacher introduced the children to the standard foot measure. Great was the excitement when it was dis-covered that the policeman's foot was exactly the same length as the foot rule!

(d) Measuring with one unit

Some five-year-olds, in their second term, measured the length and breadth of the Wendy House, of the classroom, and of the entrance hall, using yard-sticks. They made a line of yard-sticks until only a piece of a yard was left and counted the number of yard-sticks used. (At this stage they did not seem in the least troubled by the piece left over). Their answers were recorded in a book: 'How long is it'? No length greater than 8 yards was attempted. (The teacher of this class introduced yard-sticks for measurement before the smaller units).

(e) Measuring with two units

The same group of children then began to measure smaller distances, using a yard-stick and a foot rule. They found, from first-hand experience, that their yard-stick was three foot rules long (and, later, that their foot rule was 21 inches long). Working together, two boys measured the length of the three sides of the triangular section of the platform. They used one yard and two foot rules for each side (once more happily ignoring the piece left over) and were excited to discover that all three sides were of the same length, which they recorded as 5 ft.

(*f*) *Precision*

Shortly after the foregoing task was completed, one of the boys said excitedly, 'This chair (rung) just fits my ruler. Now I am going to find some other things which fit my ruler'. This led to the writing of: 'My foot-long book' on the outside of which the boy pasted a foot length marked in inches.

This group next marked their yard-stick in inches, numbering the divisions from 1 to 36. When the bookcase was measured and found to be 20 ins. wide, the children placed two rulers end to end and converted this length to 1 ft. 8 ins. They recorded this length both as 20 ins. and as 1 ft. 8 ins. Each child also recorded his own height in inches and in feet and inches.

(*g*) *Problems involving the operating of addition. subtraction, multiplication and division*

Many practical problems which arise (or can be contrived) in the classroom are, in the first instance, solved by the children by the simple method of addition or subtraction (rather than by multiplication or division). When one six-year-old wanted to find out whether the strip of coloured paper he had was long enough to go round two cylindrical boxes he was using for his model, he measured the perimeter of each, added them together, and found this combined length on his tape measure. He then compared this with the length of paper he had.

Every question such as: 'Guess and measure. How near was your guess?' results in a subtraction. Children are interested in measuring to see how near their guess was. They usually find subtraction harder than addition, until they are sure of their number trios, and therefore require much practice in problems which give rise to subtraction. At this stage, they often find the answer by addition rather than subtraction.

Two six-year-olds were asked to find the height of their hall. One of them stood on a chair and, using his yard-stick, tried to reach the top of the wall. When he found that he could not reach he sat down and looked at the wall which was covered with wall-paper. In a few minutes he said: 'I have counted the patterns, there are 11; now I am going to measure them.' He found that the patterns were 9 ins. long. He went into the playground with his partner and, using his yard-stick, a tape measure and a piece of chalk they marked out 11 lengths of 9 ins. each. They measured this length and found it to be 8ft. 3 ins.

To cover the canopy of a shop some six-year-olds decided to use coloured strips of paper 5 ins. long. The teacher asked them how many strips they could cut from a yard length of paper. They found the answer by measuring and cutting one piece at a time until a small piece remained.

The foregoing examples will serve to show the mathematical possibilities of the normal infant classroom in the field of measurement. In all the examples described the children were incidentally discovering number relationships, and particularly the number trios. These will be reinforced by using metric measures.

V. Fractions

Most children have some experience of simple fractions even before they come to school, if there is more than one child in the family. Cutting pieces of chocolate, etc. into two or three equal shares will be a familiar occurrence.

In the classroom, also, many of the children's activities will provide an experience of fractions and the use of language appropriate to the situation; for example, 'Cut it in half', 'Fold it in four (or in quarters)', 'Give Peter a quarter'. Children come to understand and to use the language of fractions long before they see the difficult written symbols.

Weights and measures provide varied experience in the use of simple fractions and also give teachers opportunities for assessing children's understanding of fractions. Some six-year-olds wanted half a yard of coloured adhesive tape for a model they were making. The boys were using a yard-stick marked, but not numbered, in inches. First they tried to count an inch at a time (one boy standing at each end of the yard-stick) to get to the middle. They lost count twice and therefore fetched two rulers which they placed one at each end; they then counted six on from the end of one ruler since they knew that six was one half of twelve. In the meantime a girl had cut a yard length in paper, folded it in half, and measured the half-yard using two rulers. When she was asked to find a quarter of a yard she folded a yard in two, and cut the fold, she then folded each half yard again and cut at the folds. She used the quarter of a yard and recorded that she had three quarters left.

Only after wide experience are children ready to understand the significance of the symbols $\frac{1}{2}$, $\frac{1}{4}$ and $\frac{3}{4}$, although they may have used the words, 'one half,' 'one quarter,' and 'three quarters' for a long time.

VI. The operations of addition, subtraction, multiplication and division

We have called these processes 'operations' because, in the first instance, they are (or should be) *actions performed* on real materials in natural situations which arise in the environment. These operations should be met in great variety, before the symbols are introduced. Children need to discuss and record in their own words the experiences which give rise to these operations before the symbols are introduced as a shorthand for the operations performed. Before we discuss each operation in turn some important points need to be made to avoid confusion.

(1) Since the symbols $+ - \times \div$ represent operations performed on a number of objects or on measures, we suggest that, in order to prevent confusion, they are taken to mean operations on what precedes them by what follows them, i.e. that the operator $+ - \times$ or $\div$ follows the number or measure on which it operates.

(2) The *mathematical names* for these symbols should be used when the symbols are first introduced:

$+$	$-$	$\times$	$\div$
plus add	minus subtract	multiply by	divide by

It cannot be over-emphasised that, if the children have had sufficient experience with real situations to be ready to meet the symbols, then they are ready for the correct mathematical terms. 'Timesing and share by' are *not* alternatives for 'multiply by and divide by': nor can correct grammatical sentences be constructed to include these terms.

For example:

> There is widespread confusion about the symbol '$\times$'. Its correct meaning of 'multiply by' is very often replaced by 'times' or 'of', in which cases the number or measure which is being operated on follows and does not precede the symbol.

For example, 3×4 means 3 multiply by 4 or 3 multiplied by 4, which is equivalent to $3 + 3 + 3 + 3$ or 'four threes' or 'four times three'. Also, 4×3 means 4 multiplied by 3, which is equivalent to $4 + 4 + 4$ or 'three fours' or 'three times four'.

In due course other notations than 4×3 for 'three fours' or 'three times four' can be used as equivalents: for example, 3.4 or, perhaps better, the use of brackets 3(4). This anticipates the eventual use in algebra of 3x or 3(x + 1).

As with addition, once a child has discovered by making patterns with real objects (or using structural apparatus) that 4×3 and 3×4 are both 12, the number of different multiplication bonds which have to be remembered is almost halved.

Teachers will find this section more valuable if they first establish what they mean by the four operations when they perform them by means of materials (that is, without resorting to written symbols). Take such suitable material as a pile of money (the basic coins, pennies, 2p, 5p, 10p would be preferable).

Separate the pile of money into two unequal heaps. Examine what operation is performed and what questions are asked when

(a) combining or adding two piles. How much have you altogether?

(b) subtracting two piles: how much more is there in one pile than the other? What must be added to one pile to make it the same as the other? These questions should then give rise to the performance of two distinct operations to find the

(c) multiplying. What do you do to find twice the amount? Three times the amount?

(d) dividing. As with subtraction there are two distinct operations depending on the nature of the questions asked.

  (i) divide (or share) the sum of money equally among four people. Must you begin with the pounds? Do you obtain the same amount if you begin with the pence? Or the 10p? How did you do this?

  (ii) to how many people could you pay 15p from your pile? How did you find the answer, using your sum of money? (or its equivalent).

In (i) the number of people is known but not the share (until you have shared out the pile). This is usually called sharing or partition.

In (ii) the share is known, but not the number of people, until you have set out the heaps of 15p. This is done by repeatedly subtracting 15p from the pile until the pile is exhausted. This is often called grouping or quotition.

It is of great importance for children to have a wide experience of the different aspects of the four operations and of the language associated with these aspects, before they meet the written symbolism. This experience should include number, weights and measures of every kind, money and capacity.

Written division presents more difficulty than the other operations, yet the situations which require the operation of division often arise in the activities of five-year-olds and should be included at frequent intervals subsequently. For example, five-year-olds can solve the following problems:

(i) *Number*

Material: a box of marbles, conkers or shells.

(*a*) share the marbles among 3, 4, ... children. (Later they can be asked: How many have you each? How many are left?)

(*b*) How many of you can have 4 marbles from this box? How many are left?

(ii) *Length*

Material: a long length of coloured ribbon, tape or braid.

(*a*) Share this among 4 children so that each has an equal share. How long is your share? (Or find a quarter of the ribbon). (Notice that folding is division and that there is no remainder in this instance).

(*b*) (A second short piece of ribbon is required.) How many pieces of ribbon of this length can you cut from the longer piece? (Later they can be asked: How many of you can have a hair ribbon 25 cm long cut from this piece? What length is left?)

iii) *Weight*

Materials: dried peas or rice.

(*a*) The sharing aspect of division is not as easy to contrive here and is more limited in scope.
Make this bag of peas into two equal bags (or four equal bags) is much less usual than

(*b*) How many 100g bags (or 50g bags) can you fill from this jar?

(iv) *Capacity*

Material: a jug of lemonade (or water), glasses.

Here again the sharing aspect of division is less easy to contrive although it does occur.

(*a*) We have all watched a number of children pouring lemonade from a bottle into glasses, trying to give fair shares.

(*b*) How many glasses can you fill from this jug? is a situation which often occurs.

(v) *Money*

Material: a collection of pennies.

Sharing and grouping are both possible here although grouping occurs more frequently.

(*a*) Share this among 6 children. What is your share? What is left?

(*b*) How much money is there in this till?

The children count the pennies in tens and set each pile of 10 aside. Every time children count money in this way they are really performing a division and answering the question:

'How many tens are there in this till?'

A simpler problem for younger children would be:

'How many children can have (for example) 5p each from this till?'

(vi) *Time*

Material: A calendar.

Again the grouping aspect of division occurs more commonly.

How many weeks were there in January? This answer will be found by counting the weeks from a calendar.

The first recordings of these experiences would be oral, but soon written recordings would be made such as:

(*a*) We shared 1 metre of ribbon between 4 children. We had 25 cm each.

(*b*) We cut three 32 cm ribbons from the piece. There was 4 cm left.

Later still the symbols $+ - \times \div$ would be introduced as a shorthand way of recording.

(*a*) would then read:

1 metre $\div$ 4 = 25 cm
and/or 25 cm $\times$ 4 = 100 cm or 1 metre

(*b*) would read:

100 cm $\div$ 32 cm = 3, 4 cm are left,
and/or 32 cm $\times$ 3 = 96, 4 cm are left.

In this way children associate the symbols for the operations with various situations long before they attempt mechanical exercises involving these operations.

There is only one way in which a teacher can find the extent of a child's number knowledge—that is by asking questions of individual children—much as she hears each individual read. This should take place at least once a month with young children and once a term with juniors. (This is also necessary for some secondary pupils.)

Teachers need to keep careful records of each child's number knowledge.

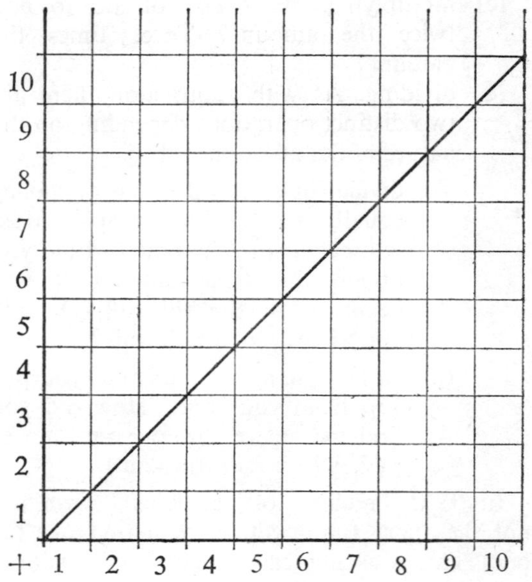

Fig. 3.3

A blank square (of the type shown in Figure 3.3) for each child's record is a quick and easy method of showing number knowledge. For example a tick (√) can be entered in the first row when a child can add and subtract 1, in the diagonal when he can double and halve, etc.

The material described in this chapter (together with the section on shapes which will be postponed until a later chapter) covers the work which most children can attempt, and the facts which they can learn, by the time they reach the age of 7 or 8. At this age, most children are ready to systemise the number relationships they have learned so far, and to learn the more difficult concept consequent upon our economical system of writing numbers: place-value. This, and other aspects of the work of the junior school, will be discussed in the next chapter.

4 Further experiences in mathematics (arithmetic)

In this chapter we shall be chiefly concerned with the development of what has been called, until recently, junior school arithmetic. Throughout, the emphasis will be on the discovery of pattern and of relationships. The underlying structure of our number system, which will emerge gradually, will be summarised at the end of the chapter.

One important objective of this chapter will be to show the place which computation should take in the mathematics of the primary school. First we must consider what we mean by 'computation'. There are two main aspects: a 'mental' agility with numbers, and written recording of the various operations and relationships. Both are important; in both there are certain facts and operations which, eventually, should be known so thoroughly that a high degree of efficiency in their use is achieved. But, as indicated in the previous chapter, such knowledge and skill must be firmly based on varied experience from which children have been able to make their own discoveries of the mathematical principles underlying the work, and must arise from the children's own attempts to record their experiences in words and symbols. Mental agility with numbers precedes written practice, and we shall try to determine the extent of number knowledge required before children are ready to profit from practice in computational processes (with particular reference to practice with 'tens and units'.)

In everyday experience many calculations are now done by machines (for example, in shops, not only in supermarkets). We must be quite clear, therefore, about out purpose in continuing to include written computational practice as a part of the primary school curriculum, as this will determine the nature and extent of this aspect of the work. There is no doubt that many young children derive pleasure from the discovery of number patterns and relationships which lead up to computation. Moreover, many calculations will need to be completed in the interesting problems which arise (or are contrived by the teacher) in the environment. But the calculations which arise from real situations will not normally involve more than two measures: for example, metres and decimetres or decimetres and centimetres or kilograms and grams, provided that the children have not been allowed to measure to an inappropriate 'degree of accuracy'. Children will therefore be faced with reasonable calculations involving the four operations, and these they ought to be able to carry out efficiently; such efficiency requires computational practice.

In Dr. Dienes's view, practice is the third stage in the learning of a concept, not the first. It is, he said, practice which fixes a concept. But there is another aspect to consider: once skill in computation has been achieved (whether in mental agility with numbers or in a written process), some systematic practice is required to maintain the skill. Two problems, therefore, to keep in mind are the timing of computational practice in order that it may be most effective, and the minimum amount of practice required to maintain efficiency.

The ground covered in this chapter will be that normally included in the arithmetic of the primary school. In brief, this comprises the operations of addition, subtraction, multiplication and division, applied to number, money and weights and measures of all kinds. The aim throughout, in the organisation and extension of the number relationships already learnt, and in the learning of written computational processes, will be to show the possibilities of discovery by the children themselves; illustrations of children learning in this way will be given wherever possible. For the purposes of this chapter it will be assumed that children have reached the stage described as desirable in the previous chapter; that they have, for example, a working knowledge of the number trios up to 20 and can recall these, in practical circumstances, without difficulty. In practice, probably about 80 to 90 per cent of the children should be able to achieve this facility in number relationships; up to 20 per cent would achieve less than this (a few might know the number trios as far as 5 only), while 20 per cent (included in the 90 per cent) would achieve more, and a few considerably more. Here, in more detail, is an outline of the concepts which will be considered in this chapter. As will be seen from the examples of children's work given throughout, the order is not necessarily significant. Some of the topics which appear later in the list can be understood by young children through first-hand experience.

I. Number relationships
   (1) *Extension of number knowledge to include numbers between 20 and 100.*
   (2) *The four operations: addition, subtraction, multiplication and division applied to numbers. Secure knowledge of number trios. Multiplication and division tables.*
   (3) *Place value number bases other than 10.*

II. Children's own problems
   Computational practice and story arithmetic.

III. Applications of the number system to the real world:
   (1) *Measurement.*
   (2) *Averages.*
   (3) *Ratio, proportion, and rate.*
   (4) *Simple statistics.*

IV. Extension of ideas of number:
   (1) *Fractions.*
   (2) *Decimal fractions.*
   (3) *Directed and negative numbers.*

V. Applications of those extensions to the real world:
   Percentages.

VI. A new look at numbers: sets. (See Appendix 4.)

VII. Summary of the laws of arithmetic.

I. Number relationships

EXTENSION OF NUMBER KNOWLEDGE

The next step, therefore, would be the extension of this number knowledge to include the numbers between 20 and 100. The following example illustrates the kind of experience which leads children to discover the number patterns and relationships within this range. In a class of fifty seven-year-olds one boy was outstanding in his quick response when asked to add and subtract numbers less than 100. For example, when he was asked to add 9 and 7 he gave the answer, 16, immediately; for 19 and 7, however, there was a pause before the answer, 26, was given. The boy explained, when questioned, that he had counted on in ones from 19 to find the answer. Fixed horizontally to the walls of the crowded classroom was the piece of structural apparatus to which reference was made in the previous chapter. This was a number strip, 100 units long, and strips 1 unit to 10 units in length, made by the teacher herself. The boy was asked to use the strips to verify his answers to 9 + 7 and 19 + 7. This done, he turned away from the strip and was asked to add 29 and 7. Again there was a pause, suggesting that he was counting on in ones, before the answer, 36, was given. Once more the boy was asked to check his answer using the strips. The questioning continued, step by step: 39 + 7, 49 + 7 and so on. Each time the boy was asked to give his answer before verifying this by using the strips. Each time he admitted that he counted on from the larger number to find the answer, until he reached 89 + 7. At this, his face lit up and he said: 'I don't need to count any more; I know. It's 96'. For the first time this boy had seen the pattern of his responses: 16, 26, 36, 46 .... Because he was very intelligent, this boy was able, at this stage, to make an abstraction, for when asked to add 8 and 3 he replied: '11, and now I can tell you 18 + 3, and 28 + 3, and 58 + 3 and 88 + 3 without counting on'.

Most children would need far more experience of this kind, with different pairs of numbers, before they would accept the result as universal. Some children might need to be asked a more direct question about the unit numeral before they could discover the repeating pattern of the numbers. All children need similar experience leading to the discovery of the pattern obtained (1) when one number is subtracted from another as, for example, 15 − 8, 25 − 8, 35 − 8, etc. and (2) when simple numbers are multiplied and divided. (For example: what are three sevens? How many sevens are there in 50? Find a quarter of 50.) These are all problems which can be solved by using the number strips.

When children can give an immediate answer to questions like 68 + 6 they need further experience with pairs of two-figure numbers, such as 68 + 26, 38 + 46, and so on until these, too, can be performed mentally by an efficient method (that is, without counting on in ones at any stage). For example, to add 68 and 26, some may add the tens first, 80, the units next, 14, and give the answer: 94. Others may add the units first and tens second. Some add 68 and 20, 88, and then add 6: 94. Now if at the last step they count on in ones from 88, this is not an efficient method and it usually means that the child is not yet ready to benefit from practice in two-figure addition (tens and units). This then, is a crucial test of readiness for practice in written computation with tens and units: the ability to add two 2-figure numbers mentally by an efficient method. To achieve this, children need a secure knowledge of place value since they have to be able to discriminate between the tens and units in the numbers added.

The following example illustrates the difficulties encountered when young children are given practice in written computation before they are ready for it. A seven-year-old boy who was doing a piece of practical work of his own choosing required to add 32 and 16. Without writing he said aloud '2 and 6, that's 8: 3 and 1, that's 4. That's 48'. An eight-year-old standing beside him, who had had a year's experience of learning by his own discoveries, corrected him, saying, 'You don't mean 3 and 1, you mean 30 and 10 make 40'. It cannot be over-emphasised that if children are given written computation of this kind to do before they are ready for it, this is not only a waste of time but can be harmful because such children are forced to use inefficient 'counting on' or 'counting back' methods which, unless discovered, may persist for the rest of their lives. Many adults and school children (primary and secondary), among them some very intelligent ones, never lose the habit of counting in ones when asked to perform a piece of computation. This is often unsuspected by the teacher and can only be revealed when the child is asked to work an example such as 37 + 25 aloud. Very often, too, some of the basic number trios are not known so that the child has a double difficulty to deal with which can only be resolved by inefficient counting methods.

Addition and Subtraction

Once children have acquired this facility with numbers, however, they are ready to benefit from written practice in addition and subtraction, first with tens and units and then with larger numbers as they come to extend their number knowledge to numbers greater than 100. Two points should be kept in mind: that written computational practice should supplement and not replace oral practice; and that it is a waste of time to give children more written practice in any one process than they require to maintain efficiency. Written subtraction presents more difficulty but here considerable flexibility of method needs to be allowed. When adults have to solve a problem in subtraction, more often than not they work this by 'Complementary addition' (or shop-keeper's addition) rather than by pure subtraction. This is often the most convenient method. Young children usually solve their real problems in the same way: by addition rather than by subtraction. When they do use the subtraction method (discovered by themselves in a real situation) they always use 'decomposition' or breaking down the next highest unit. It is most improbable that a child (or, indeed, an adult) would *discover* the sophisticated method of 'equal additions' when solving a real problem. But, once he has invented the method of decomposition for himself in a real situation, and recorded it in his own way, this can quite easily be related to the written method of decomposition. Indeed, the child's own recording may be coincident with the written method of decomposition. Similarly, when children are using structural apparatus for subtraction, the methods they discover and use for themselves are complementary addition and decomposition. Both methods, addition and decomposition, should be allowed, depending on the problem under consideration. (It is doubtful whether it is wise to introduce 'equal additions' since a child would have to be shown this method and could only verify and not discover it.)[1]

[1] See *The Teaching of Mathematics in the Primary School*, Mathematical Association, 1955.

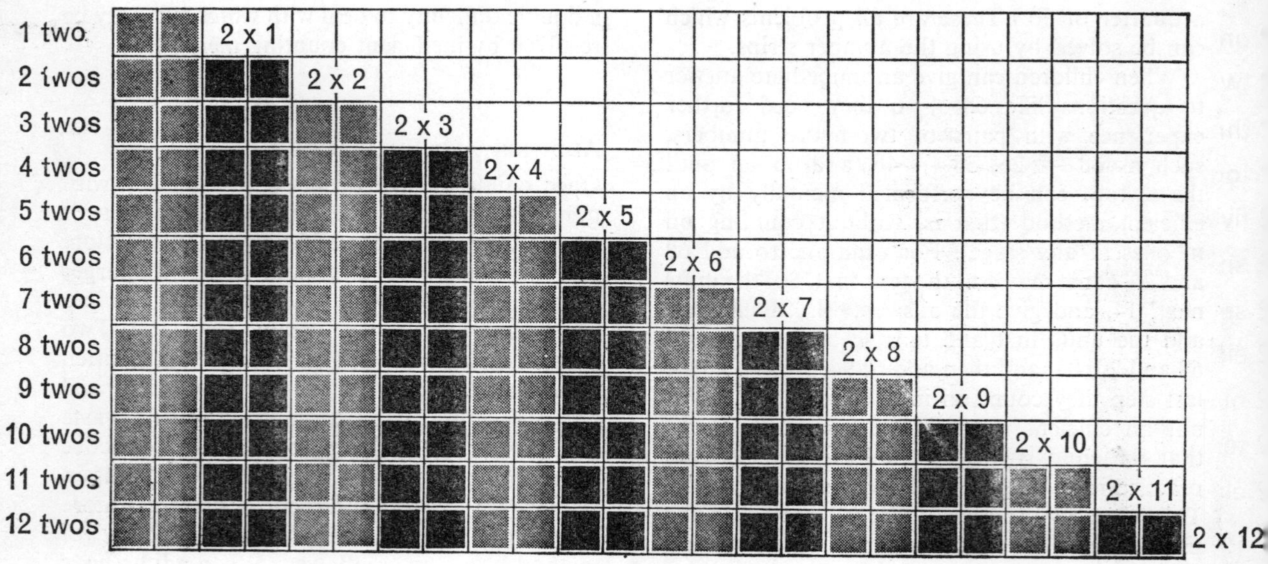

Fig. 4.1

There are two written methods of subtraction which children can be helped to devise for themselves.

1. *By addition*

(i) 62—27

```
      27 >  3
      30 > 32
      62
62—27 = 35
```

(ii) 343—158

```
       158 >   2
       160 >  40
       200 > 143
       343
343—158 = 185
```

2. *By decomposition*

(i)

```
  62   is recorded as 50+12
 —27                  20+ 7
                      ------
                      30+ 5→35
```

(ii)

```
  343→300+30+13  →200+130+13
 —158 100+50+ 8   100+ 50+ 8
                  ----------
                  100+ 80+ 5→185
```

Multiplication and Division Tables

The readiness test previously described is an important landmark in other ways also. For example, before children reach this stage, it is a sheer waste of time to try to get them to learn 'multiplication tables'. This does not mean that they will not understand the operation of multiplication. This understanding will have been based on a wide experience of multiplication (and division) at work in real situations. Nor does it mean that children will not know any of the multiplication facts. For example, they will certainly know, from first-hand experience, 'doubles' and 'halves' of numbers far in excess of 12 (why do we stop at 12?).

But it does mean that it is a waste of time to get children to learn multiplication facts systematically before they have achieved the facility with addition and subtraction implied by the readiness test. For example, if a child needs to know six 3s and already knows that five 3s are 15, provided that he understands what the operation of multiplication means, he will know that he must add another 3 to 15. But if he does not know that 15 + 3 = 18 without counting on in

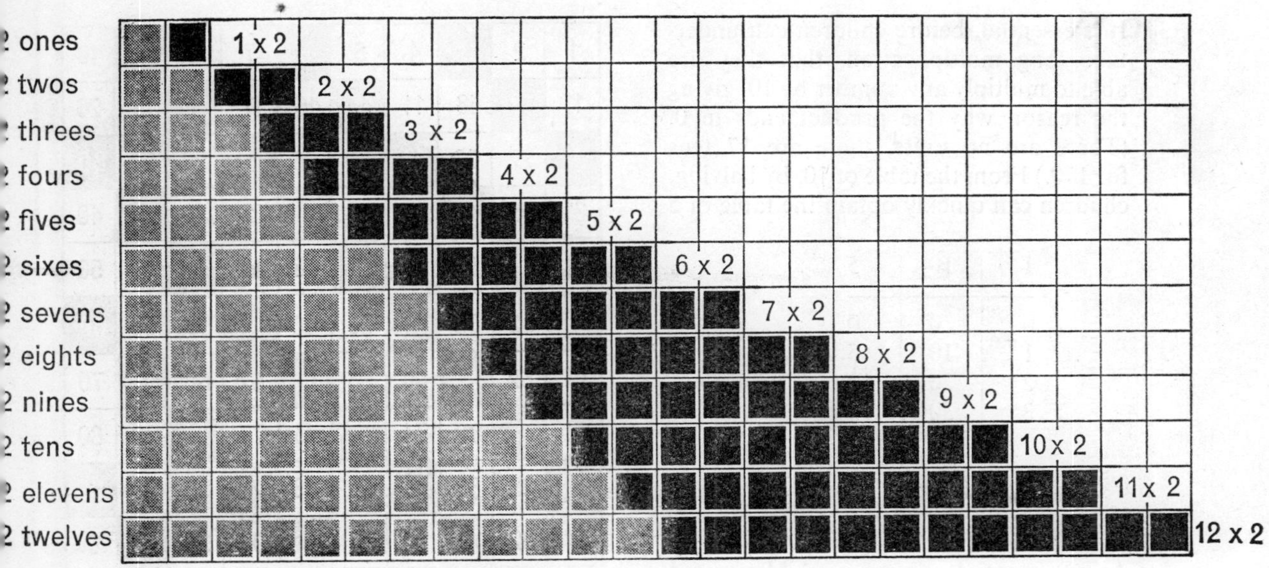

Fig. 4.2

ones, he will be forced to count on to find the answer and may establish a habit of counting on. If teachers wait until children are ready, the learning of the multiplication facts will not be a burden.

Assuming then that children have reached this stage, we are now faced with the problem of finding the best way of committing the multiplication facts to memory. This will vary from child to child, so no one way could be designated as the most effective.

Structural apparatus can be a valuable aid at this stage in the visualising and building up of the tables. Often a teacher can judge a child's progress from the way in which he is handling structural material but this does not obviate the need for discussion with the child.

The teacher needs to make sure, at this stage, that the child has discovered the commutative law of multiplication and uses it. In multiplication, as in addition, the order of the operation does not matter; 3 times 4 and 4 times 3 both give the same answer. The use of some kind of structural material (commercial or made by the teacher) is valuable in helping children to discover this law.

The following is a summary of experiences devised by teachers to facilitate the learning of the multiplication facts.

(i) *Related groups of tables*

(1) Children need to be able to double (and halve) numbers up to 50. From this they can obtain the multiplication tables of 4 and 8. Children can sometimes be asked to write tables in the following form:

1	2	4	8
0	0	0	0
1	2	4	8
2	4	8	16
3	6	12	24
4	8	16	32
5	10	20	40
.	.	.	.
.	.	.	.
.	.	.	.

(2) From the first and second columns, by addition, the table of 3s can be obtained:

1	2	3
0	0	0
1	2	3
2	4	6
3	6	9
4	8	12
.	.	.
.	.	.
.	.	.

(3) It is essential, before children can undertake long multiplication, that they are able to multiply any number by 10, giving the reason why the product ends in 0. (There are no units, there are 17 tens for 170.) From the table of 10, by halving, children can quickly obtain the table of 5

1	10	5
0	0	0
1	10	5
2	20	10
3	30	15
.	.	.
.	.	.
.	.	.

As an essential minimum, children need to know the tables of 2, 3, 10. From these, other tables can be obtained. They should also know the square of numbers up to the square of 10.

1	2	**3**	4	5	**6**	7	8	**9**	10
11	**12**	13	14	**15**	16	17	**18**	19	20
21	22	23	**24**	25	26	**27**	28	29	**30**
31	32	**33**	34	35	**36**	37	38	**39**	40
41	**42**	43	44	**45**	46	47	**48**	49	50
51	52	53	**54**	55	56	**57**	58	59	**60**
61	62	**63**	64	65	**66**	67	68	**69**	70
71	**72**	73	74	**75**	76	77	**78**	79	80
81	82	83	**84**	85	86	**87**	88	89	**90**
91	92	**93**	94	95	**96**	97	98	**99**	100

Fig. 4.3A

(ii) *Building tables by means of a graph*

This can be done at first with real objects, then as a block graph on squared paper. Structural apparatus can be very useful at this stage. Finally the multiplication tables can appear in the third or fourth year as relationship graphs as will be seen in Chapter 6.

The commutative law emerges in an interesting way where block graphs are being made of the multiplication tables: Fig. 4.1 and 4.2.

(iii) Marking in the number pattern on the 100 square. The children can discover that all the multiplication tables form some regular pattern on this square. (Fig. 4.3A and 4.3B).

This provides opportunities for asking questions such as:

12 How many 3s?
How many 4s?
How many 2s?
How many 6s? and so on.
How many factors?

1	2	3	4	5	6	**7**	8	9	10
11	12	13	**14**	15	16	17	18	19	20
21	22	23	24	25	26	27	**28**	29	30
31	32	33	34	**35**	36	37	38	39	40
41	**42**	43	44	45	46	47	48	**49**	50
51	52	53	54	55	**56**	57	58	59	60
61	62	**63**	64	65	66	67	68	69	**70**
71	72	73	74	75	76	**77**	78	79	80
81	82	83	**84**	85	86	87	88	89	90
91	92	93	94	95	96	97	**98**	99	100

Fig. 4.3B

(iv) The sieve of Eratosthenes is very useful at a later stage (Fig. 4.4).

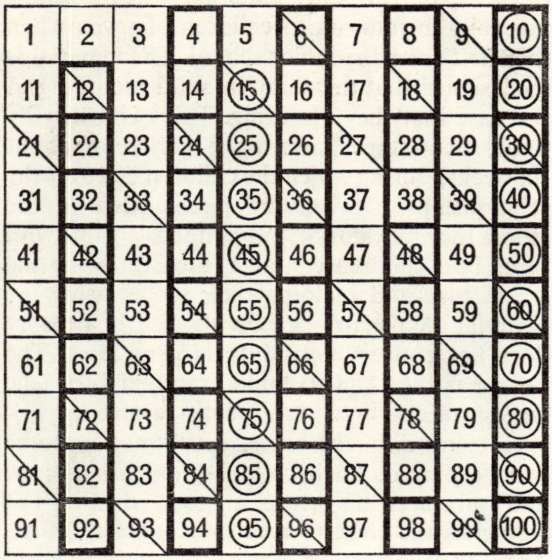

Fig. 4.4

Beginning with 2, the square containing each multiple of 2 (except 2 itself) is outlined (and must drop through the sieve). The next 'free' number is 3. Mark off all other multiples of 3. (If a different colour is used the factors of any number in the square can be seen at a glance—for example 6 = 2 times 3). These also drop through the sieve. The next free number is 5, then 7, then 11 and so on. At the end the numbers without factors are left unmarked and so the prime numbers, (and the factors of other numbers) can be seen.

Certain numbers, particularly 9 and 11, have interesting properties which fascinate children, give them much systematic practice in the four operations, and provide them with exciting opportunities for discovery. An example will illustrate this. Some eight-year-olds were asked to start counting in nines from 0 (the nine times table.) They were then asked to write the sum of the digits for each and to continue until, counting in nines, they topped 100. When they saw the pattern they were anxious to go on far beyond 108 to see whether the sum of the digits was always the same. (When 18 is obtained from 99, children can soon be encouraged to continue until they obtain a single digit). A ten-year-old boy who had found difficulty with the nine times table overcame this immediately once he had discovered that the sum of the digits of this table is always 9. He knew that six 9s were fifty-something and this enabled him to determine the last figure.

Number	*Sum of digits*
0	0
9	9
18	9
27	9
36	9
45	9
54	9
63	9
72	9
81	9
90	9
99	18
108	9

The patterns of eleven also fascinate children. Teachers are recommended to study some of the books of recreation suggested in Appendix 1 for other number discoveries.

(vi) Practice is required to fix multiplication facts, and a variety of methods is in use. It is at this stage that number games have a place. (It is important that number games should not be introduced at a stage when they would force children to use inefficient counting methods.) The clock method, in which the numbers 1 to 12 are written in any order 'round the clock' and the multiplier is put in the centre, and a group of children is asked to give responses as the teacher moves round the numbers, is still a favourite. At this stage, too, when some children require practice and some kind of incentive to make the effort to memorise the multiplication facts, games such as 'Snap' or 'Lotto' can sometimes supply the incentive. For 'Snap', cards would have such labels as 7 times 6, 42, 8 times 7, 56, 42 divided by 6, 7, 3 × 9, 27, 12 ÷ 2, 6, etc. Similar games can be devised. Such games, however, have a limited value and must not be introduced too early.

Place-value

As already indicated in the previous chapter the children will have had some experiences leading to an understanding of our number system. But the full significance of place-value will be realised only gradually and, at subsequent stages, attention needs to be focussed on place value to ensure that this is fully understood. The stages at which this should be done depend not only on the child's development but also on the kind of experiences devised.

Some teachers focus attention on the economy of our own number system by giving children (at seven or eight) opportunities of working with systems of recording numbers used by peoples in ancient times. In many cases the children are able to record numbers in a practical way, using materials resembling those used in the past, as, for example, the Babylonians with their notches in clay; the Egyptians with their single strokes and symbols on papyrus using a quill; the Chinese with their single strokes and symbols made with a brush; the Romans with the symbols that children have already met on clock faces and on buildings.

One teacher introduced children aged nine to calculations in other bases using inch cubes. For example, working in base 3:

3 unit cubes	make 1 rod (3 units)
3 rods (each of 3 units)	make 1 square (3^2 units)
3 squares (each of 9 units)	make 1 big cube (3^3 units)

The children were very quick at converting any number from our decimal system to a number in base 3. e.g. 5, 11.

Number in base 3

3^3	3^2	3	U	Decimal system
		1	2	5
	1	0	2	11
1	0	1	0	30

Fig. 4.5

Dr. Dienes's multi-base arithmetic blocks give structural experience with different bases (3, 4, 5, 6, 10). This material, when used, is normally introduced to children of seven when they first enter the junior school. The material is so designed that the children build according to the base that they are using. There is a lengthy initial play stage (covering a period of about six weeks) during which the children discover the relationships between the pieces. One of the games they play during this period is a game with dice. Two children compete, each throwing the die in turn and building their scores using the material. A penalty can be claimed if a player does not convert units into larger pieces. The winner is the child to build exactly a cube (the largest piece) first. After considerable experience using different bases, a subtraction game can be played. Each child begins with a cube and subtracts his score at each throw. The winner is the child to reach zero (exactly) first. They then enter on the stage of 'structural games' when they work and record their results in writing. The structural games include the applications of the four operations using the material. The children discover, in this way, the implications of place value. When, for example, they are 'counting in fives' they soon realise that 5 units can be exchanged for 'one rod' and can therefore be placed in the next column on the left. They are in fact writing 5 units as follows:

rods (5 units)	Units
1	0

This operation is continued for 5 rods (25 units) can be exchanged for 1 square and 5 squares (125 units) for 1 cube. For example:

cubes	squares	rods	units
2	3	4	3

would represent

$2(125 \text{ or } 5^3) + 3(25 \text{ or } 5^2) + 4(5) + 3$ units.

In other words, the greatest number of objects there will be in any column, when working in fives, will be four. The greatest number in any column, when working in threes, will be two; when counting in sixes, the greatest number will be five; when working in tens, the greatest number will be nine. The material also focuses attention on the use of zero in its most important function as a place-holder. (The symbol for zero was first invented to fulfil this function.) When, for example, the child records.

1 (5) 0 units the 0 is a place-holder.

But valuable as this structural experience is, the same experience can also be given in other ways: for example, with an abacus. Dr. Dienes himself recommends the use of the abacus as one step in the transition from structural apparatus to computation performed without the use of structural apparatus. Suppose, for example, two children are to have experience of 'counting in fives'. An abacus with two sets of four rungs would be needed, one set for each child. In the first instance coloured rings would be used, one colour for each unit. For example, blue for single units, red for 5s, yellow for 25s (5 squared), green for 125s (5 cubed), although rings of one colour will serve and later should be used. The children can use dice with numbers 0 to 4 on their faces (0, 1, 1, 2, 3, 4). After each throw they record their score on their own rungs of the abacus, adding each score to the previous total. For example, if the first throw is 3 and the second 4, the record will be as shown in Fig. 4.6

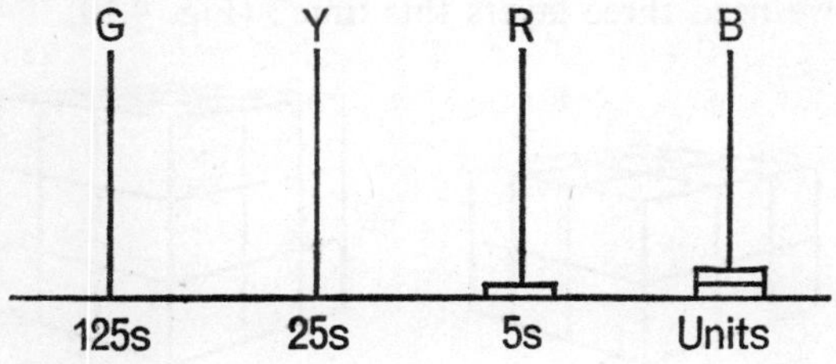

Fig. 4.6

because as soon as there are five rings on the unit rung these are replaced by 1 (red) ring on the next and so on. Various targets may be set. For example, the winner might be the child with the greatest score in a certain time, the first to obtain 1 ring on each rung, the first to obtain 1 on the highest rung, etc. Practice with any base can be given by means of the abacus, including the base in use in computers (binary or two) and the base ten. Later subtraction games can be played. Children soon find that they can work in bases other than ten without using the abacus.

Another activity, for third- and fourth-year juniors, is counting a group (e.g. 48 beans) successfully in different bases, e.g. 5, 4, 3, 2. For example, in base 5, the children will first count in 5s, then in 5 groups of 5 (25). The result will be recorded:

25	5	1
1	4	3

In base 4

16	4	1	
?	?	?	etc.

Each time the child checks by counting his recorded result to a base 10 number.

A group of ten-year-olds were so excited by working with bases other than 10 that they each chose a base and re-wrote the mechanical sums (in the four rules) from a text book used by the seven-year-olds, each in his own base. These were set as puzzles for their fellows.

The binary system is of great importance because of its use in computers. But the binary system is also important in all growth and decay.

× 2
←

... 32 16 8 4 2 1

Each cell divides into 2 cells. Each of this pair then divides into 2 cells and so on. The multiplying or growth factor is 2. A great variety of patterns will be found in different examples of natural growth: number of veins in a leaf, spirals in plants and shells, growth of animals (linear, foot area, weight).

Another activity for some older juniors is to make tables showing the equivalents of numbers in base 10 in various bases e.g. 2, 3, 4, 5 and 10. (A long strip of centimetre graph paper would be convenient for this.) They can then place the tables in order, side by side, to study the patterns. Here is the start of base 4:

64	16	4	1	Base 10 numbers
			0	0
			1	1
			2	2
			3	3
		1	0	4
		1	1	5
		1	2	6
		1	3	7
		2	0	8

Here, then, are parts of the sequence of the number systems we have mentioned:

1000	100	10	1	base 10
125	25	5	1	base 5
64	16	4	1	base 4
27	9	3	1	base 3
8	4	2	1	base 2

These can be written in various forms and extended in both directions e.g. base 2

$$\times 2 \longrightarrow$$
$$\longleftarrow$$
$$16 \quad 8 \quad 4 \quad 2 \quad 1 \;\Big|\; \tfrac{1}{2} \quad \tfrac{1}{4} \quad \tfrac{1}{8}$$
$$\longrightarrow$$
$$\div 2$$

In base 2, $0{\cdot}1 = \frac{1}{2}$, $0{\cdot}01 = \frac{1}{4}$, etc.
or the sequence can be written

	$2\times2\times2\times2$	$2\times2\times2$	2×2	2	1
or	2^4	2^3	2^2	2^1	2^0
	$\frac{1}{2}$	$\frac{1}{2\times2}$	$\frac{1}{2\times2\times2}$		
or	2^{-1}	2^{-2}	2^{-3}		

Some older juniors would find the pattern and continue this for themselves. Index notation is used in abbreviations in the metric system and knowledge that $10 \times 10 \times 10$ can be written as 10^3 and 10×10 as 10^2 will help children to understand why cubic centimetre is abbreviated to cm^3 and square centimetre to cm^2.

Long Multiplication and Division

Once children know their multiplication facts they are ready for computational practice to fix these facts. Multiplication with multipliers up to 10 is the first step. Long multiplication, in which the multiplier consists of a number of two or three figures, needs more careful preparation but here, too, children can (and should) discover the recording process for themselves, as the following example will show. The incident occurred in a rural school in a class of 28 children of ages seven and eight years.

On the mathematics table were two boxes, each containing eight 1 inch cubes. It was evident, from conversation with the children, that they understood what a cube was. A small group of girls was asked to make a cube whose edge was 2 inches. They first made one layer, using 4 cubes to make a square base of 2 inch edge, 1 inch high (Fig. 4.7).

They seemed quite satisfied with this until the teacher inclined her head to look at the height. The girls then followed suit and one said: 'Of course, we need another layer', at which they put four small cubes on top of the first layer to complete their cube of 2 inch edge (Fig. 4.12).

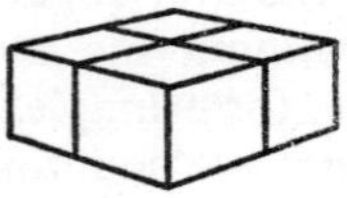

Fig. 4.7

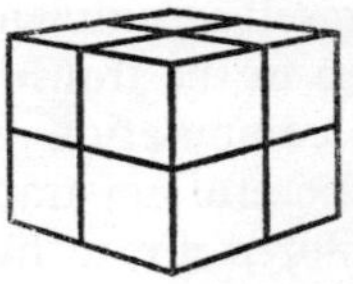

Fig. 4.8

They were then asked to make a cube whose edge was 3 inches. At once one of the group said, 'We haven't enough cubes, I'll get some more'. When this girl returned the group set to work to make the 3 inch cube. They used 9 cubes to make the square base of edge 3 inches and, determined not to make a mistake this time, they immediately added another layer of 9 cubes, making two layers in all (Fig. 4.9). At first they seemed satisfied with this, until one girl looked at the height and said, 'Of course, we need three layers this time'. (Fig. 4.10).

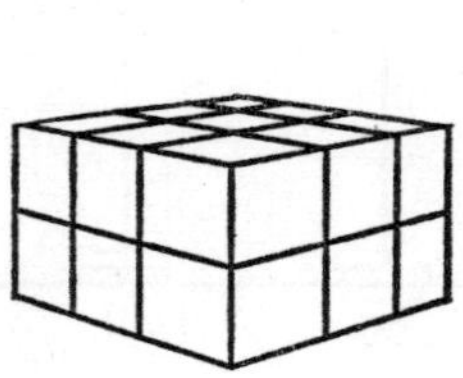

Fig. 4.9

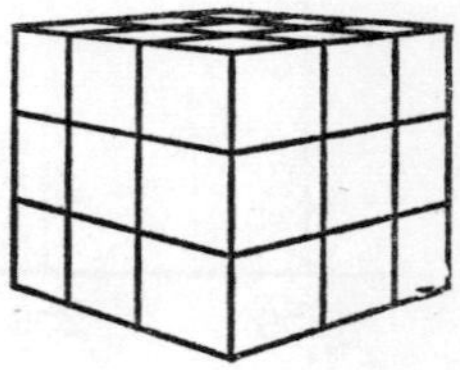

Fig. 4.10

The girls were then asked if they could make a cube whose edge was 4 inches. At first they were silent, then one girl said, 'You know what you are asking us; you are asking us our 16 times table, and we don't know that'. When she was asked how many layers of 16 cubes they would need she replied, 'Four 16s'. After some persuasion the girls agreed that, although they did not know their 16 times table, they could work out four 16s, 'If you give us time'. The first answer given was 54, but this was immediately corrected by another girl who said that it must be 64 because it was four 10s and four 6s which make 64. After this success the girls were asked if they could find the answer to 17 times 16.

Not unnaturally they asked for some paper. They said (each at their different stages):

	16 × 17
Ten sixteens	16 × 10 = 160
Seven sixteens	16 × 7 = 112

(They worked this as seven tens and seven sixes.)

Then they added, and obtained 16 × 17 = 272. With very little direction these girls had discovered the method of long multiplication for themselves. Here was nothing they did not understand and nothing they might forget, because they had invented a method for themselves.

Since then, some teachers have succeeded in encouraging children to discover a method of long division for themselves. In one example the problem of division arose when the children (aged eight) wanted to find the number of weeks there were in 137 days. A group undertook to find the answer. One boy began by subtracting 7 successively. Another began by subtracting 70 because he knew this was the number of days in 10 weeks. He wrote:

137	
70	10 weeks
67	
63	9 weeks
4	19 weeks
days	

137 days are 19 weeks 4 days

This boy's method, with a little refinement, led him to the usual method of long division. Each child in the group worked the problem in his own way. Some used more efficient methods than others. Each explained his method to the group and there was a general discussion to decide whose method was the best. By this time the group was thoroughly prepared for the next problem the teacher set them. There had been a boxing match the night before and she drew their attention to the weights of the boxers which had been given in pounds. She asked them whether their fathers weighed more than the boxer who weighed 160 lb. The children solved this in various ways. One boy subtracted 112 lbs. because he knew this was a hundred-weight, or 8 stones, and then subtracted 28 and 14 successively. Another first subtracted 140 lb.

1st boy

lb.	
160	
112	8 stones
48	
28	2 stones
20	
14	1 stone
6	11 stones
lb.	

2nd boy

lb.	
160	
140	10 stones
20	
14	1 stone
6	11 stones

He weighed 11 stones 6 lb.

Again this method is close to the normal method so that when the group of children was asked to work a more difficult problem, involving the division of 4,000 by 72, they tackled this with confidence. The problem had been made up by a nine-year-old boy. 'A burglar broke into a sweet shop and stole 4,000 sweets. Could he carry these away himself or did he need a mate'? After much discussion the children weighed a $\frac{1}{4}$ lb. of fruit drops and found that there were 18 sweets in a $\frac{1}{4}$ lb. and therefore 72 sweets in one lb. One girl subtracted 720 successively and then 72, until she had discovered the weight of the stolen sweets. A boy refined this method by subtracting 40 times 72 or 2,880, then 720 and so on. He eventually decided he could have subtracted 50 times 72 straightaway and wrote:

Boy

4,000	
3,600	50 times 72
400	
288	4 times 72
112	
72	1 times 72
40	55 times 72

Teacher

	55	
72	4,000	
	3,600	50 times 72
	400	
	360	5 times 72
	40	

4,000 sweets weigh more than 55 lb.

At this stage the teacher showed the boy the usual way of working long division with a refinement which he appreciated. (Since the teacher was able to lift this boy, who weighed 4 stones, the boy decided a burglar could easily carry the sweets unaided.)

Teachers are urged to provide similar opportunities for the children they teach so that all may have the advantage of first attempting a solution for themselves. It cannot be over-emphasised that, provided the children's first attempts at written computation are made as records of their own experience, when an efficient method is eventually reached, far less practice will be required to attain and maintain efficiency in this process.

II. Children's own problems

Once the stage has been reached when children are fully aware of the implications of our place-value number system, and are also confident in the computational processes, they usually show a tendency to enjoy the use of large numbers, introducing them for the sheer pleasure of working with them. When given the opportunity to invent problems for themselves (they will often do this of their own accord) they frequently produce problems of greater interest than those they are set. For example, a class of ten-year-olds was asked to find any interesting fact and to make a problem about this fact. (These problems were collected in a book called 'Fact and Fancy' which contained problems of special interest; the large majority involved very large numbers). One boy wrote: Fact: 'The sun is 93 million miles from the earth. Fancy: how long would a man, running at a speed of 1 mile in 4 minutes, take to run to the sun'?

The boy worked the problem and found the answer to be 707 years, 278 days, 8 hours (sic), and wrote: 'But he would have been dead long before that'.

Another group of ten-year-olds set out to find the number of grains of wheat demanded by the inventor of the game of chess who asked, as his reward, for 1 grain of wheat on the first square of the chessboard, 2 on the second, 4 on the third, and so on, doubling the number on the previous square until the 64th square was reached. The children were not daunted by the problem but, as the number they obtained was so unexpectedly large, they decided to have this checked by a computer. It was six months before they received the answer, and they wrote 'We got our answer right but the computer took longer than we did'. They also determined the necessary length of a granary to store the wheat if it were a mile wide and a mile high. They found that it would stretch for 200 miles.

There are two fairly simple methods of finding out whether children at this stage (between seven and ten) understand computational processes when they are given these to do. These are: writing a story to embody a given piece of computation, and doing a piece of computation in several different ways. In fact these methods may precede (as well as accompany) the practice stage.

The two pieces of written work which follow describe and illustrate these methods. Both were written by girls at schools in Staffordshire. The first was written by an able girl of ten. The second was written by a girl of I.Q. just over 80.

1. Story Arithmetic

At the end of every sum we write a story, no matter what kind of sum, add, subtract, divide or multiply. It has to be a sensible story to describe the numbers we have used.

Just setting numbers down as numbers means nothing, but writing a story makes them mean something. For example, $46 - 8 + 7 = 45$, that means nothing, but if I write a story and say that 46 people were on a bus, 8 people got off and 7 people got on the bus and there were 45 people then on the bus, that means something. We have had some very funny examples in our class sometimes. One pupil said two children weighed themselves on the scales, one weighed 3 lb. 8 oz. and the other child weighed 4 lb. 9 oz., altogether they weighed 8 lb. 1 oz., and our teacher wrote on this person's book: 'What clever babies'! Now, if you write a story like that you cannot understand the meaning of the sum[1]. You know how to do the sum but you do not know why you did it. Two years ago it would just be another sum in the Mechanical Book IV, but now that sum has a meaning for us. If you know you have to write a story at the end of the sum, you are thinking of the story as you do the sum, so it makes sense. Besides writing stories about sums, sometimes we also explain how we have done a sum, and do the sum in as many different ways as we can.

[1] What the girl did not appreciate was that such a story sum showed lack of experience with real situations and not lack of understanding.

2. Ways of Multiplying

2s. 11d. × 6 = 17s. 6d.

The first way: [2/-] + [11d.] × 6 =

2s. 0d. × 6 =	12s. 0d.
11d. × 6 =	5s. 6d.
	17s. 6d.

The fourth way:

s.	d.
2	11
2	11
2	11
2	11
2	11
2	11
17	6
5	66

My Story

One day my father went to put 2s. 11d. on a horse and the man times it by 6. So there was 17s. 6d. to come back to my Dad because the horse won. I don't like this story because my Dad would put 3s. 0d. on a horse, not 2s. 11d.

For 2s. 11d. I could get a pair of stockings but I don't want six pairs at once so that would be silly. I have seen a cake for 2s. 11d. and I could buy six for my party. The last way I added it takes long. I couldn't have multiplied 2s. 11d. + 2s. 11d., + 3s. 11d., but they were all 2s. 11d. so I could.

The last example shows, without a shadow of doubt, that the second girl had complete insight into the operation of multiplication. It also underlines the need to allow flexibility of method. This is not to say that children should not know one efficient method of performing each kind of operation but it does mean that, in the learning stage, variety of method may help towards understanding. Therefore children should be encouraged sometimes to solve a problem (and even a piece of computation) in a variety of ways.

Discussion of the methods used would of course follow to focus attention on the most efficient methods.

III. Applications of the number system to the real world

1. Measurement

Experience with money, weight and measures will continue throughout the junior school, experiences increasing in scope and variety. In general, very rarely are more than two successive units used in real situations. A gram does not normally matter to an elephant and probably a kilogram does not matter either! The experiences involving measurement which are devised by the teacher for the children should, therefore, serve to illustrate the distinction between a count (made in answer to a question such as: How many children are there in this class? pencils in this box? children in the school?) and a measurement (made in answer to a question such as: Is this room a square? How heavy are you? What is the difference in weight between the lightest and the heaviest in the class?). The children need experience of the widest possible range of measuring instruments. For example, in length, they need to find the width of thin things like a post card and a sheet of paper, as well as finding longer lengths such as the distance across the playground, the distance they walk to school, the distance to the next town, the distance to London and the distance round the Equator. From such experiences children will come to realise that there is an appropriate unit for the different ranges of lengths and that to give an answer involving kilometres and centimetres is not usually sensible. They can only discover this through their own personal experiences. Similar experiences can be planned for weight, for time, etc. Too many questions in selection tests have been set involving days, hours and minutes or hours, minutes and seconds!

These varied experiences should cover the operations of addition, subtraction, multiplication and division. There is no reason why all of these experiences should be real, once the children show that they understand fully what they are doing. They will then, of course, require some problem practice and computational practice to fix the concepts and to maintain facility.

Before passing on to other important mathematical ideas which can arise out of children's real experience with weights and measures, we include a sequence of events which took place

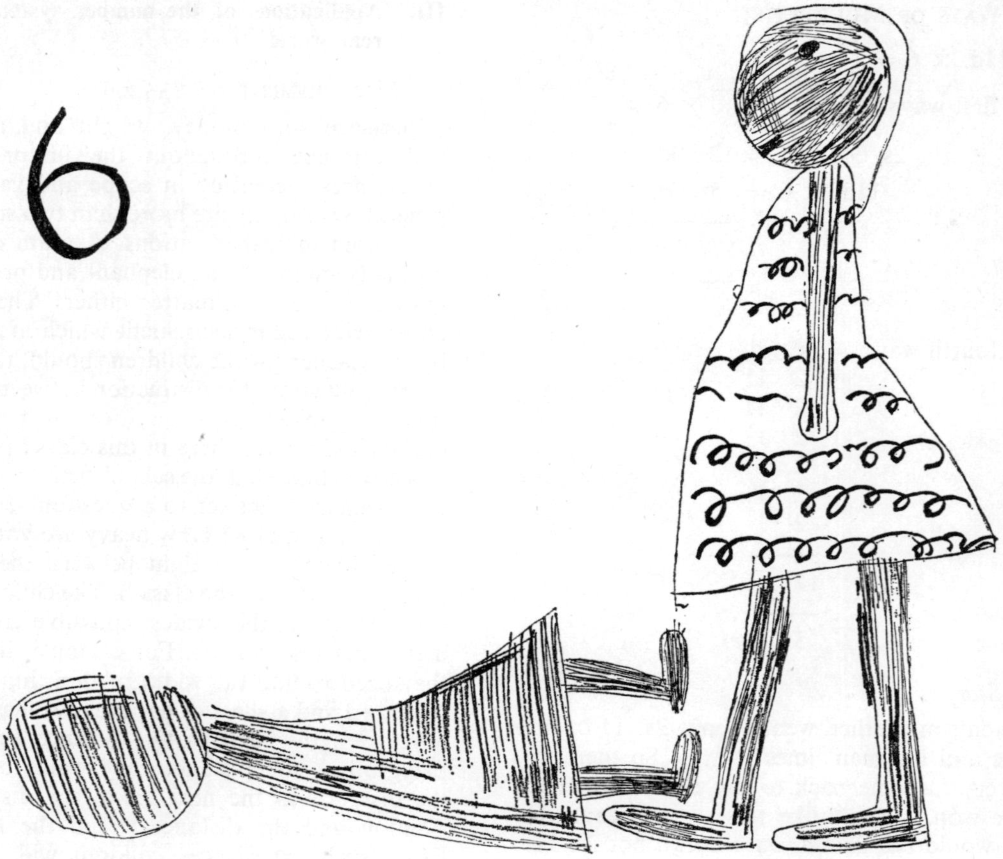

Fig. 4.11

with children of different ages concerned with the same topic: 'shadows'. This sequence is important because it shows how the same topic, tackled by children of very different ages, will be pursued as far as the children's abilities and development allow, provided the teacher gives the right kind of encouragement and guidance.

The first example occurred with some young five-year-olds who had been chasing their shadows one day. Noticing their interest their teacher suggested that they should chalk in the shadow of a pole in the playground at each hour during the day. At nine o'clock they all watched one boy draw a line along the shadow. They then chose two boys to draw the shadow at ten o'clock. An hour later the teacher was hearing a girl read when she was disturbed by an angry voice saying: 'You moved it'. 'Moved what?' she asked. Ignoring the question the angry voice repeated: 'You moved it. I'm going to sit here and watch you for an hour so that you can't move it next time'. With some concealed amusement the teacher collected the children together and they sat in the sunshine for some time. watching the shadow of the stick move. At this stage wisely she did no more.

A six-year-old girl made the following record:

Me and my shadow.

	Me	*Shadow*
10 a.m.	4′ 4″	4′ 10″
11 a.m.	4′ 4″	3′ 10″
Noon	4′ 4″	3′ 8″

Figure 4.11 is taken from the illustration which accompanied this. As the record suggests, this six-year-old actually measured her height each hour to make sure that she had not grown during the interval.

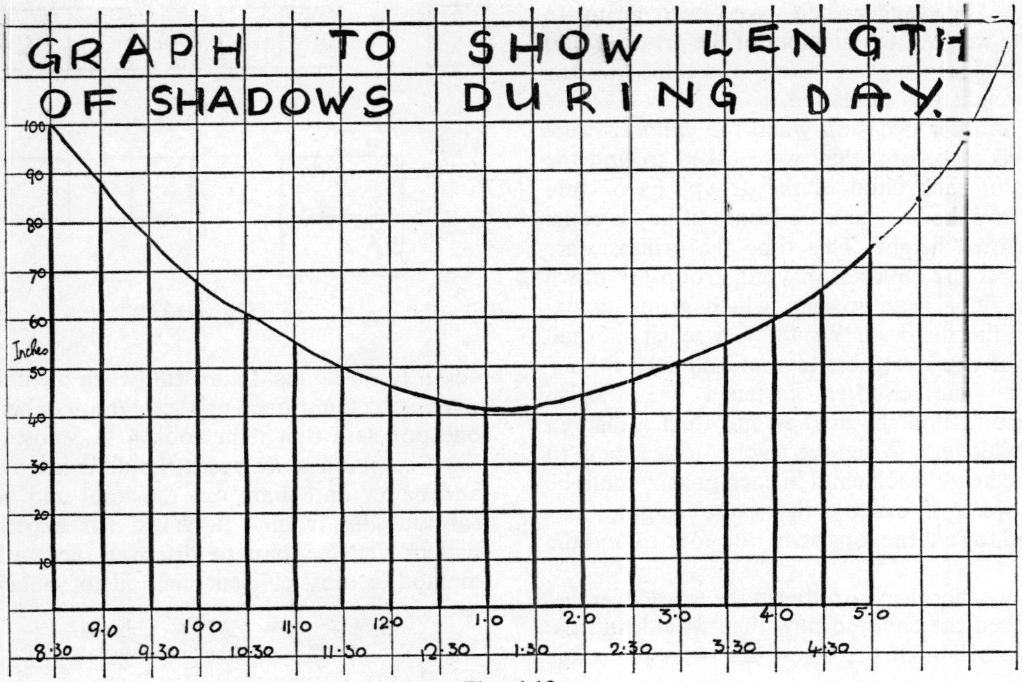

Fig. 4.12

The third example, 'Measuring the smallest boy's shadow' was written by a nine-year-old boy. It begins: 'At ten o'clock I measured the smallest boy's shadow it was 57 ins. His proper height is 50½ ins. His shadow was 6½ ins. longer. At quarter past ten his shadow was 54½ ins. It had gone down 2½ ins. I used the exact spot every time. I am measuring his shadow every quarter of an hour' . . . The results were represented on a block graph showing the length of the boy's shadow from 10 a.m. to 2.30 p.m. at 15 minute intervals. The booklet also contained 17 questions with the statement: You will find that the answers to these questions can be found on the graph.

1. At what time was his shadow smallest?

   What is the difference between the lowest height of his shadow and his proper height?

The final piece of work, 'The Sun's Shadow' was the work of a ten-year-old. It begins with an illustrated account, obviously adapted from a book, of the sun's 'passage' across the sky on December 21st and June 21st. This was followed by a scale diagram showing the measurements and direction of the shadow of a stick taken from 8.30 a.m. to 5 p.m. at half-hourly intervals. The work concluded with the line graph reproduced in Fig. 4.12. An attempt had been made to continue the curved line joining the extremities of the columns as though the child had tried to predict what would happen after observations ceased. (Fig. 4.12).

2. Averages

Children can experience the meaning of an average without first being told what to do. For example, each of a group of four seven-year-olds was given a few wrapped sweets, the teacher taking care that each had a different number (e.g. 3, 5, 6, 10) and that, in the first instance, the total was divisible by 4. She then asked the children what they could do so that each would have the same number of sweets. Unhesitating they collected the sweets together and shared them equally amongst the group.

Some ten-year-olds were asked to group themselves in fours. Each child was weighed and the teacher asked them which group was the heaviest. Naturally, to find the answer, each group added the weights of the children in the group. They found the heaviest group, the lightest group, and the difference between these groups. The teacher then asked each group to find the weight each member of the group would be if they all weighed exactly the same and the total weight was unaltered.

On another occasion when the children were grouped as before, they were asked to find the height of each child in the group. Each child was then asked to cut off a length of paper equal to his own height. This time the groups were asked, 'If the children in your group lay down on the floor head to foot which group would stretch the farthest? Would you reach the hall ceiling if you were able to stand on each others' heads?' The children fastened their strips together to find the answer and then measured the total length. When the teacher asked them to find the height each child in each group would be if all were of exactly the same height, they decided to fold the long strip into four to find the answer.

The teacher then introduced the word 'average' and asked the children how they would find the average height of the whole class. At this stage the children themselves suggested first finding the total height and then dividing by the number of children in the class. They then took their strips, and arranged them in order, beginning with the smallest, and fixed them to a piece of brown paper on the wall. They marked in the average and each child worked out how much below the average or above the average his height was. They were given a shorthand way of writing this, — for below and + for above the average. When the children were asked what they thought the average height meant, they were able to say it was the height each would be if they were all the same height. The teacher next asked them if they could suggest a way of testing whether the average height they had found for the whole class was really the height each would be. They cut off the pieces of paper above the average and fitted them into the spaces left by the strips which did not reach the average, dividing them where necessary. They were delighted to find that the pieces fitted exactly.

Later this experience gave the children an idea to save themselves some work. They noticed that the shortest child was 4 ft. 6 ins. and so decided to add up all the heights above 4 ft. 6 ins., divide this by the total number of children, and add it to 4 ft. 6 ins. Later still, when the children were being questioned on their 'graph of heights,' one boy said that if he took 4 ft. 9 ins. as his 'line' he could write down the differences above and below and share out the total and add or subtract this from 4 ft. 9 ins. His experiences had in fact led him to discover the statistical method (a most efficient method) of calculating averages.

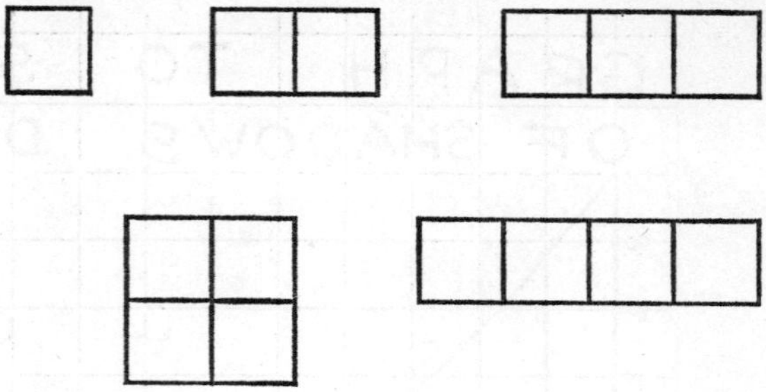

Fig. 4.13

3. Ratio, Proportion and Rate

These three related topics form a familiar part of everyday experience and yet ratio and rate are usually avoided until the secondary stage and proportion is often taught merely as a method (the 'unitary' method). In consequence these topics cause unnecessary difficulties partly because of an inadequate (or even misleading) vocabulary.

We often use the concept of *ratio* when we need to compare two (or more) numbers or quantities (frequently lengths) as the following examples show. Some six-year-olds made a model to illustrate the incidence of birthdays in the class. They marked the months in order on a piece of paper and put one match box in the appropriate column to mark the birthday of every child in the class. One six-year-old wrote: 'There are twice as many birthdays in November as in July'. This was a comparison of the number of birthdays in the two months and was therefore a natural use of the idea of ratio.

One teacher used squares of the same size to introduce a group of children to the idea of ratio. The children made rectangular shapes with one, two, three, four squares (and so on) (Fig. 4.13). After some discussion the word ratio was introduced.

PLATE V
Infants: Preparing number trays.

PLATE VI

Infants: Weighing ingredients for making toffee.

PLATE VII

Young infants: One-to-one exchange at the milk bar.

PLATE VIII

Making the net of a cube by trial and error.

PLATE IX

Young juniors: Use only the apparatus on the table to find a quarter of:

1. *the sugar on the plate.*
2. *the water in the jug.*
3. *the apple.*
4. *the distance across the table.*

PLATE X

Using one square, the ratio of the length to the width is one to one (written $\frac{1}{1}$ or 1 : 1).

Using two squares, the ratio of the length to the width is two to one ($\frac{2}{1}$ or 2 : 1),

and the ratio of the width to the length is one to two ($\frac{1}{2}$ or 1 : 2).

The use of the word ratio is much simpler here than the alternative which the teacher first used: how many times the width is the length? (She also asked: What fraction of the length is the width?) The word ratio should be used naturally and frequently in such comparisons.

Some nine-year-olds enjoyed recording the 'ratio of rotundity' for the children in their class and for the adults they knew—for this they compared each person's height with his waist measurement. (They soon discovered that to make these measurements to the nearest inch was a sensible degree of accuracy). For example, the teacher's height was 5 ft. 10 ins. and his waist measurement was 30 ins. The children recorded:

His ratio of rotundity is $\frac{70}{30}$ or $\frac{7}{3}$ or $2\frac{1}{3}$.

One boy's measurements were:
height 4 ft. 10 ins., waist 2 ft.
He found his ratio of rotundity to be $\frac{58}{24}$ or $\frac{29}{12}$ or $2\frac{5}{12}$.
At the end of a series of recordings the boy wrote:

'Although all the people we measured were different ages and sizes their ratio of rotundity was almost the same'.

A girl added: 'The answer always came to between 2 and 3 whole ones'. (It would have been interesting to record also the ratio of the weights of the people measured, for example of the teacher and the boy.)

A group of ten-year-olds were making arrows for a performance of Robin Hood. Some arrows (willow sticks with 'feathers' of cardboard) flew through the air much more effectively than others. The children began to examine the 'balance' of each arrow, using their hands to find the point of balance. The arrows were of different lengths and they wanted to make a comparison—but they had difficulty in describing what they wanted to compare. They demonstrated that it was the two lengths into which the point of balance divided the length that they needed to compare. To help them the teacher chose the smallest girl (of known height 52 in.) and asked them if she, the teacher, was twice as tall as the girl. There was much merriment as they realised how tall this would make the teacher whose height they knew to be 5 ft. 10 inches. The teacher then introduced the word ratio and the children suggested that the ratio of their heights would be about 70 to 50 or 7 to 5.

Many similar examples, using numbers, money and measures of all kinds, will arise naturally or can be contrived easily. Some important illustrations of ratio will be found in Chapter 6 (the circumference/diameter ratio of a circle) and in Chapter 7 (a simple approach to density).

Proportion is another familiar topic in the environment. Children ask many questions which involve the idea of proportion and often solve these in their own way, using their common sense. Such problems as the following, asked by teachers of their children, have all been solved by children of primary school age.

(1) How heavy is a pint of water?
How heavy is a gallon of water?
(One weighing only was done).

(2) What weight of water is wasted in 24 hours by the dripping tap in the cloakroom?

This is how an eight-year-old described what she did.

'First I got a measuring tin. Then I put it under the tap. A $\frac{1}{4}$ of a pint was wasted in $\frac{1}{2}$ an hour. This weighed 5 ozs. 10 ozs of water in 1 hour. 10 ozs. $\times$ 24 = 240 oz. I then divided 240 by 16. There are 15 $\times$ 16 in 240. So the answer is 15 lb. in one day'.

(3) Find the distance you cover in 8 even paces. How long is one pace (assuming your paces are all of the same length)?

Some slow nine-year-olds who were tackling this problem could not see what to do to find the length of one pace. So they were asked to measure the length of 2 paces. They immediately suggested halving this to find the length of one pace. They then measured the length of 4 paces and suggested dividing by 4 to find the length of one pace. This additional experience helped them to see that they must divide 19 ft. 8 ins. (the length of 8 paces) by 8 to find the length of one pace: 2 ft. 4 ins. The children's next exercise was to 'pace' the length of the playground and, using the length of pace they had worked out, to find the length of the playground (which they afterwards measured using a surveyor's tape).

Many similar examples, involving money, weights and measures, will be suggested by the children, as well as by the teacher. The concept of proportion is also of great importance in geometry; this is discussed fully in the next chapter as 'mathematical similarity'.

Children's first experience of the third of the three related topics, *rate*, is price, and the second is usually speed. Two variables are associated with rates. For example, price is the rate of buying a commodity, e.g. 10p for 100 grams of sweets or of tea; 5p for 1 litre of petrol. Speed is the rate of covering distance so that the two variables are the distance covered and the time for the journey. Children have many experiences with money and with the price of various commodities. We shall therefore confine our illustrations to those concerning speed.

There are two ways of considering speed; the simplest aspect is that used in athletics. How long does it take to run a measured distance? This is usually the aspect which young children first consider, as the following example will show. In a class of six-year-olds Timothy, a tortoise, was brought to school one morning. Someone asked Peter, his master, 'How fast does Timothy go?' Peter put a yardstick on the floor and held Timothy at one end. The teacher had a watch with a second hand which she allowed the questioner to use. When he said, 'Go', Peter released the tortoise. Surprisingly Timothy walked obediently beside the yardstick. He completed the measured yard in 2 minutes 55 seconds.

It happened that in the next class a second tortoise had arrived that day. The children decided to find out which tortoise moved faster. They asked the other class to find out how long their tortoise would take to travel a yard. These children marked a chalk line a yard long on the floor and started the tortoise at one end. The second tortoise ignored the line altogether and took its own course. At first the children wondered what to do. Then its owner drew its path with a chalk line while another child cut a piece of string a yard long, and covered the chalk line with the piece of string. Unfortunately this tortoise became discouraged before he had completed the course and the problem was not solved.

Some nine-year-olds conducted a similar (but more systematic) investigation after they had collected some insects on a nature walk. They decided that they would find the time taken to cover a foot by all the insects they had collected. A piece of work on the caterpillar is quoted in full. (The children have assumed 'constant speed'.)

The Caterpillar

To go 1 foot the Caterpillar takes 45 seconds.
To go 1 yard it takes 45×3 seconds, which is equal to 135 seconds.
1 mile is equal to 135×1760 seconds.
Then you divide by 60 to get minutes and then by 60 again to get hours.

Answer = 66 hours.
66 hours = 2 days 18 hours.

It is a mile to the Guildhall and if the Caterpillar sets off at twelve o'clock on Monday it will reach the Guildhall at 6 o'clock on Thursday morning.
This does not allow for meals or sleeping.

The examples quoted are those in which the time taken to cover a measured distance is found. The second aspect, the more usual measure of speed, is to quote this in km per hour. This is done by finding the distance covered in a measured time. An eight-year-old wrote a book, as a record of her own experience, which she called: 'In two minutes I can'. The record contains such interesting and varied items as

skip round the hall 13 times
skip through a hoop 106 times
kick the ball round the hall 10 times.

The girl had made up problems on this for other children to do. One of these was: 'How many times can I skip round the hall in 12 minutes?'

Two girls aged eleven became interested in the speed of trains.[1] Their interest started with an electric railway with which they were playing at school. They decided to try to find the speed of a goods train which passed the school. On a

[1] *Science in Primary Schools*, HMSO, 1961.

map they marked two places half a mile apart on a straight length of rail. They first synchronised their watches and then took up their places at the appointed spots. As the train reached the first girl she noted the time. The second girl recorded the time as the front of the train reached her. Their record read that the train had taken 90 seconds to cover a half mile. They therefore said that in 3 minutes the train would cover a mile and since there were 3 minutes $\times$ 20 in an hour the train was therefore travelling at 20 miles an hour.

Now these girls were fortunate in that the time taken to cover the measured distance was an easy unit. If the time had been, for example, 1 minute 19 seconds the girls might well not have been able to work out the result. But using a ready reckoner graph of the time taken to cover a measured distance, the distance travelled in a simple unit of time could be read from the graph (to ensure that the calculation would be an easy one). Speed (or distance-time) graphs are an important aspect of mathematics and will be considered in Chapter 6.

4. Simple Statistics

In a subsequent chapter contributions to the work in mathematics from other aspects of the curriculum will be considered. These will be seen to have relevance to the topics discussed in the present chapter. There is one branch of applied mathematics which has particular relevance to the work of young children: this is usually known as statistics. The scope and importance of the work can be judged from the following examples in which the simplest statistical methods were used.

The first example occurred in an infants' school with a large class of six-year-olds. The children had decided to count the number of dandelions on part of the lawn. The teacher discussed with them the difficulty of keeping count and asked them how they might mark the dandelions they had counted. One boy noticed that there were some white poppet beads on the teacher's desk (deliberately left there) so he suggested using these, putting one bead on each dandelion. After the children had set to work they discovered that there were several plantains on the lawn also. They wanted to include these in their count and to find out whether there were more dandelions than plantains. They found some yellow poppet beads to mark the plantains. At the end all the beads were collected and strung together. When the teacher held the two strings of beads for the children to see they said at once that there were more dandelions than plantains because the white string was longer than the yellow one. At that moment the teacher noticed that the white beads were slightly larger than the yellow ones. He did not point this out to the children but said, 'Are you sure that there are more white beads than yellow?' Most children maintained that there were more white beads, but one boy noticed that the beads were of different sizes and he said he was not sure, because the beads were not the same size. Even then many children stoutly maintained that there were more dandelions but a few said they thought they ought to count the beads. This proved very difficult (there were more than 60 of each of the beads on the two strings). Eventually the children decided to count the beads in tens and by a method of matching discovered that there were in fact seven more plantains than dandelions. These children had happily suggested and accepted the one-to-one correspondence involved in making their count.

A group of ten-year-olds undertook a simple sampling experiment. The children decided to investigate the incidence of weeds on a patch of lawn. The lawn was a large one and it was decided that to count the weeds on the whole lawn would be impossible. They identified four weeds and wrote their names in their notebooks. The teacher discussed with them ways of preventing the choice of those patches where most weeds occurred. They borrowed some wire frames, each made into a square foot, and used these to enclose a piece of lawn. They decided to drop the frames over their shoulders to prevent any tendency to choose a weedy patch. To avoid using the same piece of lawn more than once they each worked on one strip. If a weed was enclosed within the square it received a tick. (Only one tick was recorded for each square however many times the weed occurred.) Altogether fifty squares were examined by the group and the number of ticks against each weed was counted. A column graph of the result was made on squared paper so that the lengths of the lines showed the relative incidence of the four plants. When asked which weed was most abundant, the children unhesitatingly gave the right answer. They said that there are about seven times as many clover as yarrow. When the teacher asked them 'If we could have counted all the clover plants on the lawn and all the yarrow plants, how many times as many clover as yarrow plants would there have been?' The answer came immediately: 'Seven times'. (A big assumption was made here—one which it would have been interesting to substantiate using a smaller patch). The next step was to examine the football pitch which was a continuation of the lawn. There the children found that the proportions of the same four weeds were quite different.

Similar methods were used by another class of ten-year-olds in their investigation into the creatures contained in a pond. Twenty samples were taken in different parts of the pond (in the sun, in the shade, in the weeds, in moving water). Each small group chose a creature and recorded how many times in their twenty samples the creature was present. In this way they were able to determine which conditions their chosen creature preferred.

Sampling is a difficult idea and it is very doubtful whether the full implications can be realised until the children have had a very varied experience over a considerable period of time.

IV. Extension of ideas of number

1. Fractions

So far, the children's knowledge of number has been mainly concerned with whole numbers (integers) which they first used to describe situations in their environment, and later learned to combine in different ways according to the operation demanded by the specific problem in hand. Gradually, through recording their experiences, they learned to relate the different operations—addition, subtraction, multiplication and division—to the appropriate symbols ($+ \ - \ \times \ \div$) and eventually arrived at an efficient way of solving the different computational operations.

When, often at the same time as this growing knowledge of the way whole numbers behave, children meet parts of wholes or fractions, these occur so early and so frequently in their real experiences that they invent their own ways of dealing with them (and usually their methods are quite efficient). When they meet the written symbols for fractions, they are experiencing, for the first time, pairs of numbers used in a different way; number pairs which appear to behave differently from integers when combined by any of the operations addition, subtraction, multiplication and division. The symbolic way of writing fractions is more difficult than is sometimes supposed. Children can deal with fractions orally long before they can record their results in symbolic form. For example they know that three quarters and one quarter make four quarters or one whole before they are able to record it as $\frac{3}{4} + \frac{1}{4} = \frac{4}{4} = 1$. Once they have met the symbolic form and recorded their results in this way they need to be asked, at intervals, the meaning of the numerals such as 8 and 5 in $\frac{5}{8}$ to ensure that they thoroughly understand what they are doing. A variety of regular geometric shapes (in two colours) is often used for giving children varied opportunities for recognising the common fractions. In most of their experiences the fractions they meet should be the simple ones of everyday life and should therefore normally be restricted to those in common use: $\frac{1}{2}$, $\frac{1}{4}$, $\frac{3}{4}$, $\frac{1}{3}$, $\frac{2}{3}$, $\frac{1}{10}$, etc.

But sometimes children devise and enjoy experiences in which they come across far more complicated fractions as the following example shows.

A class of nine-year-olds were asked by their teacher to find the weight of a laurel leaf. A girl solved this problem by weighing an ounce of laurel leaves. She wrote:

41 of our leaves make 1 oz.
So 1 leaf is $\frac{1}{41}$ oz.

This investigation fired the imagination of the whole class and, between them, the children found the weights of a wide variety of small objects from a marble to a drawing pin. The recording was precise for one boy wrote:

4 similar marbles weigh 1 oz.
1 marble weighs $\frac{1}{4}$ oz.

and another wrote:

44 sweets make 1 oz.
So one is $\frac{1}{44}$ oz.

The children then turned their attention to finding the thickness of a variety of strands which they wound on card until the inch was obtained. A girl recorded:

24 strands of wool to 1 inch.

So thickness = $\frac{1}{24}$ inch

and a boy:

Thread 52 to 1 inch.

Thickness $\frac{1}{52}$ of 1 inch.

The finest strand was found to be nylon ($\frac{1}{92}$ of 1 inch) for which strands wound to $\frac{1}{4}''$ only were counted. The children concluded this investigation by finding the thickness of every type of paper in the stock cupboard.

The value of these experiments was not only in the excitement which they caused (and competition also—to find the lightest object and the finest thread). The children gained insight into the meaning of fractions and, in particular, an understanding of a difficult idea: although 40 is much greater than 4 (for example) $\frac{1}{40}$ is much smaller than $\frac{1}{4}$. This is an example of inverse proportion.

Once the nature of a fraction is understood, the only other concept concerning fractions which children need to discover and to understand is the equivalence of fractions. Again, this is a novel idea for them. Hitherto there has been no ambiguity about the recording of their experiences. When they make a count of five they record the answer verbally or in writing by the numeral. Now they find that $\frac{3}{4}$ can be represented by more fractions than they can count. Children are normally given wide experiences from which they can discover this equivalence of fractions. Much of this experience will concern measurement. The most usual way of focusing attention on equivalence is by means of a fraction board.

That young children can solve quite difficult examples mentally is illustrated by the following example. A seven-year-old, working on a model of Coventry Cathedral, decided to find the corresponding lengths in the original. The scale was 1/16th of an inch to 1 foot. He measured the height of the model chapel and found it to be $3\frac{3}{4}$ inches. He said, 'Each inch is the same as 16 feet, so 3 inches will mean 3 sixteens, that is 48. Half of 16 feet is 8 feet; that is 56 feet. One quarter of 16 feet is 4 feet; that is 60 feet altogether'.

Experience is needed in problems leading to all four operations in fractions. As already suggested, the methods will be varied and the recording will be done in an informal way. For example:

$$\begin{aligned} 3\tfrac{1}{2} + 1\tfrac{3}{4} \text{ will be worked as } & 3\tfrac{2}{4} + 1\tfrac{3}{4} \\ &= 3 + \tfrac{5}{4}\ (\tfrac{4}{4} = 1) \\ &= 4\tfrac{1}{4} \end{aligned}$$

The advantage of this simple method over the 'common denominator' method is even more striking when a difficult subtraction is performed.

$$\begin{aligned} 3\tfrac{1}{2} - 1\tfrac{3}{4} &= 3\tfrac{2}{4} - 1\tfrac{3}{4} \\ &= 2 + \tfrac{4}{4} + \tfrac{2}{4} - 1\tfrac{3}{4} \\ &= 1\tfrac{3}{4} \end{aligned}$$

Children will also solve simple problems involving multiplication and division of fractions in their own direct way. For example, an eight-year-old was asked to find the total length of five short lengths, each of $3\frac{1}{2}$ inches, and was asked to check this by an experiment. The girl said: five lengths of 3 in. is 15 in., five of $\frac{1}{2}$ in. is $2\frac{1}{2}$ in. The total length was $17\frac{1}{2}$ in. She then put the lengths end to end to see whether they would stretch to $17\frac{1}{2}$ in.

Even more complicated examples such as $5\frac{1}{4} \times 3\frac{1}{2}$ can be solved in this way. Once again we must be careful about our interpretation of the symbols in this operation and of the possible confusion between 'of' and 'multiply'. (See p. 22)

$5\frac{1}{4} \times 3\frac{1}{2}$ means $5\frac{1}{4}$ multiplied by $3\frac{1}{2}$ or

$$\begin{aligned} 3 \text{ of } 5\tfrac{1}{4} + \tfrac{1}{2} \text{ of } 5\tfrac{1}{4} &= 15\tfrac{3}{4} + 2\tfrac{5}{8} \\ &= 15\tfrac{6}{8} + 2\tfrac{5}{8} \\ &= 18\tfrac{3}{8} \end{aligned}$$

The 'top heavy' fraction method comes later:

$$\begin{aligned} 5\tfrac{1}{4} \times 3\tfrac{1}{2} &= \tfrac{21}{4} \times \tfrac{7}{2} \\ &= \tfrac{147}{8} \\ &= 18\tfrac{3}{8} \end{aligned}$$

Similarly, and more simply, we know that

$$\tfrac{1}{2} \text{ of } 3 = 1\tfrac{1}{2}$$

$$\text{and } 3 \times \tfrac{1}{2} = \tfrac{3}{2} \text{ or } 1\tfrac{1}{2}$$

Area problems will provide many useful examples which require multiplication of fractions.

In division, a girl who was not yet nine years old invented a very efficient method for dividing fractions. She was working a problem: $3\frac{3}{4} \div 1\frac{3}{4}$. She wrote: These are all quarters

$$15 \div 7 = 2\tfrac{1}{7}$$

When asked what she would do if she had to work $3\frac{3}{4} \div 1\frac{3}{8}$ she said, after some thought, 'I could turn them all to eighths couldn't I?'

She wrote: $3\frac{6}{8} \div 1\frac{3}{8}$

These are all eighths

$$30 \div 11 = 2\frac{8}{11}$$

This method obviates any need to teach children to 'turn upside down and multiply' and will meet any normal needs of the children, provided the fractions given are commensurate with reality.

When children are given problems such as: 'How many lengths of balsa wood, $1\frac{3}{4}$ in. long can be cut from an $11\frac{1}{2}$ ins. length?' The remainder sometimes creates a problem unless a simple method is used.

$$11\frac{1}{2} \div 1\frac{3}{4}$$

$$11\frac{2}{4} \div 1\frac{3}{4}$$

These are all quarters of an inch.

$46 \div 7 = 6$ and 4 quarters or 1 inch over.

Such a simple problem can always be checked by measuring. If this example is worked by the 'turn upside down and multiply' rule, the answer comes to be $6\frac{4}{7}$. It is difficult for children to understand that this $\frac{4}{7}$ relates to the length of $1\frac{3}{4}$ in. The simpler method is obviously better here and it is certainly one which children can discover for themselves.

Measurement will provide many opportunities for work with fractions and in the use of the four operations applied to fractions.

2. Decimal Fractions

Now that we use a decimal money system, decimal fractions are likely to be introduced earlier than the correct norm (10 years old). The use of metric units of measurement will contribute to this. Some teachers introduce decimals once place-value is thoroughly understood, and as soon as children can extend our number system to the right.

1000	100	10	1	$\frac{1}{10}$	$\frac{1}{100}$
Shorthand forms:				0·1	0·01

It is important that decimals should be be introduced from their use in real situations. Children will already be accustomed to buying records at £1·25, £1·05, but, as with their counterparts in the U.S.A. will probably translate this to one pound 25 pence. They will, however, know that there are 100 pence in £1, so that the equivalence 25p or £0·25 or £$\frac{25}{100}$ will soon be established. But they will need to use tenths before hundreds and here equivalence in measurement will supply examples,

e.g. 1 metre 7 decimetres as $1\frac{7}{10}$ metre or 1·7 metres or 3 decimetres 4 centimetres as $3\frac{4}{10}$ dm or 3·4 dm.

Measurement of area will give additional examples in hundredths

e.g. 1 square decimetre 55 square centimetres can be written as 1·55 dm^2 (about the area of an adult's hand).

Later the third place of decimals can be introduced through measurement in grams and in millilitres

e.g. 1 kg 675 g as 1·675 kg
2 litres 25 ml as 2·025 litres.

Children who can perform calculations in the four operations with understanding will not have difficulty when calculations are extended to include decimal quantities (provided the operator is a whole number in multiplication and division). Multiplication by a decimal fraction will need careful development. A few top juniors will meet problems requiring division of decimals, e.g. How many records at £1·35 can I buy with £5? How many dress lengths 2·25 metres long can be cut from a 22 metre roll? for which they will devise their own methods if they have complete understanding of the problem.

The introduction of the second place of decimals can be made through weather observations. In official records and newspaper reports rainfall and the number of hours of sunshine are normally quoted to two decimal places. Again, provided the children understand what they are doing, the transition from one to two places is made without difficulty. There is no point in extending the use of decimals beyond those experienced by the children unless they happen to come across these (as in using the micrometer to measure the thickness of very thin things such as a sheet of paper or a hair). If a child is able to discover what the graduations on a micrometer mean, and how to use it without being told, there is no reason why the micrometer should not be used in this way. On the other hand there is no reason why it should be introduced unless it is needed.

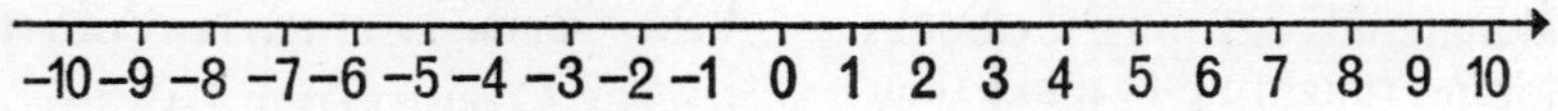

Fig. 4.14

3. Directed and Negative Numbers

The next extension in the field of number which some children experience is obtained by extending the positive number line through zero to include the negative numbers. If they are already familiar with the number line (the positive numbers set out in order) the extension backwards (to the left) is not difficult. (Fig. 4.14). As will be seen in the section on graphical representation the suggestion to extend the field of numbers backwards sometimes comes from the children themselves. The questions they asked (after they had realised that the positive numbers seemed to go on for ever) were 'What about the other way? Do the numbers stop at zero?' The teacher replied, 'Can you count backwards? If so, continue the line'.

Raised signs e.g. $^{-}5$, $^{+}3$ used to mark points on a number line, have been found very helpful in the early stages of teaching directed numbers to distinguish between the position on the line and the operations of addition and subtraction.

V. Applications of extensions of ideas of number

Percentages

A small unit is chosen, % or $\frac{1}{100}$, so that 1 is 100 of these units, (100%), 2 is 200 of these units (200%), $\frac{1}{2}$ is 50 of these units (50%) and so on.

Nine-year-olds and ten-year-olds, who have become aware of the mathematical possibilities of the environment, will soon come across percentages in their shopping expeditions (real and imaginary). A group of ten-year-olds in a rural school first encountered percentages when they were studying the germination of wild flower seeds. They were given packets of wild flower seeds containing different numbers according to the type of seed. They planted all the seeds and wanted to find out which gave the best return. At first they tried to solve this problem by expressing the number of seedlings grown as a fraction of the number of seeds planted but this was too complicated. They then began to turn these fractions to decimals and at this stage the teacher told them about percentages.

Another group of ten-year-olds discovered references to percentages in the Saturday shopping page in a newspaper. Once they had discovered what a percentage was they used this knowledge in the books of problems they prepared for each other.

VI. A new look at numbers: sets

An increasing number of teachers may feel that they want to introduce the notion of sets to junior children. The difference between the mathematics of sets and traditional mathematics is largely one of vocabulary and new symbols. Those interested will find a brief section on this topic in Appendix 4.

In this chapter an attempt has been made to indicate the place which the knowledge of number relationships on the one hand and computational practice on the other hand should take in primary school mathematics. It has been emphasised that children can make their own discoveries of number relationships, of quantity relationships and of the operations, through their own first-hand experience with the real materials of their environment (supplemented by structual materials, home-made or commercial). This way of learning is sound and conforms to the latest research on children's learning but it is, of necessity, apparently slower in the early stages when measured by traditional computational achievement alone. By the age of nine years, however, (and by eight for some children) those children who have learnt by their own discoveries are able to hold their own in traditional computational processes also. And there can be no comparison where ability to solve problems (with real materials or from a textbook) is concerned. Children brought up to make their own discoveries in mathematics have complete confidence in their own abilities and show an evident enjoyment and appreciation of mathematics, even when it begins to become, as it must, more abstract. They, like Archimedes, can use their imagination in problem solving when materials are not available or when they no longer need these. (Archimedes said, 'When I have a problem to solve, in imagination I weigh and measure . . .')

There is another advantage which this method of learning brings. Those teachers who have already organised the work so that the children learn by their own efforts all bear testimony to the decrease in the amount of computational practice children require in order to attain and maintain computational efficiency. Many teachers have found that they can safely reduce this practice to two periods (and some to one) each week and that the children's efficiency in computation has improved and not declined in consequence. With this in mind, the suggestion that other aspects of mathematics be included in the primary school programme becomes a reasonable one, and we shall turn our attention to recent developments in this field in the next chapter.

The present chapter has been chiefly concerned with number and quantity relationships of all kinds. The infiltration of ideas from modern mathematics has caused us to take a new look at the underlying structure of our own number system.

Here is a summary, in more mathematical form, of the various relationships which should be explicit to the child from his discoveries. It cannot be over-emphasised that these will become explicit only as a result of discussion between the teacher and children and as a result of real experience and subsequent recording. (The reader would be well advised to test the validity of each of these statements, using numbers instead of letters.)

VII. Summary of the laws of arithmetic

1 THE COMMUTATIVE LAWS OF ADDITION AND MULTIPLICATION

$A + B = B + A$
$A \times B = B \times A.$

(Does this apply to subtraction and division? Consider $A - B$ and $B - A$ and $A \div B$ and $B \div A$.)

2 THE ASSOCIATIVE LAWS OF ADDITION AND MULTIPLICATION

$A + (B + C) = (A + B) + C$
$A \times (B \times C) = (A \times B) \times C.$

3 THE DISTRIBUTIVE LAW OF MULTIPLICATION

$A \times (B + C) = AB + AC$

For example, we work 16×17 as $16 \times (10+7) = 16 \times 10 + 16 \times 7$.

4 SUBTRACTION IS RELATED TO ADDITION

$A + B = C, A = C - B, B = C - A.$

5 DIVISION IS RELATED TO MULTIPLICATION

(Does this make sense of $\frac{3}{4} \div \frac{5}{7} = \frac{3}{4} \times \frac{7}{5}$?)
$AB = C, C \div A = B, C \div B = A.$

6 THE ZERO ELEMENT

$A + 0 = A$

The number is unaltered by the addition of zero.

Notice also $(+A) + (-A) = 0$
i.e. $(-A)$ is the additive inverse of $(+A)$.

7 THE UNITY ELEMENT

$A \times 1 = A$

The number is unaltered by multiplication by unity.

Notice also $A \times \frac{1}{A} = 1$ i.e. $\frac{1}{A}$ is the multiplicative inverse of A.

5 Children, shapes and space

In this chapter we shall be concerned with geometrical ideas which young children can discover for themselves. All the ideas included are possible for children of primary school age; and all are of fundamental importance mathematically and therefore deserve a place at this stage. It will be seen from the illustrations which follow that these mathematical ideas can arise from the normal activities of the classroom. But if teachers are to make the most of these activities for the learning of mathematics they must themselves be familiar with the mathematics involved. Ideas which have normally been thought to belong to the later years of the primary school or the early years of the secondary school can be learned much earlier, provided children are given opportunities to discover these for themselves. It is therefore reasonable to ask, in these circumstances, how far the oldest and brightest juniors can progress with the topics included. Throughout the chapter, therefore, the idea of progression will be kept in mind. The ground covered will include the properties of shapes themselves, dimensions, symmetry and similarity and mathematical limits.

An important point must be made at the outset. The introduction into primary schools of such investigations with common mathematical shapes as will be described in this chapter is very recent, too recent for anyone to say, with certainty, the optimum stage at which the opportunity for each discovery can be presented to young children. The investigations are included here in full in the hope that teachers will be encouraged to try some of them with the children they teach, observing, and sometimes recording, their responses. A good deal of research of this kind is necessary and the experiences of teachers willing to experiment with this material would be a valuable guide in planning the work. Teachers who would be willing to undertake such work are referred to the 'research' section in chapter 8.

I. Shapes

Children learn, at an early age, to distinguish one shape from another and the sorting of objects according to shape, by handling them, is a normal activity of young children. More recently it has become usual to associate the correct names with the objects and to introduce a quite extensive geometrical vocabulary at the infant stage. For example, a six-year-old's book of shapes contained drawings and names such as cube, block, ball, cylinder and cone. This was followed by the names of the shapes of the faces of these solid objects and each was accompanied by a drawing. The names included: rectangle, square, circle, diamond, triangle, and oval. Descriptive adjectives such as curved, straight, round (and also adjectives of texture such as smooth and rough) were included. Underneath the names of the shapes were the names of objects the child had seen which had these shapes.

One of the first activities of children when they come to school is often the making of models from cardboard boxes in a wide variety of shapes and from materials they find in the junk box. This activity can be an important one in the development of mathematical representation, as is shown by the following example. In one school model-making occupied a good deal of the time, for, when the children were satisfied with the model (and they sometimes made two or three attempts before they reached this stage), they then wrote a book about the making of the model, describing their difficulties and the materials they used. All models were covered by the children by cutting newspaper to fit, pasting it on the model, and then painting the whole with a thick layer of paint. This activity directed the child's attention to the shapes as he made them and also demanded the matching or measuring of shapes as the model was covered. A boy who had made a rather unusual house was asked if he could draw the house as he would see it if he flew over the house in an aeroplane. Without hesitation he produced a good free-hand drawing of the ground plan including the chimney shown as a square (Fig. 5.1). When

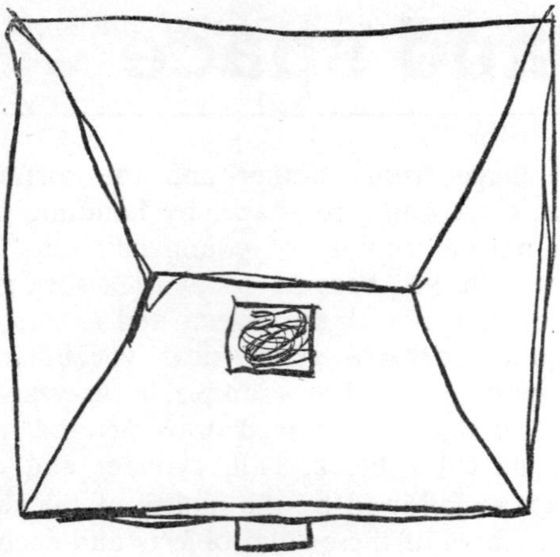

Fig. 5.1

encouraged to do so he drew each elevation in turn, giving great attention to detail. Although the drawings could not be full scale, proportions were good. Other children in the same class, with this lengthy experience of model making, also proved themselves able to draw a good free-hand plan and elevation drawings of their models. This ability is unusual in children of six years old unless they have this wide experience of detailed model making. (They must often have stood over their models as they were making them.) When the children were subsequently asked, in turn, to draw a picture of a table as it would be seen from above they were all able to do this correctly. This, too, is unusual for children of this age; frequently the four legs of the table are included. Such experience, and that provided by doll-making and dressing, is of value mathematically since the child not only looks closely at the shapes themselves but also intuitively strives to maintain the correct relationships in the shapes concerned so that the finished result is 'in proportion'.

Mathematical shapes (particularly if these are gaily coloured) have a fascination for young children. Once their attention is attracted to mathematical shapes they do not need much encouragement to discover a variety of relationships from patterns of tiles on floors, from wallpaper and fabric patterns, and from natural forms as well. The shapes of cardboard boxes, the way in which these fold flat, and the way in which they can be fitted together to pack into large containers are matters which have been found to appeal to children of seven and eight years old. From these 'investigations' a variety of interesting properties of some of the uncommon as well as of the common shapes emerge. Some of these are described in the pages which follow.

Cubes, Blocks, Squares and Rectangles

From the child's point of view, since we live in a three-dimensional world, solid shapes are recognised before flat shapes and should therefore be introduced first. We, as teachers, are conditioned to working on a sheet of paper or on a blackboard but young children are more accustomed to looking at the world 'in the round' as the following example shows.

A teacher of seven-year-olds had provided the class with sheets of square inch paper. She asked the children how many sides a square had and what they knew about squares. Most children declared that a square had four sides and that these were all equal. But one girl insisted that a square had six sides. To demonstrate her point she took a closed box and touched its six faces, counting as she did so. The teacher said, 'But a sheet of paper hasn't six sides!' 'Oh, yes it has,' said the girl, and she counted the four edges of the paper and its upper and under sides. The teacher then realised that the cube was perhaps more familiar to the children than the square. She showed them a cube and one girl was able to invent for herself the 'net' of a cube: a way of cutting a pattern from her sheet of square inch paper so that when folded it would make a cube when she fastened the edges together with sellotape (Fig. 5.2).

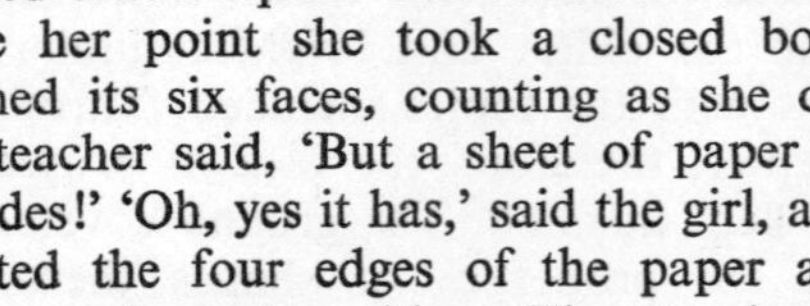

Fig. 5.2

After the children had handled and examined the cubes they subsequently made, and had decided that the six faces of a cube were all squares and were all the same shape and size, they were able to select the squares from a group of squares and rectangles of different sizes. They were then able to discover some of the properties of squares which follow.

Squares and rectangles have 'square corners' or right angles. A mixed class of young children in a rural school (the group included children of five, six and seven) had each made a right angle by folding a rough piece of paper carefully into four (first one fold was made and the second fold was made by placing the folded edges together). The children then began to test the corners of the room using their home-made 'set squares' to see whether the walls were at right angles. They tried the corner of the blackboard, the corners of pictures and the corners of the tiles. It was a five-year-old who first discovered, from a tile pattern, that the diagonals of a square cut at right angles. It was some time later that an eight-year-old discovered that the diagonals of a rectangle are not at right angles to each other.

A class of nine-year-olds was given some coloured squares and given opportunities to fold these and to talk about the shapes they made. Among their discoveries were: 'The diagonal cuts the square into two equal triangles.' (This fact was never questioned whatever the position of the square). When they folded the square into four triangles and flattened the square out again they were equally sure that the four triangles now made were all exactly the same size and shape. They were then each given a sheet of duplicating paper and left to experiment once more. They were asked to draw in the longest line. They found that their rules would not stretch from one corner to the opposite one so that, in order to put in the longest line, they had to fold the sheet of paper along its diagonal. When they smoothed the paper out again to restore the rectangle they were asked if they could say anything about the two triangles into which the rectangle was divided by the diagonal. They immediately said that the diagonal cut the rectangle into two equal triangles. When, however, they folded the rectangle along the diagonal again they were surprised to find that the triangles did not cover each other. Many of them decided that the triangles were not the same. A few still maintained that the triangles were the same and when challenged by the teacher to show this they cut the rectangle along the diagonal. It was not long before some of the children had discovered that it was possible to turn one triangle round so that it exactly fitted the other.

FRAMEWORKS: *Squares, rectangles and triangles*

Although children begin to recognise different shapes, they do not, at first, think of rectangles, squares and triangles as frameworks, although later objects such as bridges and pylons (containing triangles) begin to appear on the lists. But subsequently, children seem quite able to recognise frameworks of this kind, as the following example shows.

Some eight-year-olds were using meccano strips of equal length and bolting these together at the corners to make shapes of three and four sides. They discovered that the triangle was a firm (rigid) shape which could not be pushed out of shape. When they made a square, however, they found that, however tightly they screwed the nuts and bolts at the corners, the square could be pushed out of shape. In order to make it rigid they found they had to put a longer strip from one corner to the other. They recognised they had now made two triangles. They then tried making other regular shapes and found that in order to make these rigid they always had to put in enough strips to make the components into triangles. They called the triangles 'the strong shape.'

Some ten-year-olds spent a long time in constructing a 'girder' bridge made of balsa wood in order to run an electric railway track over it. The sides were made of regular triangular frameworks. When the bridge was finished the children discovered that it was very light and the train, by comparison, was very heavy. Thereupon they refused to allow the train to run over the bridge. They weighed the bridge and found its weight to be $3\frac{3}{4}$ oz. The engine and coaches weighed nearly 2 lb. This convinced the children more than ever that the bridge would not bear the weight of the train. The teacher then suggested they should make a replica of one side of the girder bridge and test its strength. This they did and, supporting the ends of the bridge, they hung a pound packet of plasticine from the centre. To their surprise the framework withstood the weight (Fig. 5.3). They then tied together the

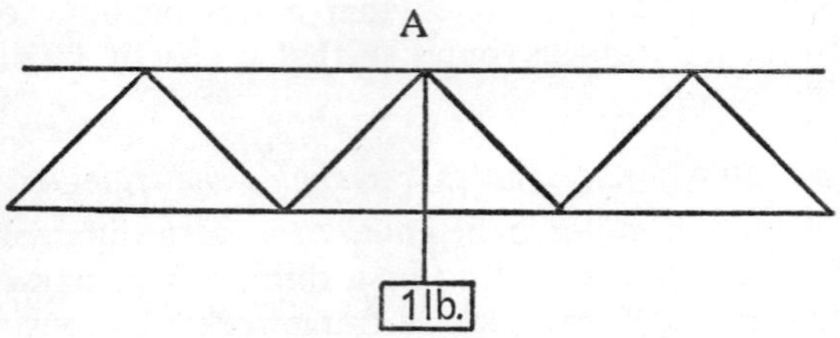

Fig. 5.3

equivalent in balsa wood of all the pieces they had used in the construction of the bridge and, once more supporting the ends, they suspended the pound of plasticine from the centre.

The pieces of wood immediately snapped under the weight. A girl explained the strength of the framework which had supported the pound weight as follows. 'When the weight is hung from A it is shared by all the pieces of wood at A so the triangles are strong shapes'. After this experiment the children happily let the train run over the bridge.

Angles

A group of eight-year-olds had been experimenting with meccano frameworks to discover the properties of the different shapes they made. They noticed that when they pushed a square out of shape the corners were no longer 'square'. The teacher then suggested that each child should fasten at one end two cardboard strips of different lengths. They started with the strips together, the teacher then asked them to rotate the smaller one until it was back again in its starting position. In this way the children were experiencing an angle as a rotation with one revolution as the unit of measuring an angle. She next asked them to rotate the smaller strip until the two strips appeared to make a 'square corner'. She asked what fraction of a revolution this was and they told her a quarter. She told them that this was called a right angle and they were able to associate this name with the rectangle. By paper folding the children then made the eight points of the compass and met, for the first time, half a right angle.

Another group of eight-year-olds using equal strips of cardboard fastened with paper fasteners, also found that the square could be pushed out of shape however tightly they fastened the corners. The children called these new shapes 'diamonds'. They fastened the opposite corners with shirr elastic and were able to discover various facts about the diagonals, including the exciting fact that the diagonals of a diamond are at right angles. They next explored the properties of a rectangular framework, once more putting in the diagonals to see what they could discover.

Triangles

A group of nine-year-olds discovered by folding a square along a diagonal that the triangle they made had, as its angles, one right angle and two half right angles. (They had already commented on the symmetry of this triangle).

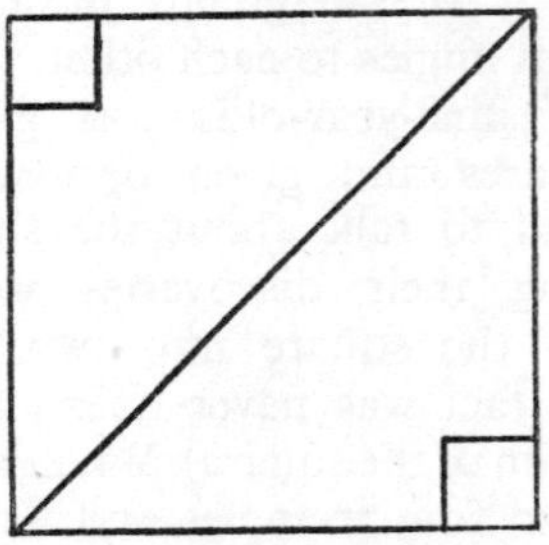

Fig. 5.4

They next folded a rectangular sheet of paper along the diagonal and cut along the diagonal so that they had two triangles.

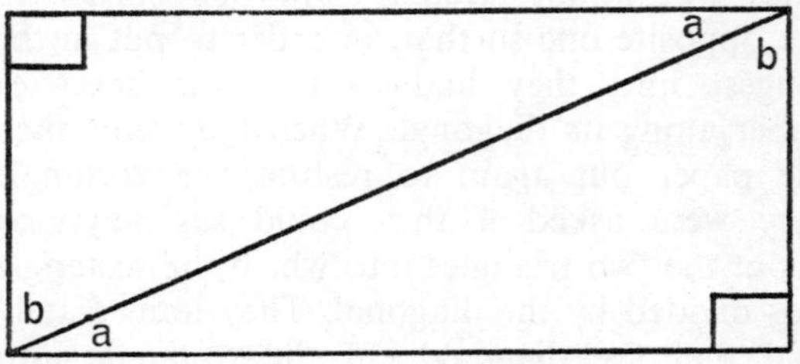

Fig. 5.5

The teacher asked them if they could discover anything about the angles of these two triangles. One child immediately said that the three angles together must make two right angles because a rectangle had four right angles and they had cut two equal triangles from the rectangle. This group of children had, therefore, discovered that the sum of the angles of right angled triangles was two right angles.

The teacher had also collected some of the triangular containers from a brand of chocolate. The children found that they could fix six of these together to make a new kind of shape. (Fig. 5.6)

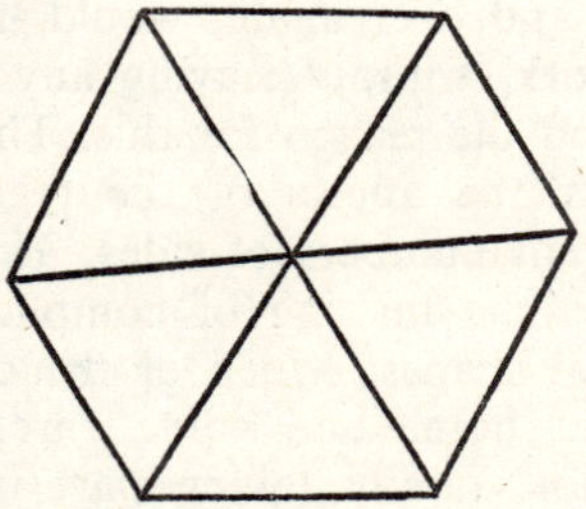

Fig. 5.6

and that they could stand three together on the table as in Figure 5.7.

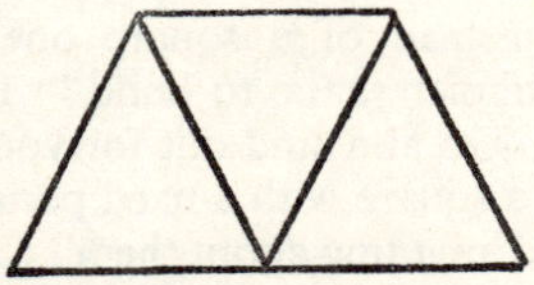

Fig. 5.7

This showed them that each of the equal angles (they had discovered that the angles were equal quite quickly from the symmetry of the figure) was a third of two right angles and that, once more, the sum of the three angles was two right angles.

The teacher then asked the children if they could discover whether there was anything interesting about the sum of the angles of a triangle of any shape they liked to draw. She suggested that they draw and cut out several triangles of different shapes, asking them to mark in the angles at the corners (Fig. 5.8). After unsuccessfully trying to fold the triangles so that the angles came together, some of them tore the angles off, and others cut them off, and placed them as in Figure 5.9.

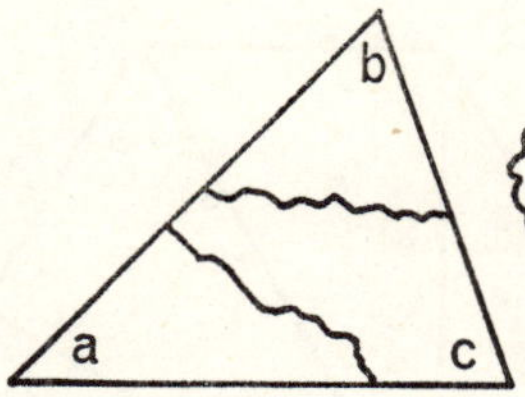

Fig. 5.8

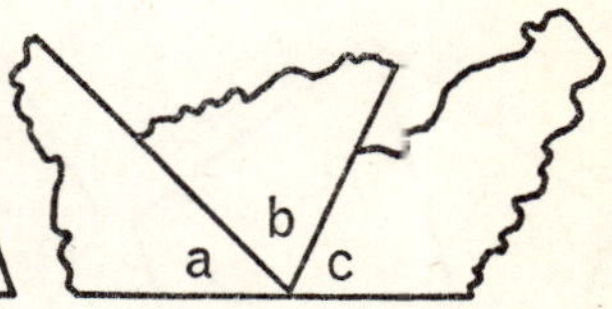

Fig. 5.9

They discovered that the outer arm did in fact make a straight line. Some of the children spent a good deal of time trying to discover whether they could find a triangle the sum of whose angles was not two right angles. Finally the teacher suggested that instead of drawing a triangle on a piece of paper, they draw a triangle on a ball. They were delighted to find that, on a ball, many triangles could be drawn with two right angles and some could be drawn with three right angles.

Other Regular Shapes

Some ten-year-olds who had discovered the sum of the angles of the triangle in a similar way realised that they could then find the sum of the angles of any polygon. They made their polygons from equal strips and discovered that, in order to make each polygon rigid, a series of additional strips had to be inserted until the polygon consisted of triangles.

The table these children drew up is given:

Number of Sides	*Number of Triangles*	*Sum of angles in Right angles*
3	1	2
4	2	4
5	3	6
6	4	8

The children completed the table as far as 12 sides.

In making these frameworks the children had taken great pains to keep the outer frameworks regular in shape (Fig. 5.10).

In order to do this they had used long strips of cardboard punched with a series of holes at

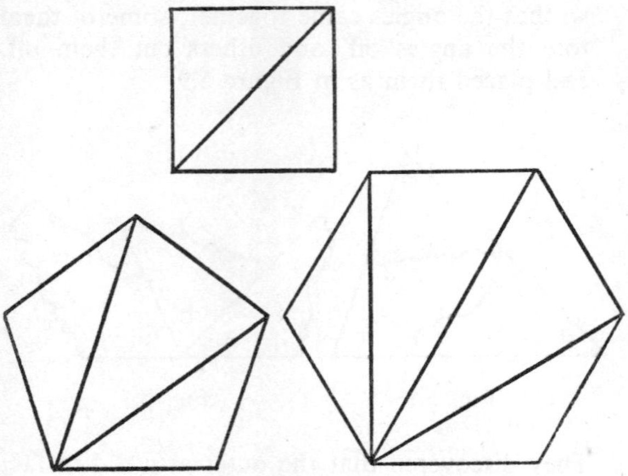

Fig. 5.10

half inch intervals so that they could use that length of diagonal which would leave the outer framework in the shape of a regular polygon. When they had drawn up the table the teacher asked them if they could discover a means of finding the angles of these different regular shapes. They had realised, in their efforts to keep the shapes regular, that in order to do this, the angles of any one figure must be kept the same. Since these children had already come across and used the 90° in a right angle, they now began to draw up a second table to show the individual angles of frameworks with differing numbers of sides.

Number of Sides	*Sum of Angles in Degrees*	*Angle*
3	180°	60°
4	360°	90°
5	540°	108°
6	720°	120°

These children at first continued up to 12 sides. This time they were unable to detect a relationship from the pattern of the numbers. The teacher then suggested to them that they should make a graph showing the number of sides the shape had, and its angle. This story will be continued in the next chapter.

Another less able group of ten-year-olds made similar discoveries about the angles of regular shapes from a series of tile patterns and shapes they had collected. They became interested in making various regular shapes themselves and even began to use these in their pattern making and painting. They discovered that they could make a regular pentagon (and from this make a five-pointed star for decorations) by tying a single knot in a strip of paper. They found that some packets of biscuits were sealed with hexagons. They experimented to see which regular shapes, used over and over again, would fill space, as in patchwork, without leaving any gaps. They tried to find the reason for this. This led them to discover the angles of the regular shapes with different numbers of sides. The investigation led to the making of complicated three-dimensional shapes. Much of the construction went on at home and some parents testified to the whole family taking part in this. The interest of some children spread to shapes of crystals.

Peter, aged 11, set out to discover why bees and wasps used hexagonal cells. Here is the account in Peter's own words of his experiment.

I said, 'Why does the bee build a hexagonal honeycomb instead of a square one because the square is a simpler shape to build?' He (the headmaster) said, 'Go and find out for yourself; draw a hexagon and a square with a fixed perimeter and see if you can find anything about them'.

There followed a detailed account of Peter's method of drawing a hexagon and of the counting process he used to find the area. He recorded:

'A hexagon with a perimeter of 1 ft. has an area of $10\frac{3}{8}$ sq. ins. A square with a perimeter of 1 ft. has an area of 9 sq. ins. . . . I have come to the conclusion that with the same length of wall and the same amount of material the bee gets more area and therefore more volume in building a hexagonal honeycomb than if it builds a square one. . . . I think that shapes with more sides and the same perimeter have more area so I tried an octagon with a perimeter 1 ft. It has more area but octagons do not fit together.'

Here are some of the patterns made by younger children in the school who were interested in Peter's investigation, in their attempts to fit regular shapes together.

It is clear from the foregoing examples that the study of these regular shapes is a fascinating one for the children.

Fig. 5.11

PARALLEL LINES

When young children begin to look for interesting shapes and patterns they very soon discover the incidence of parallel lines, and, in particular, the parallel lines on their exercise books. One group of nine-year-olds discovered, when they placed a ruler across the lines in their

ks, that the successive angles (corresponding
es) are all the same (Fig. 5.12).

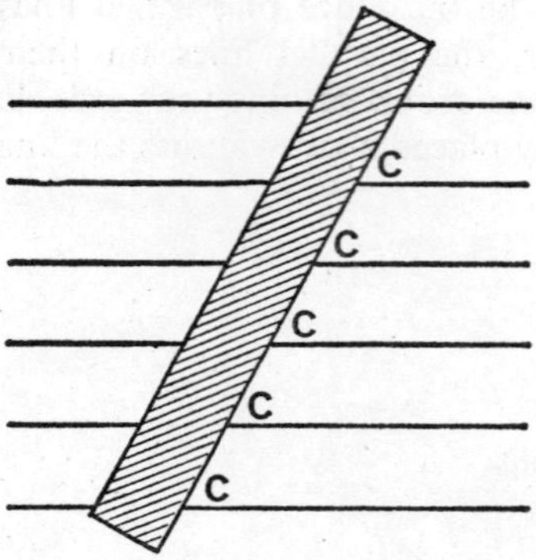

Fig. 5.12

In order to get the children to make other discoveries about the angles formed when a cutting line (transversal) meets a set of parallel lines, one teacher asked the children to make shapes using three strips bolted together as shown in Figure 5.13. The children discovered that when the strips were in the position as in Figure 5.14 the opposite lines were parallel and the angles marked 'a' were equal. They called these the 'Z' angles (after 'Z' cars). When the lines were not parallel, as in Figure 5.13, the angles marked 'b' and 'c' were not equal.

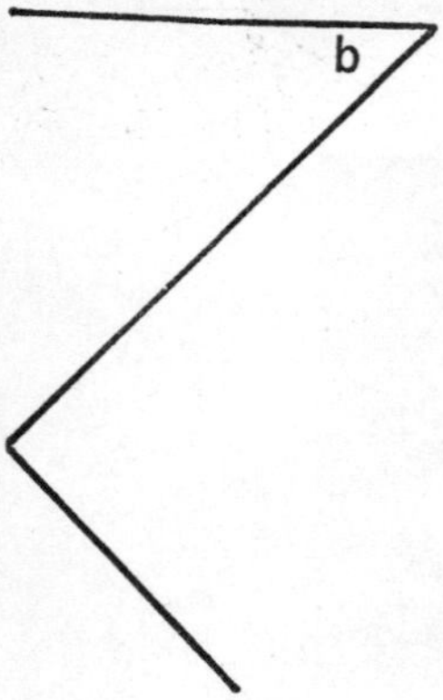

Fig. 5.13

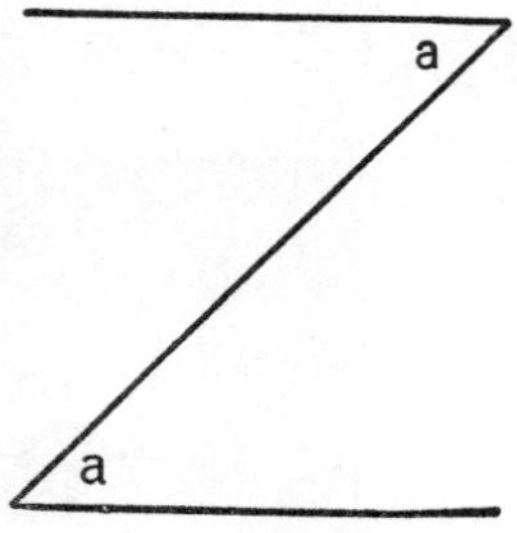

Fig. 5.14

Spheres, Cylinders, Circles and Cones

Probably the first mathematical shapes a young child uses are a cube (a building brick) and a sphere (a ball). As he plays with these shapes he comes to realise their essential differences—the comfortable curved shape of the ball in his hand but its disconcerting habit of rolling away on sloping ground. Cylinders (tins) too, are familiar shapes to young children and they soon discover for themselves in model making, that they can make a chimney, for example, from a roll of paper. In this way and by many other means, (clock faces, wheels, plates, coins) children become aware of the circle as a shape. Their first attempts at drawing circles should be their own; probably drawing round a penny or a plate; or using a pencil in a loop of string held taut and pivoted about a drawing pin; or, out of doors, using a length of string anchored to a post. (They should *not*, at first, use compasses for drawing a circle for this instrument obscures the most important property of the circle, that its radii are all equal.)

When young children cut out a circle they have drawn and are asked to find its centre, they will almost certainly begin folding the circle. In this way they soon discover for themselves not only a good method of finding the centre but also the symmetry of a circle when it is folded about a diameter.

Some eight-year-olds, who had folded a circle into four equal sections and then cut out one section to show that the remainder was three quarters (Fig. 5.15), discovered that they could use this shape to make a cone to fit on top of a model they had made. A cone is

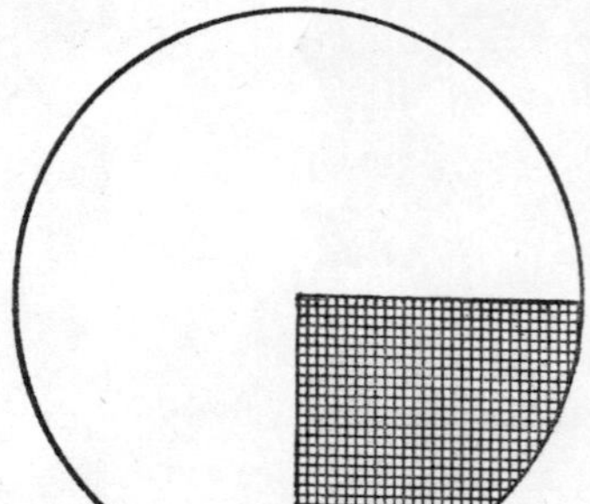
Fig. 5.15

not an easy shape to make. Children and adults often begin by cutting out an isosceles triangle and are surprised to find that this cannot be made into a cone.

PLATE XI
A class of seven-year-old juniors working on a variety of mathematical assignments.

PLATE XII

A fourth year "C" class (of more than 40 children in all) at work on a mathematics project "Life at the Mitchells". This project soon spread to other subjects.

PLATE XIII
Older juniors: These girls are working on areas. Those in the foreground are finding "how squares grow" (i.e. finding the relationship between the areas and sides of squares using square inches).

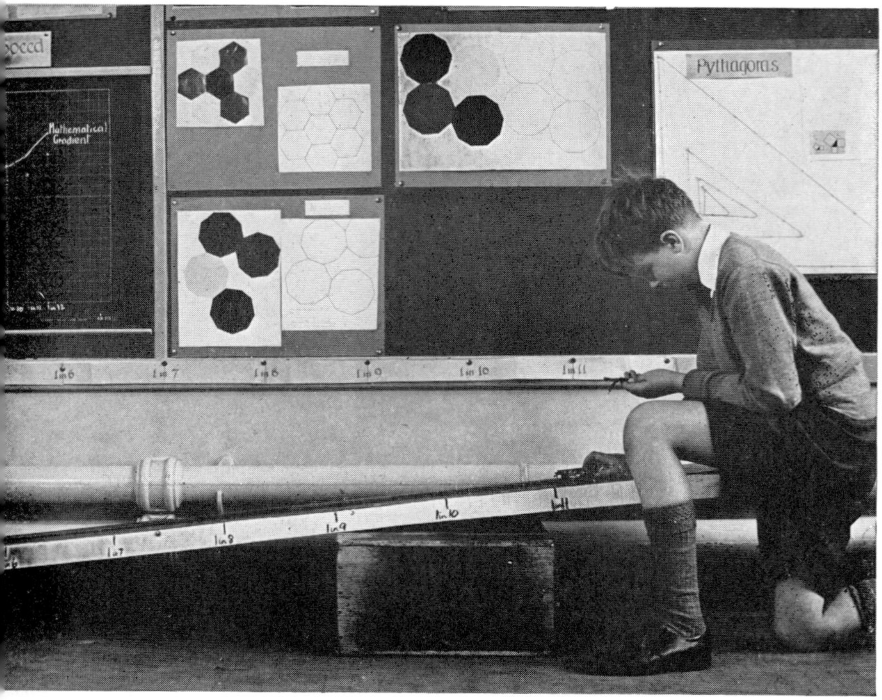

PLATE XIV

Older juniors: This boy, of his own volition, is trying to find the relationship between the gradient and the time taken by a truck to run down the slope.

PLATE XV

These boys are finding the thickness of a sheet of blotting paper by counting the number of sheets in half an inch.

The next important property of a circle which children can discover for themselves is the circumference/diameter relationship. But if the children are to discover this for themselves care must be taken to ensure that the calculations involved are not so complicated that they obscure the result. It is worth waiting until a collection of circular objects has been made of diameters 1″, 2″, 3″, 4″, etc.

Some nine-year-olds were asked to make such a collection. This took some time and entailed a good deal of measuring. When the collection was made a small group of children was asked first to guess the circumference of each circle and then to measure this. The children then suggested using tape measures to measure the circumference. Their first guesses were always twice the diameter. They soon found, however, that the perimeter was about three times the diameter. They amended their guesses accordingly. Some ten-year-olds solved this problem graphically and this will be elaborated in the next chapter.

Another group of able ten-year-olds was asked to find if there was a relationship between the diameter of a circle and its area. In order to do this they drew circles of diameter 1″, 2″, 3″ up to 10″ on squared paper with $\frac{1}{4}$″ squares and decided to find the area by counting the squares. They were not, of course, able to see the relationship for the numbers they obtained. They represented their results on a graph and used the smooth curve they obtained to find the areas of circles of different diameters. The same group of children became so interested in shapes that they decided to investigate the properties of an ellipse. Once again they represented their results graphically, and reference will be made to this in the next chapter.

Further properties of shapes which have been investigated by young children of primary school age will be found in the sections which follow on the topics: dimensions, symmetry, similarity.

II. Dimensions

Perimeter

A group of six-year-olds was working on some coloured shapes drawn on square inch paper (Fig. 5.16). When asked what they were doing, a girl replied: 'This is where we find perimeters'. Asked what she meant by perimeter, the girl answered: 'It's all the way round'. The girl was then given a cylindrical container and asked if she could find its perimeter. She hesitated and then said, 'No, because we measure perimeter with a ruler and I haven't got a round ruler'. Now on the wall there was a recording of a rather unusual piece of work for an infants school. There was a coloured picture made by one of the children of a path through the wood at the back of the school. With this there was the following record, written by a young seven-year-old: 'We went for a walk through the little wood. We measured the path. It measured 9 chains, 4 yards'. (See Fig. 5.16.)

$$\begin{array}{r} 22 \times 9 \\ 9 \\ \hline 198 \\ +4 \\ \hline 202 \text{ yards} \end{array}$$

Fig. 5.16

Hanging underneath this record was the rope chain the children had made by marking each yard on a piece of skipping rope, 22 yards long. It was obvious from the drawing that the path was a curved one. The questioner went over to the drawing, hoping that this might suggest to the girl a way of measuring the perimeter of the cylinder. Before anything was said, however, the girl, who had been watching, ran off saying, 'I know. The string bag!' The girl returned with the string bag, and a ruler. As she began to measure the perimeter of the cylinder a group of children became interested and immediately made their own collection of objects of various shapes (most of them circular). The group of children used string and rulers or tape measures to find the perimeters. The teacher suggested that they should make a record of their findings. It was quite evident that these children were very clear about the meaning of perimeter, and that it was a length, as they were all using string or a tape measure to measure the perimeter.

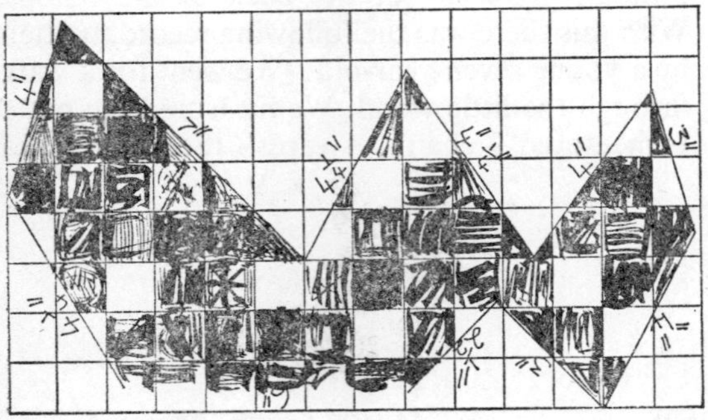

Fig. 5.17

AREA

As will be seen from Figure 5.17 the shapes the children had been measuring previously were all closed and were made with straight lines and drawn on squared paper. When the children were asked what these squares were, a girl replied, 'Square inches, of course,' and explained, 'You use them to cover things.' The children were then asked to go to the wood and to make a collection of leaves. When they returned the teacher asked who had the largest leaf. Immediately a boy replied, 'Mine is the largest because it is the longest'. It was an iris leaf. Rather hesitatingly a girl replied, 'He does not mean the longest. He means the biggest perimeter,' and this girl began to use her piece of string to find the perimeter of her largest leaf. But a girl with a large simple sweet chestnut leaf and a pinnate mountain ash leaf looked from one to the other and said, 'I don't think you mean perimeter.' A minute later she replied: 'If I draw round this leaf in my square-inch book, I could count the squares.' This she did and some other children followed suit. This done, each child began to number the whole squares carefully 1, 2, 3, 4 and so on. They stopped when the whole squares were numbered and began to discuss what to do about the bits of squares. At last they decided to pair these off, big and little, and a triumphant voice said, 'Mine is 19 square inches'.

These young children had not only discovered for themselves the basic method of measuring area but they had also devised a means of dealing with the added difficulty of fractions of units. They were then in a position to find the area of any shape they came across. They were most unlikely to confuse area and perimeter because they were familiar with the units of area and the units of perimeter from first-hand experience.

A class of eight-year-olds dealt with a similar problem in a still more mathematical way. The teacher had cut some square inches from Fablon backing and had painted them in gay colours with household paint. The children were asked to take a handful and to make and sketch different shapes, using all the squares they had taken. It was quite evident, from conversation with the children, that they realised that each of their different shapes had the same area, according to the number of square inches taken. It was interesting, too, to see that none of the children made a rectangle with the square inches. These children were then asked if they could find which of their own paintings of 'My imaginary island' was the largest. They began to guess but could not decide which was the larger of two. They were then asked if they could devise a means of finding the area of these two islands. A boy suggested that they could pin square inches all over the islands to determine area. This they did, using unpainted square inches, and gave the area of one, with evident delight, as 277 square inches. Now they had failed to cover some small areas round the shores of the island. When questioned about this a boy removed one of the square inches at the edge, saying as he did so, 'You see this one covers a part which is not really there, so we thought it would all even up in the end'. In fact these children had discovered a very mathematical way of solving the problem of counting the part squares round the shores. They had first paired off the half squares. They then covered with square inches those parts of more than half a square inch in area and left uncovered (and therefore uncounted) those parts of less than half a square inch. This method invented by the children, can be compared with that of giving an answer to the nearest whole number. (If the figure in the first decimal place is more than five, one is added to the unit figure. If the figure is less than five the unit figure is left as it is.)

It seems, from these examples, that once children are familiar with the units of perimeter, area and volume they should first be confronted with finding the perimeter, area or volume of an irregular shape and not, as was normal until recently, be given the deceptively easy rectangle to consider in the first instance. Since the formulae for the perimeter and area of a rectangle are both concerned with the length and breadth, these are frequently confused by adults, as well as by children. Once the concepts of perimeter, area and volume are understood, children are able to apply these to any shape. When they do come across the rectangle, they are able to discover the 'quick' method for themselves without any help from the teacher. It is clearly best to avoid the simple shapes in the beginning and to avoid giving a rule for the area of a rectangle.

VOLUME

It is becoming more usual to find inch cubes available in infant classes as well as inch squares. Some six-year-olds were asked to make a variety of shapes using a handful of inch cubes. But, if they had not been asked a specific question by the teacher, the fact that they had made a variety of different shapes with the same collection of cubes might well have escaped them. Conservation of volume is a concept of which children need considerable experience before they accept it. Many of the activities of young children can be used to give the necessary experience. Modelling with clay provides a valuable opportunity in this respect, an opportunity which is rarely taken. Every time a child makes a different model with the same lump of clay he is really experiencing the principle that many different shapes can have the same volume. Discussion between teacher and children is essential if this experience is also to be used as 'conservation experience'.

The following pieces of writing by six-year-olds give an insight into young children's early ideas on volume. These children had been asked to put some containers in order of size. They used small cubes to fill the containers. After they had arranged the containers in order on a large sheet of $\frac{1}{2}''$ graph paper, they piled the small cubes contained by each, one on top of the other in separate columns. Finally they recorded on the graph paper the number of cubes in each column by colouring one half inch square for each cube (thus making a block graph).

Here are the records of three different children:

'We had lots of fun deciding what was a container and what was not, philip said a house. I said some rings piled on top of one another, simon said a pieace of paper but a flat pieace of paper won't do, you would have to fold it in a box shape and that would be right, a pocket is a container and so is a rocket, ramond said a leg is because it holds blood and bones but thinking of blood and bones put me of my tea.'

'Finding out the volume of a container means measuring how much it will hold. We used small cubes to measure the volumes of these boxes. But you can use sand, and then weigh it, or pebbles or liquids, or lots of other things to measure volume.'

'This graph shows how many small bricks each box will hold. Each small square equals one brick. Can you see that boxes 3 and 4 hold the same number of bricks, and boxes 7 and 8 hold the same number of bricks, but they are not the same shape of box. When we made this graph we were finding out the Volume of the boxes.'

The seven and eight-year-olds described in the last chapter, who were building cubes of dimensions 2 inches, 3 inches and 4 inches, were also gaining valuable experience of using the units of volume. They, too, one day, from this experience, will have little difficulty when they have to determine the volume of various shapes made with inch cubes.

If, then, children in infant schools become familiar with the units of perimeter, area, and volume and also have some simple experience of measuring these quantities, what can be expected of children of nine and ten years old? The following example will give some idea of the possibilities with older juniors. A large class (48 ten-year-olds) became interested in geometrical shapes. At their teacher's suggestion they made a collection of containers of all kinds from their mothers' larders. They sorted these and found that, although there were some interesting shapes among them, by far the greatest number were cylinders or rectangular boxes. They set themselves to try to discover why containers were the shape they are. For example many packets, like packets of detergents, were tall and thin (although one in its 'square deal' offered an interesting variation). Many large cardboard box containers, however, had a square cross section. The children decided that the tall boxes were tall because they could be held easily in the hand but they were still curious about some of the square sections. They were therefore given this problem to solve: 'Find the largest shape you can enclose with a yard of string'. It was suggested to them that they should begin by finding the largest rectangular shape. The teacher discussed this with them and they decided that, although they could take many more values for the width and length, they would restrict themselves to whole numbers of inches. Each child drew up a table for himself. The teacher asked them for the narrowest rectangle. A girl said it would be one inch wide and seventeen inches long, so that the area would be seventeen square inches. A boy then said he could make a smaller rectangle with his yard of string. He folded the string in two and held the two ends together in one hand. He said the width was nothing at all, the length eighteen inches and the area nothing at all. He insisted on putting this rectangle in the first place in his table. The third entry in the table was then declared to be width two inches, length sixteen inches and area thirty-two square inches.

Width in inches	*Length in inches*	*Area in square inches*
0	18	0
1	17	17
2	16	32
3	15	45
and so on.		

After this the children were left to find the largest rectangle for themselves. There was some discussion as to whether the largest, a square (of side nine inches and area eighty-one square inches), could be allowed to be a 'rectangle' but eventually the children decided that a square was a special rectangle. This discovery delighted the children and they renewed their efforts to collect examples of the economical square shapes. One boy discovered that dry stone wall sheep pens made by farmers are often square in shape. (Reference will be made in the next chapter to the graph which resulted from this investigation.)

A boy then drew attention to the fact that although they had discovered the largest rectangle which could be made with a yard of string, they had not yet discovered why so many containers were cylindrical in shape. The children therefore decided to find the area which a circle made with a yard of string would hold. Their first attempt was to superimpose over a square made with a yard of string a circle made with a yard of string as shown in Figure 5.18.

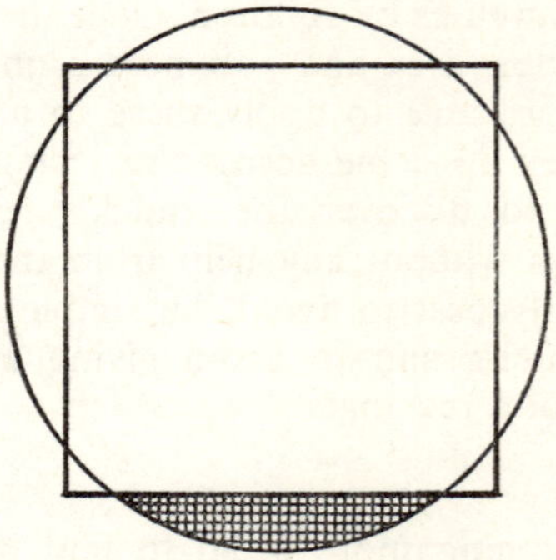

Fig. 5.18

Even by these somewhat crude methods the children were able to appreciate at once that the circle was larger than the square. They attempted to find out how much larger the circle was than the square by marking the enclosed spaces out in small squares. This was not very satisfactory, so the teacher gave them the formulae for circumference and area of a circle. From this they calculated the area of a circle of circumference one yard. They were surprised to find how much larger the circle was than a square of perimeter one yard. (Subsequently the teacher realised that it had been unnecessary to give the children the formulae for the circumference and area of a circle.) The children drew two graphs, first to show the relationship between the circumference and diameter of circles, and secondly to show the relationship between the area and the diameter of circles of different diameters. They used the first graph to find the diameter of the circle of circumference one yard and the second to find the area of a circle with this diameter.

In these examples we have seen that children with wide experience of perimeter, area and volume use these ideas with great confidence to solve the problems they come across. Another group of ten-year-olds came across the statement: 'The pressure of the atmosphere on every square inch is about 15 pounds'. They immediately enquired what the pressure of the atmosphere would be on one of them. They decided to find the surface area of one of the group: a girl. They made her lie on her back on a large sheet of paper and drew round her. They then made her lie on her side and drew round her again. They marked out, in square inches, the profile of the front and the back and counted the number of squares and doubled the result. They found the total area to be 1,962 square inches. (The children were so excited by this piece of work that the teacher decided not to discuss the advisability of approximation with them.) From this result they calculated that the atmospheric pressure on 'Alison' was about 13 tons. An infant from the school enquired anxiously of Alison one day: 'How do you carry it about?'—which shows what a difficult concept atmospheric pressure is for young children!

ELLIPSES

Some children of ten found from a book how to draw an ellipse using two drawing pins and a loop of string (Fig. 5.19). They discovered that they could vary the shape by fixing the pins farther apart or nearer together. The teacher suggested they should find the smallest and the largest ellipses they could draw with the same

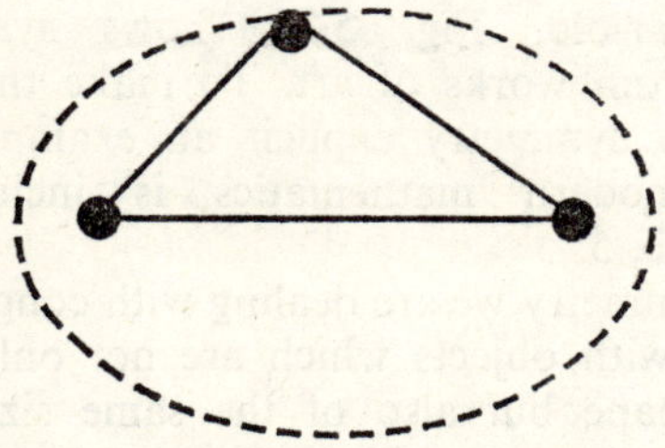

Fig. 5.19

loop of string. For the smallest they soon found that they had to fix the drawing pins as far apart as possible (Fig. 5.20). For the largest

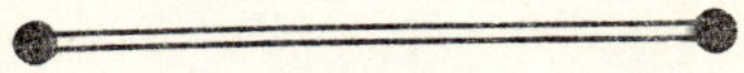

Fig. 5.20

they had to have the drawing pins as close together as possible—in fact, one on top of the other. They were interested to find that a circle was really a special ellipse. This lead them to investigate the properties of the ellipse and in a book called 'Research on the Ellipse' they recorded their findings about the perimeter and area of an ellipse.

III. Symmetry

Many of the activities of the primary school provide excellent opportunities for giving children experience of different types of symmetry and for drawing their attention to properties which can be deduced when shapes are symmetrical.

A five-year-old boy in his first term spilt some paint on a sheet of paper he was going to use. He folded it in two and walked across to throw it in the waste paper basket. On the way he opened the paper out and looked at it (Fig. 5.21). He was so excited by the pattern he saw that he took it to show his teacher. His teacher appreciated his discovery and sent Stephen to show the older infants and the headmistress. Soon the walls were covered with 'Stephen's patterns'. These children became aware of the simplest kind of mathematical symmetry.

Some six-year-olds had been making symmetrical patterns by Stephen's method (with one axis of symmetry) and by folding a sheet of paper into four and cutting patterns through the four folds of paper using scissors (giving two axes of symmetry). They began collecting leaves and flowers which were symmetrical in shape. At their teacher's suggestion they sorted their collection as follows:

1 Those which could be cut into halves in one way (one half is the mirror image of the other).
2 Those which could be cut into two halves in two ways.
3 Those which could be cut into two halves in more than two ways.

In fact their collections of flowers took them into three-dimensional symmetry.

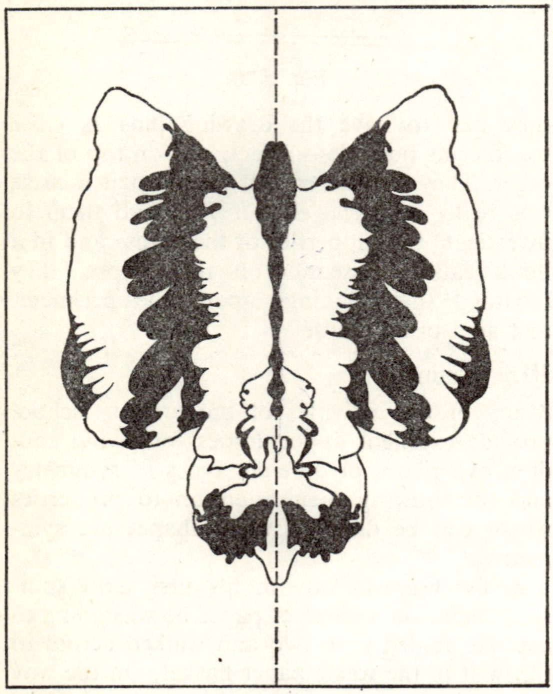

Fig. 5.21

Some nine-year-olds made a collection of interesting shapes: of hexagons (from biscuit packets), of octagons from tile patterns, of three-penny pieces (dodecagons). They recognised the symmetry of these regular shapes, saying 'The shapes are the same whichever way up you hold them' (Figure 5.22) and that all the angles must be equal. From this they were able to calculate each angle by the method already outlined in the previous section.

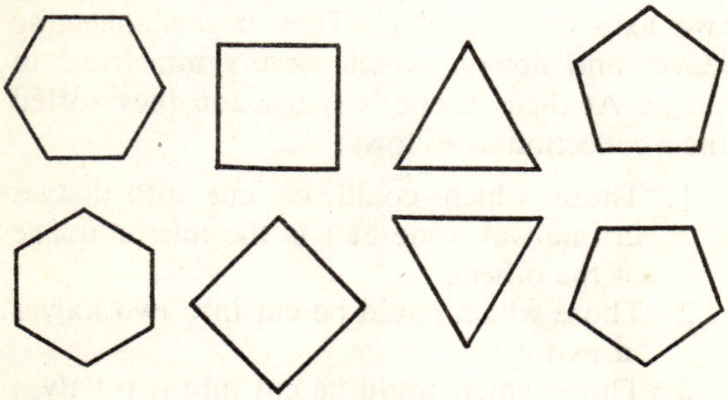

Fig. 5.22

Some ten-year-olds investigated the working of the kaleidoscope. They found that, using two mirrors hinged with sellotape, and a drawing pin with large coloured head as the object, they could vary the number of reflections by altering the angle between the mirrors. They then set about, systematically, to see if they could discover whether there was a relationship between the angle between the mirrors and the number of pins they could see altogether (one real, all the others reflections). They made some interesting discoveries which they represented on an unusual graph.

Symmetry is a powerful and far reaching mathematical concept with applications in many fields, traditional and modern; there is a symmetry in number patterns, in algebraic expressions, and in geometry, ancient and modern. Usually the recognition of symmetry permits a far more elegant and concise mathematical solution to a problem as the following two examples of 'dynamic' geometry will show.

(i) Fold a rectangular sheet of paper in half. Cut off a corner of the fold by a straight cut. Unfold the corner you have cut off and describe all the properties of the shape made.

(ii) Fold a rectangular sheet of paper in half and in half again. Cut off a corner of the double fold by a straight cut. Unfold the corner and describe all the properties of the shape made.

It is most important that teachers should make the most of the activities of children which give them varied experience of symmetry, and help them to abstract the mathematical consequences. Mathematically speaking a symmetry is any transformation which leaves the shape as a whole in the same position. This can be effected by translation, rotation and reflection. Fig. 5.23 overleaf was the work of an eight-year-old. Fig. 5.24 shows symmetries taken from works of art. To make the varied types of symmetry explicit an example taken from modern mathematics is included in Appendix 5.

In symmetry we are dealing with congruences, that is with objects which are not only of the same shape but also of the same size. Wallpaper patterns provide interesting examples of congruences of shapes. Some examples of

Fig. 5.23

congruences or repetitions in number patterns will be found in the previous chapter in modulus arithmetic. We now turn to another mathematical idea of first importance. In this case the shapes are the same but the sizes are different.

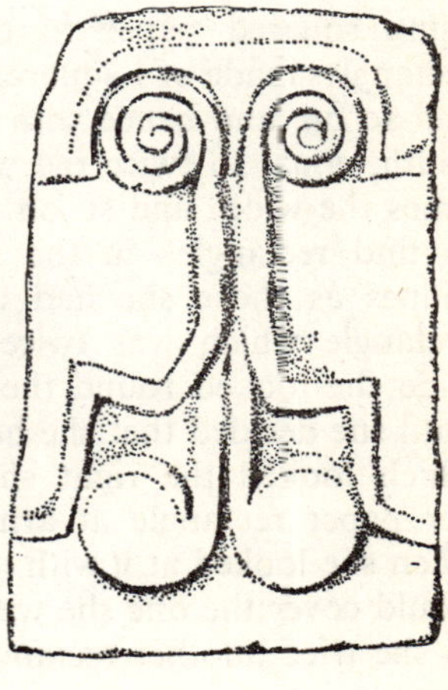

Fig. 5.24

IV. Similarity

Mathematical similarity has a more definite meaning than the 'similarity' of everyday use. Objects are mathematically similar if one is a scale model of the other; that is, if they are of identical shape but different in size. To speak more mathematically, objects are mathematically similar if corresponding angles in the two figures are of the same size and if corresponding sides in the two figures are in the same ratio. Words which will frequently occur in mathematical similarity are ratio and proportion.

Once more this topic has its beginnings in the infant school. When five-year-olds are making clay model animals, vegetables and different fruits for their 'shop' they instinctively strive to make these of the shape that looks right to them and, in comparing one fruit with another, in the right proportion.

A class of five- and six-year-olds became interested in making a map of the houses and streets in which they lived. They used blocks of wood for the houses, each writing his name on a block of wood. They constructed their map on the floor and told the teacher where to draw in the roads. She wrote the names on the roads and drew in the river and the children (after a lot of discussion) placed the houses in the roads in which they lived. When this map was finished and they had enjoyed it to the full, they wanted to make a real 'map'. So the teacher put a very large sheet of paper on the floor and she and the children painted in the roads and the river and named these. Then each child drew, painted and labelled his own house and stuck it in the right place on the map. As time went on, more and more land-marks were entered on the map until by the end of their second year in the infant school the children had produced an attractive and most instructive map of their district.

In the same school a seven-year-old boy and an eight-year-old had made a model of Coventry Cathedral. Reference has already been made to the competence with which these boys were able to determine the actual measurement of different parts of the Cathedral from the model, using the scale of 1 ft. to $\frac{1}{16}$th of an inch. They had a thorough working knowledge of scale models (and therefore of mathematical similarity).

Two eight-year-old boys were working on a 4 inch to the mile map of the district. They enquired of visitors who arrived by car their starting point and undertook to work out the shortest route to the school. They did this, using a piece of string and converting the length to miles with the aid of a ruler, taking 4 inches as 1 mile. When they had found the shortest route they asked to see the car's milometer, triumphantly recorded the result and told the visitors how far out of their way they had travelled.

Some idea of the intuitive understanding young children have of mathematical similarity and of their direct and simple approach to this topic in solving real problems is shown by the following examples. (Probably this results from experience outside the school with plastic model making.) An eight-year-old girl was using squared paper to cut out a series of rectangles made of 1 square, 2 squares, 3 squares and so on, and hence with lengths equal to the width, equal to twice the width, equal to three times the width and so on. She was then asked to find rectangles in the school of the same shapes as those she had cut out. Taking the rectangle which was twice as long as it was wide she looked round the classroom carefully until she decided that she had found a rectangle which looked the right shape. She then held her paper rectangle at arm's length to see if, when she looked at it with one eye, the rectangle would cover the one she was testing. It did not, so she tried another rectangle until she did discover one of the proportion she was looking for.

A boy of nine, faced with a similar problem, solved it in a different way. He was asked to discover whether a set of three match boxes of different sizes were of the same shape or not (i.e. whether they were scale models of one another).

He put one match box on top of the other (Fig. 5.25) and tried to see if the four corners A, B, C and D would all lie on the edge of his ruler. This proved too difficult for him, so he removed the top two boxes and drew round the largest one. He then removed that, placed the second-sized box with one corner at A and drew round that. He repeated this with the smallest match box also. He was then able to use the edge of his ruler to test whether the four corners A, B, C and D were in a straight line. They were

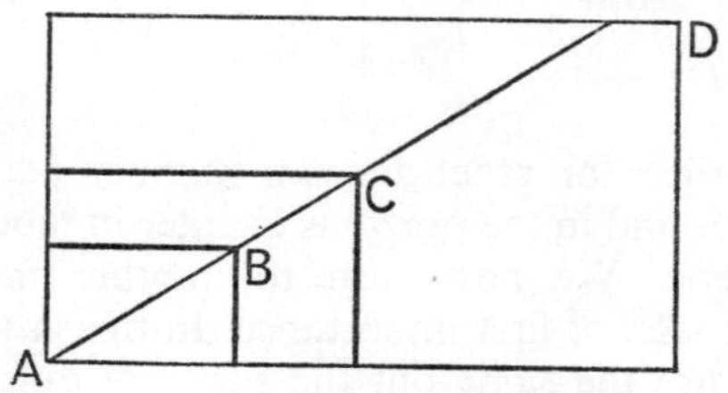

Fig. 5.25

not, so the boy said at once: 'The match boxes are not the same shape'.

A teacher gave his eight-year-olds experience of mathematical similarity by asking them to draw a lorry on squared paper with squares of different sizes. A teacher of nine-year-olds, after giving them this kind of experience, suggested that the children should draw mathematical caricatures. Each child drew on squared paper any object he chose (for example a face, an aeroplane and so on). They retained one dimension as it was and magnified the other by 2, 3, 4 or 5 times as they chose. When they came to use a pantograph to enlarge a map, they realised that the original and the one they had drawn were in fact scale models of each other. They were asked to work out the ratio of the areas of the two maps, the original and the one they had drawn. Now the scales of their two maps were in the ratio of 1 : 2. The teacher suggested that they should first try to find out what would happen if they doubled the edge of various simple shapes, beginning with the square (Fig. 5.26). When they had found the answer to this they repeated the experiment with a rectangle and with a triangle (Fig. 5.27). Some of them were more adventurous and tried to discover what would happen if they doubled the edges of regular shapes with six sides, eight sides and so on. They then decided that they could now give the answer to the ratio of the areas of their maps. They also turned their attention to the shapes they had already considered and found out what happened to a square when its side was trebled, quadrupled and so on.

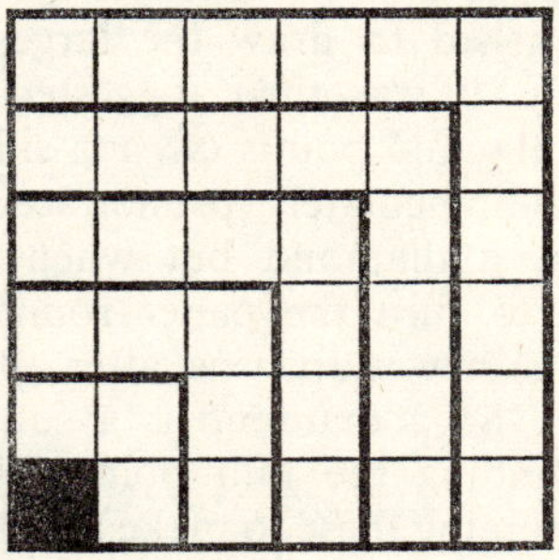

Fig. 5.26

The teacher suggested that they should draw a graph showing how the area of the squares varied as the side increased.

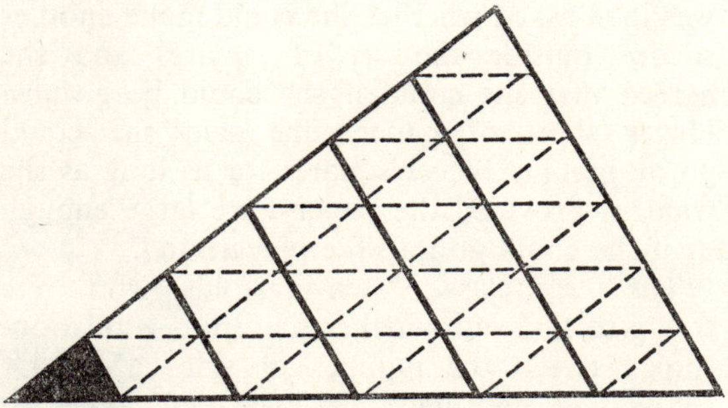

Fig. 5.27

Some bright ten-year-olds were able to solve an interesting problem which gave them a clear insight into the meaning of mathematical similarity in three dimensions. In a book they found a quotation which interested them: 'A man has to eat one fiftieth of his weight in food every day. A mouse has to eat one half of its weight in food, just in order to keep alive.' The children discussed this with their teacher. She asked them why they needed to eat. They decided that they ate so that they could have energy and that they dissipated the energy again by such means as running and getting hot. This meant that they lost the heat through their skin. As a result of this discussion, the children decided that they would compare the surface area of the mouse with its weight and the surface area of a girl in the class with her weight. It was easy enough to weigh the mouse but the determination of its surface area was more of a problem. Eventually they made a clay model of the mouse and 'squared it up' to find the surface area in square inches. They had already found the area of 'Alison' and so determined the number of square inches of Alison's surface there were for each quarter pound of her weight. They found the number of square inches for each quarter pound of the mouse was about 23 to 1 and the number of square inches for each quarter pound of Alison was $5\frac{1}{2}$ to 1. The children were still puzzled and their teacher discussed the result with them and eventually suggested that they should examine what happens when a simple mathematical shape, such as a cube, increases in size. The children decided to take a one inch cube as their unit and to calculate the number of square inches of surface per cube as the cube grew in size. (They decided that the overall result would not be affected if they used the ratio of area to volume instead of area to weight since the former would give them an easier unit.) The table they made began as shown in Fig. 5.28. A cube has six faces and therefore the surface area of a 1 inch cube is 6 square inches. A 2 inch cube has six faces, each of area 4 square inches. Its volume as shown in the previous chapter, is 8 cubic inches (2 layers of 4 cubes). The children continued as far as a cube of side 6 inches. They realised from the table that small creatures have a much larger surface area for their volume than large creatures and hence understood why a mouse needed to eat so much more than a man. To complete the problem they drew a graph showing the relationship between the area and the volume. They also applied these results to a baby of length 24″ and a man of height 6 ft.

This complex problem required an understanding of the underlying principles of mathematical similarity and their effect on the areas and volumes of similar shapes.

Length of edge in inches	Area of 6 faces in sq. ins.	Volume in cubic inches	$\frac{A}{V}$ sq.ins. per cubic inch
1	6	1	6
2	24	8	3
3	54	27	2
4	and so on		
5			
6			

Fig. 5.28

The $\frac{\text{skin area}}{\text{volume}}\left(\frac{A}{V}\right)$ relationship is another example of inverse proportion

Edge length	1	2	3	4	5	6
A/V	6	3	2	?	?	?

When the edge is doubled, $\frac{A}{V}$ is halved.

When the edge is trebled, $\frac{A}{V}$ is divided by 3.

V. Mathematical limits

This is a concept which comes within the understanding of quite young children as the following examples show. An eight-year-old girl was making heavy weather of long multiplication, addition and subtraction. She was asked to name the largest number she knew. After some hesitation she said 'a million' but added 'I don't know how many noughts though. It might be three or it might be six'. A nine-year-old boy said slowly: 'That was a silly question to ask. If I tell you, this moment, the biggest number I know, the next moment I can tell you a number one larger and the next moment a number one larger than that and so on for ever'. Now these children had made a model of the seaside with sand and shells. They were shown how to draw a shell pattern, using two pencils tied one at each end of a piece of string; the string was wound tightly round one of the pencils, which was held fast upright on the paper. The other pencil was moved so as to keep the string taut as it unwound, and the pencil point drew a curve. When the string was fully unwound the children were asked if they could make a large shell pattern. They immediately asked for a longer piece of string and a larger sheet of paper. The girls suggested that they should go outside in the playground and use a very long piece of string and finally said that, if the playground were large enough, the shell pattern could be made as large as required. To give children further experience of a limit each was given a large sheet of $\frac{1}{4}$ inch graph paper and asked to draw the largest possible square on it. It was then suggested that they should find the mid points of each side and join these. They immediately pronounced the new shape to be a diamond but when they were encouraged to turn the paper round they decided that the new shape was, after all, a square. A boy said, 'So a diamond is a square'. They continued finding the mid points of the new square and joining these to make another square. When they had a series of six squares one inside the other, a girl said, 'I can see what is going to happen. We are going to get nearer and nearer to the middle but we shall never really get there'. She obviously had a clear idea, from this experience, of a mathematical limit. She was then asked whether she could make another square outside the set of squares and she agreed that she could if she could be given a bigger sheet of paper. She said she could go on making bigger squares for as long as she wanted, provided the paper were large enough or if she could go into the playground.

The large class of ten-year-olds, who were trying to find out whether there was a relationship between the number of sides a regular shape had and its angle, was left alone to solve this problem because their teacher had influenza. Initially it was suggested that they should continue to twelve sides but their interest in the problem drove them to continue first to 240 and eventually to 450,000,000 sides. (Their description of this piece of work is quoted in full in the following chapter.)

No specific reference has been made to the introduction of algebra. This is not because we do not think this is a suitable subject for primary school children but because this subject is probably best introduced incidentally. Many of the illustrations discussed in the chapter might well have been extended to include algebra. For example, after the children had discovered the number of triangles in a rigid framework, they might have been asked: 'How many triangles for 10 sides? 20 sides? n sides?' and given the answer n — 2. Further reference to algebraical applications will be included in the next chapter on graphical applications.

Summary of spatial relationships and concepts discovered by primary school children

1 Angles. Square corners (or right angles) of squares and rectangles. Angles by rotation. Compass directions. Intersecting lines and vertically opposite angles. Parallel lines and intersecting line and angles so formed.

2 Geometrical shapes and the relationships between sides, angles and diagonals.

(a) Solid shapes: cubes, cuboids (rectangular boxes), cylinders, cones, spheres. Making the regular solids.

(b) Regular flat shapes: square, rectangle, triangle, hexagon, octagon, pentagon, shape fitting, tiles. Circle.

3 Conservation of area, volume.
Perimeter, area, volume of irregular shapes. The relationship between the perimeter and side of a square; circumference and diameter of a circle; the area and side of a square; the area and diameter of a circle; the volume and edge of a cube; the volume and diameter of a ball.

4 Symmetry. Recognition in 3 dimensions and 2 dimensions. Recognition of the types of symmetry: reflection, rotation, translation. (Appendix 5).

5 Similarity. Maps, scale models, caricatures. Recognition of the precise relationship: angles equal, sides in the same ratio.
How squares grow; how cubes grow.

6 Mathematical limits from shapes: spirals, contracting and expanding squares.

6 The place of graphical representation in the learning of mathematics

Graphical representation makes an immediate appeal to children of all abilities and helps them to see relationships which they might not otherwise be able to appreciate. In this chapter the development and interpretation of graphical representation by young children will be shown by illustrations taken from the work of children of various ages. The mathematical implications of the ideas included in this chapter, and the unification of mathematical ideas which graphical representation makes possible, will form the second part of this chapter; this will not be drawn from children's work.

Pictorial representation

Graphical representation frequently begins in infants schools, where it normally takes the form of vivid pictorial representation, but at this stage such representation is simply a way of recording results and, in general, involves a one-to-one correspondence of one kind or another. The headmaster of a large junior school, where the children had taken to graphical work with great enthusiasm, was on his way to visit the infant school when he saw some infants lying on the ground, side by side, with their feet against a wall. One of his juniors was drawing round the infants with a piece of chalk. They greeted the headmaster and he inquired what they were doing. 'Playing at graphs', was the rather surprising answer and the children jumped up to show the headmaster that each one had been 'drawn round' in chalk.

Children of six and seven enjoy collecting their own numerical data and making pictorial graphs of their findings. In a small village school the children made a census of the traffic passing during the morning. The five-year-olds used model toys to make their record of the census; they arranged the right number of cars, lorries, cyclists and G.P.O. vans in rows on the table, adding to the collection as each vehicle passed the school. The seven-year-olds labelled some inch cubes with the name: car, lorry, bicycle etc. and made their record as each vehicle passed the school, adding the cube to the correct row. The older children took the census first and then represented their results by a block graph.

This type of vivid pictorial representation usually arises naturally at this stage, as the following examples show:

1 Some five-year-olds kept daily records of the growth of a tadpole; they fished it out in a teaspoon in order to make a drawing of it each day.

2 Some six-year-olds kept a pictorial record of the growth of a sweet pea plant. Each day they matched the length of the stem in their picture with the actual length of the stem of the plant. As the leaves appeared in pairs they kept a numerical record as well.

3 A class of six- and seven-year-olds became interested in the colour of eyes and colour of hair of the children in the class. For the record each child drew and cut out two pictures of his own face with hair and eyes coloured. The children decided to keep separate records for boys and girls so that they were able to compare the results for the sexes. They had (a) fair hair, dark hair, brown hair for boys and girls on one sheet and (b) blue eyes, brown eyes, grey eyes for boys and girls on the second sheet.

4 Some six-year-olds took a great interest in the thermometer which they learnt to read. The teacher drew a thermometer on the left-hand side of a large sheet of paper and marked in an enlarged version of the gradu-

ations of the thermometer. Each day, at midday, the children read the temperature and entered the result on the graph by drawing a red column to the correct graduation on the thermometer. Of course this column had to be coloured red to resemble the thread of alcohol in the real thermometer. Each day a child added a comment about the temperature in one part of the room or another and compared the temperatures on different days.

The last two examples emphasize a vital function of graphical representation: the use of the graph to obtain further information. It is of the utmost importance that, once a graph has been made, it should then be used for further discoveries.

The transition from the type of vivid representation described in the preceding examples to the symbolic block graph, in which the symbol used, a square on a piece of paper, does not resemble the object it represents, needs to be a gradual one to ensure that children fully understand the more abstract representation. The different ways of recording traffic already described illustrate the transition very clearly (but here as always, unless discussion followed the completion of this piece of work, the children might well have been unaware of the mathematical implication of it).

Children of seven and eight can often take the step for themselves from the pictorial method to the symbolic. It is most important that children should undertake their own investigations for graphical representation. Sometimes, as in a traffic census, a group of children may be concerned with a particular piece of work, but some individual personal investigations should be encouraged. In the beginning the teacher may need to provide suggestions to keep the numbers within the children's capabilities. But as soon as possible children should be encouraged to make suggestions for themselves. It is at this next stage, when children are planning their own investigations, that large numbers become involved and children begin to tire of drawing pictorial units and resort to shorthand symbols (such as a cross or coloured square); the following example illustrates this. A girl decided to make a graph of the number of pairs of shoes belonging to each member of her family. She drew the appropriate style for each person on her sheet of ½ inch graph paper, 8 pairs of stilettos for her mother and 2 pairs of large black shoes for her father! These drawings were a vivid substitute for reality. A boy in the same class found out the number of pets of various kinds kept by the children in his class. The number of budgerigars (26) and of cats (22) were so large that he decided to use one square (which he coloured blue) for each budgerigar and one square (which he coloured black) for each cat.

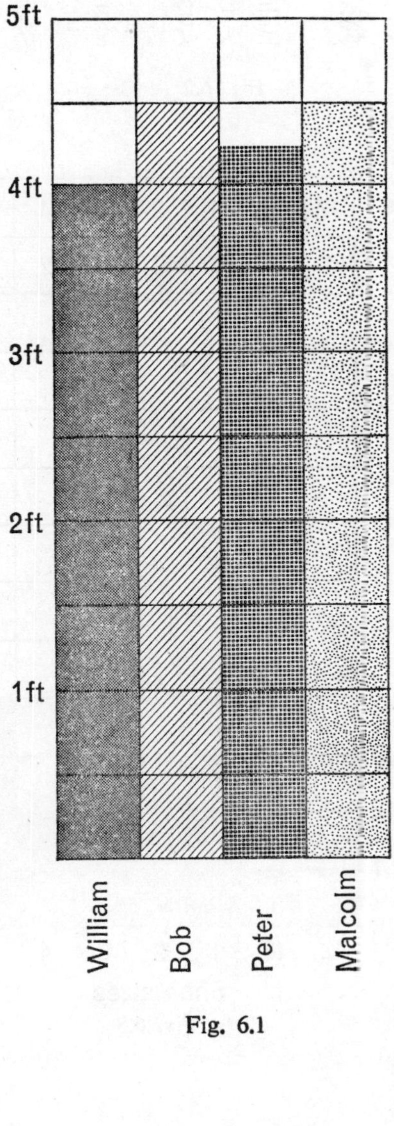

Fig. 6.1

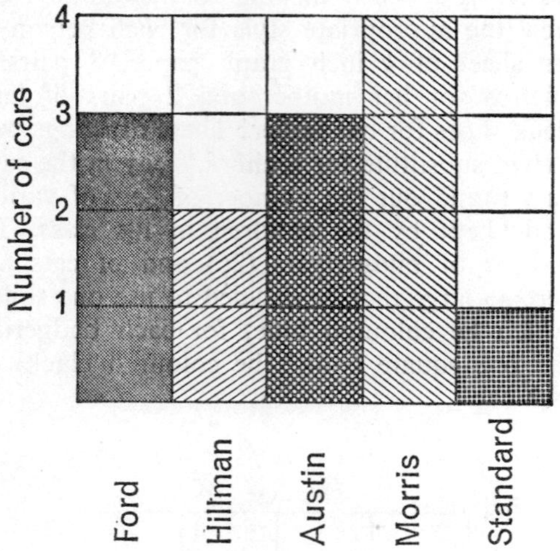

Fig. 6.2

Block graphs

It is important for us, as teachers, to distinguish between the different types of block graphs which the children will meet.

I. (a) The height of four boys. (Fig. 6.1).
   (b) Number of different kinds of cars owned by our fathers. (Fig. 6.2).
   (c) How I spend my Sunday.
   (d) Favourite T.V. Programmes.

In this type the 'units' on the horizontal axis need not be in any special order.

II. (a) Sizes of shoes worn by children in 3A.
   (b) Number of children in families in 4A.

In this type the 'units' on the horizontal axis are numbers and are set out in order. (Figs. 6.3, 6.4). Not only must the information be collected, it must also be put in order before the graph is made. Weather observations and data from scientific experiments are examples of this type although column graphs are often used instead of block graphs for representing such data. It will be seen from the section which follows that in column graphs points on the horizontal axis are numbered (instead of spaces—the width of the blocks—as in block graphs).

Shoe size	12	13	1	2	3	4	5
No. of children	1	1	7	9	8	2	4

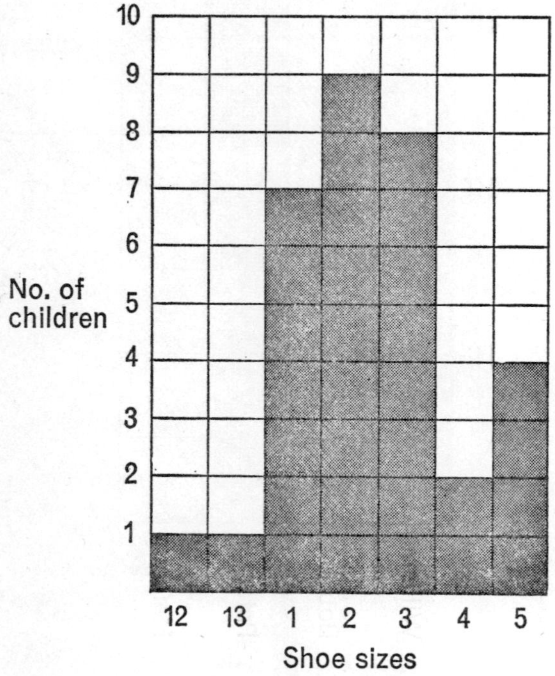

Fig. 6.3

No. of children	1	2	3	4	5	6	7
No. of families	2	4	3	2	0	1	1

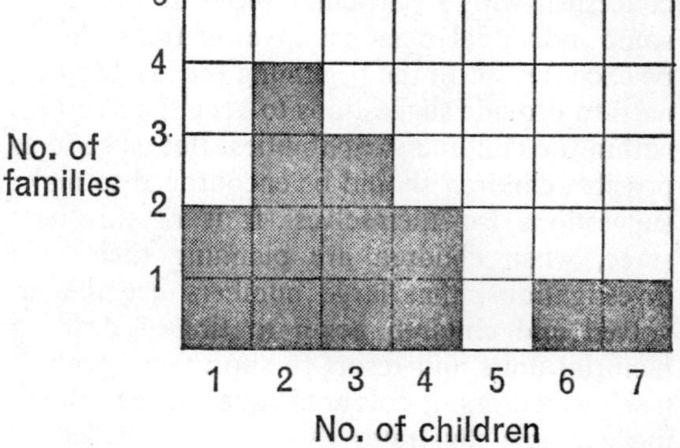

Fig. 6.4

Graphs showing algebraic relationships

If, subsequently, children are to be helped to discover relationships from graphs it is essential that they should first have a very wide experience of making and using graphs in which there is no apparent and easy relationship to be seen between the quantities or numbers (called variables) represented. The transition from the pictorial or block graph to one in which a definite relationship is represented needs to be a gradual one. The essential differences between a block graph and one which represents an algebraic relationship will be evident from the examples which follow.

A graph can be regarded as a visual means of recording data collected, such as those provided by weather observations, rainfall day by day or week by week, temperature kept hour by hour or day by day, the speed of the wind taken daily at a certain time, the number of hours of sunshine each day; or data from scientific experiments. Such data should be recorded by means of a block or column graph because the recordings are made at intervals and are not in any sense continuous. A graph normally shows the variation between two sets of numbers or of quantities. In graphs made to record data collected in simple scientific experiments, the independent variable (that is the one chosen by the children or suggested by the teacher) is normally represented along the horizontal axis. The second variable (which is then dependent on the first) is marked on the 'vertical' axis. The examples quoted will make this point clear.

The examples which follow are all illustrations of those in which an algebraic relationship exists. Such relationships, if derived from the children's experiences, are limited in type and will occur over and over again.

Straight lines

The first example[1] shows that children can recognise a relationship from the recordings of experimental data. A class of 46 ten-year-olds was investigating the stretched length of elastic bands under different conditions. Four girls in one group were adding weights (at 2 ounce intervals) to a light scale pan at the end of an elastic band suspended vertically. They were recording their results on a prepared graph with weights (in ounces) marked along the horizontal axis (because the children had decided for themselves that they would observe the lengths as they added 2 ounces, 4 ounces, 6 ounces, etc.). The actual length of the elastic bands as each weight was added was therefore marked on the vertical column. They had made four recordings and it was clear to their teacher that these were almost on a straight line. When a further 2 ounces was added, the reading was taken and a girl entered the result on the graph; it was clear that the fifth point was right out of line, as shown in Fig. 6.5. The girl who had taken the last measurement said immediately, 'I must do it again: I must have made a mistake'. It was quite evident that the girls had noticed that the tops of the columns appeared to be in a straight line; in other words, although nothing had been said to the children, they had become aware from their recordings of the relationship which was emerging.

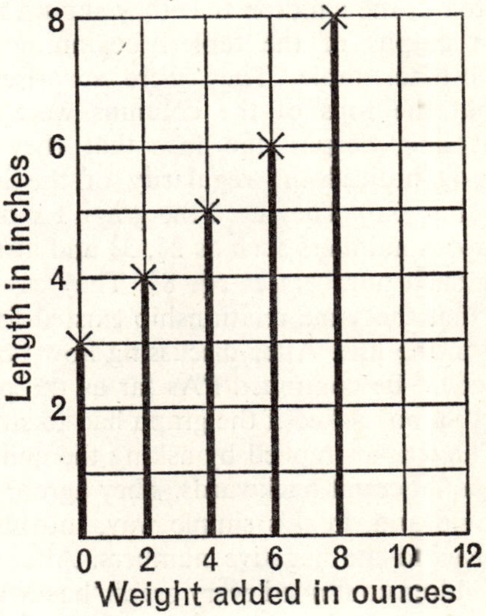

Fig. 6.5

A straight line relationship is obviously an easy one to recognise. Even so, when data have been collected from an experiment, because of human errors as well as unavoidable inaccuracies of measurement, the points will not lie exactly on a straight line. In such cases (and they will be many) the 'line of best fit' is most easily obtained by stretching a piece of string so that

[1] *Science in Primary Schools*, HMSO, 1961.

the points are well balanced on either side of the line. If children are encouraged to use a piece of string to test whether or not their recordings appear to lie on a straight line they may themselves suggest drawing in the 'line of best fit' in order to use the graph to predict other results. Some examples of experiments which should give a straight line relationship are given at the end of this chapter.

The illustrations which follow focus attention on the distinction between a block or column graph and a straight line graph. They also provide a transition from one type of graph to the other.

Some ten-year-olds (with little previous experience of practical work) were asked to draw graphs of some of the multiplication tables. Their first attempt was a block graph from which they were able to see that the blocks increased regularly so that successive steps were equal (see Chapter 4, Figs. 4.1, 4.2). The graph gave the appearance of a staircase. It was next suggested to the children that they should make column graphs of the tables, beginning with the two-times table. They were surprised to find that the tops of the columns were in a straight line, despite the fact that they had previously noticed the regularity of the block graph. (Fig. 6.6). They used the graph for doubling various numbers such as $2\frac{1}{2}$, $3\frac{3}{4}$ and also for halving such numbers as $5\frac{1}{4}$, $8\frac{3}{4}$. They came to realise that the same relationship existed for all points on the line. After discussing how far the graph could be continued ('As far as the paper allowed') a boy asked if the graph had to stop at zero. The teacher replied by asking the children if they could count backwards. They agreed that they could and, in this simple way, introduced themselves to the negative numbers. After that these children continued every graph 'backwards' whenever possible.

One day, when putting in the axes, the teacher substituted an x for one of the numbers on the horizontal axis. The children protested so he replaced x by the expected number. He was apt, at any time, to write x for any number along the horizontal axis. The children noticed that when he substituted a letter for a number on the vertical axis, he always used y. Soon the children themselves were referring to the numbers along the horizontal axis as the x numbers and those

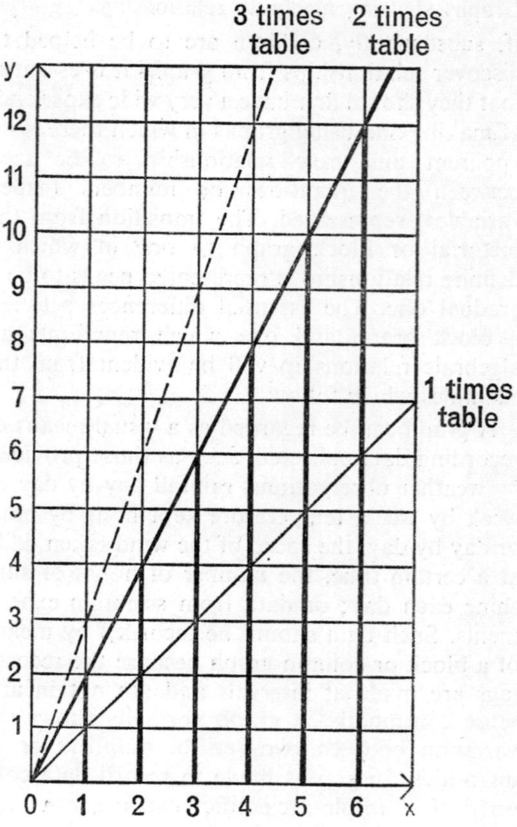

Fig. 6.6

along the vertical axis as the y numbers. When, one day, the teacher asked the children to tell him the relationship between all the y numbers and the x numbers, without hesitation they replied, 'The y numbers are always twice the x numbers'. This statement was soon abbreviated to $y = 2x$. This experience was repeated with the three-times table, the four-times table and so on. The children labelled each line with its algebraic relationship $y = 2x$, $y = 3x$, $y = 4x$ etc. One boy insisted on drawing the graph of the one-times table, $y = x$.

The teacher sometimes encouraged the children to write these relationships in the form $\frac{y}{x} = 1$, $\frac{y}{x} = 2$, $\frac{y}{x} = 3$ and called these the *constant ratio* or ready reckoner relationship.

The materials used for learning should look attractive to the children

PLATE 1 *Weighing small objects*

PLATE 2 *Finding the English equivalent of a homemade litre measure*

PLATE 3

Curve stitching

When a girl discovered that, starting with a circle, she obtained a circle within it (Plate 3), she decided to find out what shape she would get if she started with a semi-circle (Plate 4) and an ellipse (Plate 5)

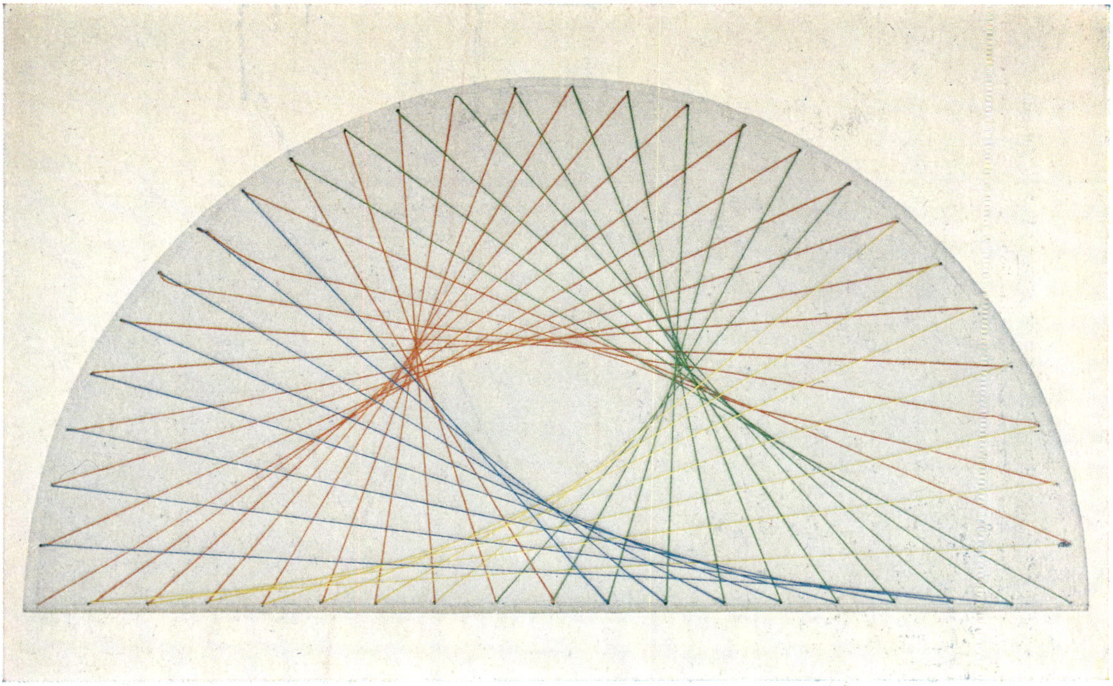

PLATE 4

PLATE 5

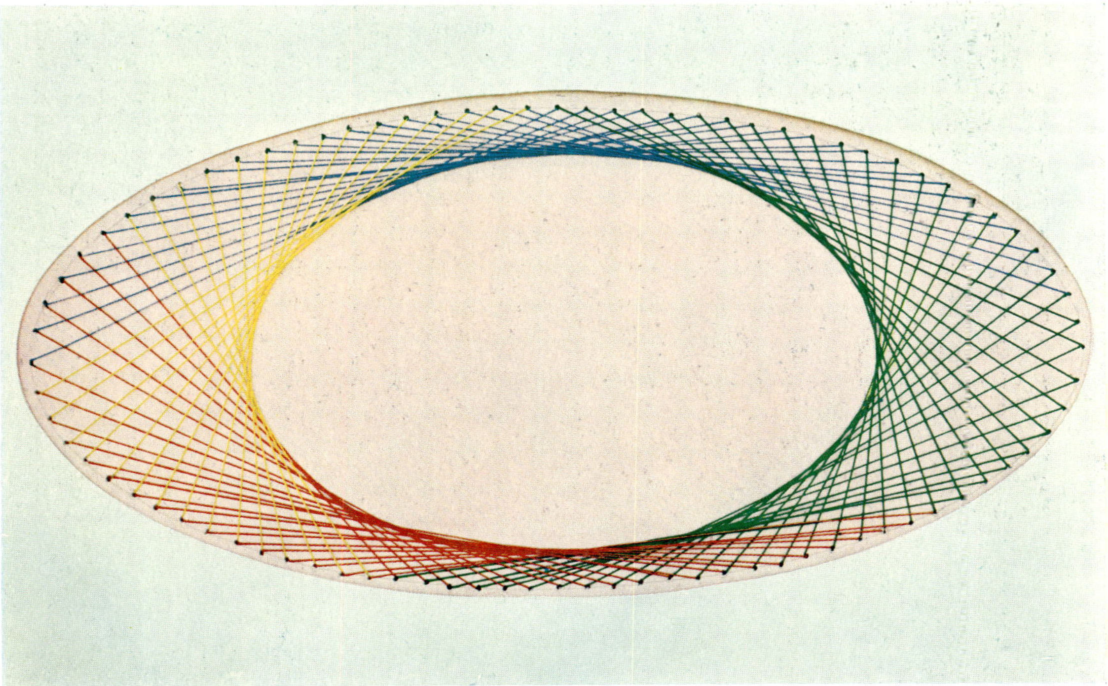

PLATE 6 *Finding actual distances from a map*

PLATE 7 *Finding the circumference/diameter relationship of circles from a graph*

The children noticed that the lines became steeper with each table and the teacher introduced them to the word gradient. (Fig. 6.7). They found the gradient for each table (e.g. in the 2-times table, the gradient is 2 in 1 or $G = \frac{2}{1}$).

This led the children to take an interest in road gradients (which they discovered from a book were measured in a different way i.e. a steep slope of 1 in 3 means 1 unit up in 3 units measured along the road. (Fig. 6.8). They collected the gradients of the steepest hills from the road book of one of the motoring associations and wrote of their personal experiences on these hills.

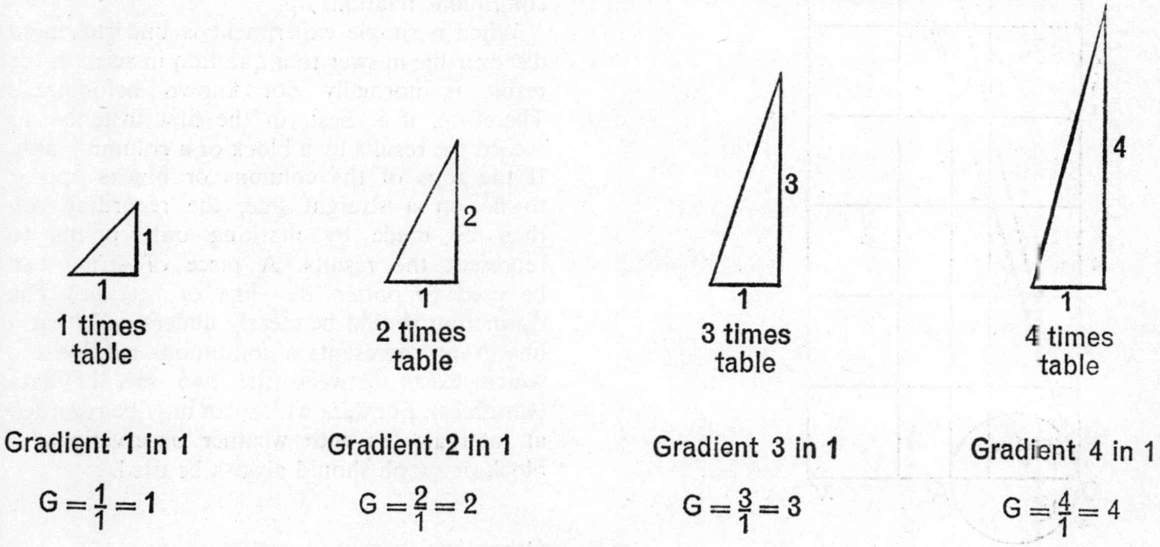

Fig. 6.7

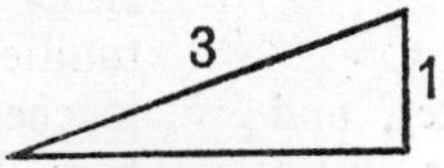

Fig. 6.8

These same children were next given another example of this kind of relationship. The teacher interested them in circles and asked for suggestions as to the magnitude of the circumference/diameter ratio of a circle. At first they guessed that the circumference was twice the diameter. Using a piece of string of length twice the diameter of the circle they soon convinced themselves that the circumference was more than twice the diameter. Some guessed three for this ratio.

The children then made a collection of tin lids of all sizes. To avoid the difficulties of awkward measurements (which frequently obscure simple relationships) the children recorded their results as follows. They drew two axes at right angles on a large sheet of paper. They then placed each tin lid in turn with one point at O and moved the tin until, as nearly as they could judge, the diameter was along the horizontal axis OX (Fig. 6.9.) They marked A, the other end of the diameter, on the axis. They then wrapped a piece of coloured sticky tape round the tin lid and so cut a collar to fit around the lid exactly. They removed the collar and stuck it carefully on the graph as shown (AB with one end on A.) This experiment was repeated with the collection of tins which each pair of children had made. Even using this rather crude method the children were able to discover for themselves that the tops of the 'columns' seem to lie on a straight line.

They took a piece of string and found that they could stretch it along the tops of the columns and that it passed through their zero mark (O). (A more accurate method can be obtained by

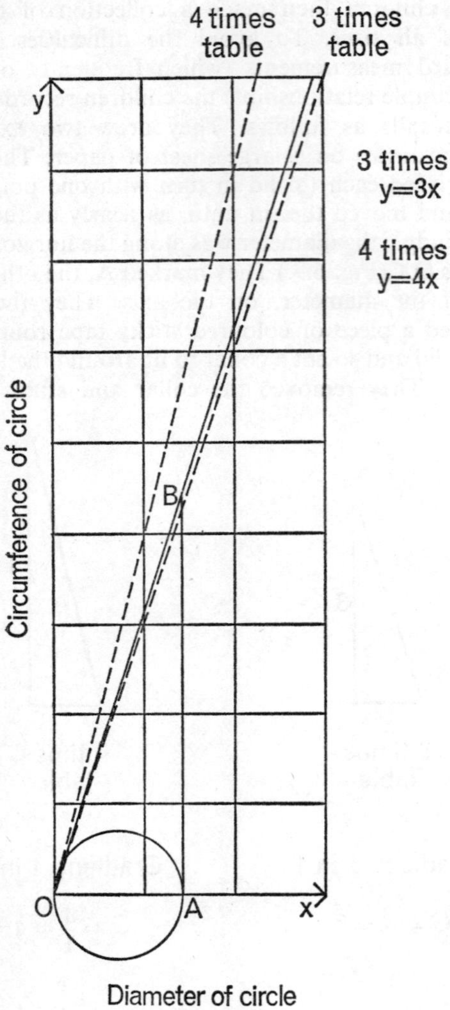

Fig. 6.9

using calipers to mark off the diameter, and making the collar with a strip of paper and a pin hole to mark the ends.) They used their graphs many times to read off the circumference of circles whose diameters they measured. They also used it to find the required diameter of the click wheel they wanted to make (to click every yard so that its circumference had to be a yard in length).

In order to focus attention on the circumference/diameter relationship itself the teacher then suggested that on the circumference/diameter graph, the children should put in the two-times table, the three-times table, the four-times table, etc. to see where the circumference/diameter relationship came. The children found this line came in between the three-times table ($y = 3x$) and the four-times table ($y = 4x$) but that it was considerably nearer to the former. (Fig. 6.9).

This graph can provide an excellent transition from a block graph to a line relationship graph. If the 'collars' are made of fine string, the graph becomes a column graph. If the tops of the columns only are marked, the graph becomes a line graph. The children appreciated that they could in fact collect many more tins of varying diameters to fill in many of the intermediate spaces. In other words, this represented a continuous relationship.

When a simple experiment is undertaken to discover the answer to a question in science, the result is normally not known beforehand. Therefore, it is best, in the first instance, to record the results by a block or a column graph. If the tops of the columns or blocks appear to lie on a straight line, the recording can then be made by marking only points to represent the results. A piece of string can be used to obtain the 'line of best fit'. The distinction should be clearly understood, that a line graph represents a continuous relationship which exists between the two sets of data (variables). For data which can only be recorded at intervals (as with weather observations) a block or graph should always be used.

Other than straight lines

Of the types of relationships which follow, either might occur first according to the opportunities which arise in the classroom or the teacher's inclination. The experiments described here have been undertaken successfully by children well below average ability as well as by average and very able children. In each case, the children have been questioned about the graphs they have drawn and their answers showed, without doubt, that they understood the experiment which gave rise to the graph and that they derived a meaning from the graph which could not have been conveyed to them by other means. Initially children may need help from the teacher as to suitable scales to be used on the axis. At first graph paper can be cut in convenient sizes anticipating the children's needs. At a later stage the children, particularly the able ones, can be left to plan their work entirely on their own including the choice of graph paper and scales. A variety of graph paper should be available in several sizes: 1″ squares, $\frac{1}{2}$″ squares, $\frac{1}{4}$″ squares, $\frac{1}{8}$″ squares and $\frac{1}{10}$ ″squares.

Squares and cubes

The ten-year-olds who discovered the largest rectangle which could be enclosed with a yard of string were persuaded to draw a graph showing the relationship between the widths and the area of the rectangles made. (The teacher had conveniently prepared graph paper marked with tenths of an inch graduations and of dimensions 10″ by 9″ so that the children were able to choose their own scales.) The graph is shown (Fig. 6.10)

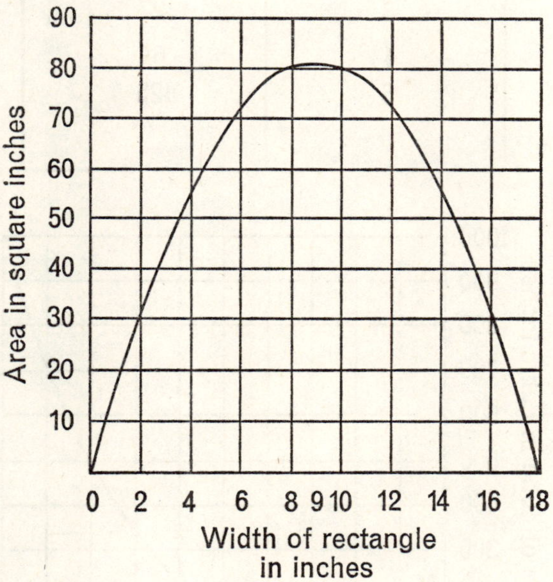

Fig. 6.10

as a continuous curve because intermediate values could, the children decided, be calculated if required. The children discussed the shape of the curve with their teacher and she encouraged them to look for this shape outside the classroom. One child noticed that the jet of water from a hose pipe made this shape. Several mentioned the shape traced out by a ball when thrown between two children. A boy brought a toy air pressure rocket to demonstrate the curve.

The children discussed the chief features of the graph: the turning point at the top and the levelling off at the turning point.

The teacher then gave the children two more graphs of this type. The first she called: 'How squares grow'. Using squared paper the children drew up a table showing the area of squares, with sides 1″, 2″, 3″, up to 9″. A boy reminded them all that they should enter the square of zero width in the table. When each child had drawn the graph its shape was discussed (Fig. 6.11). The children noticed its similarity with the

Length of side of square in inches	Area of square in square inches
1	1
2	4
3	9
4	16
5	25

N.B. Tables are left incomplete to give readers the opportunity of continuing for themselves

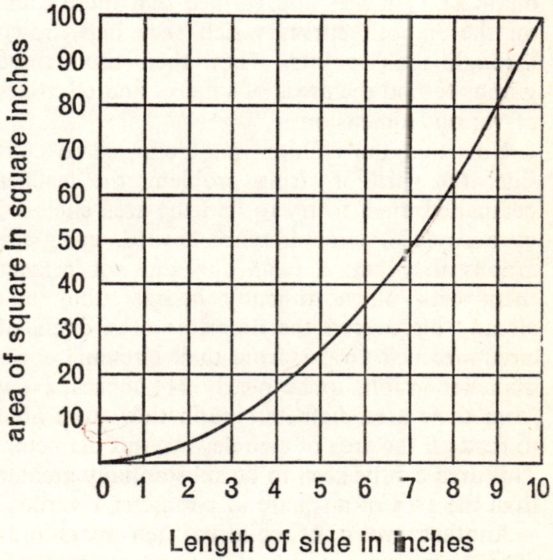

Fig. 6.11

'rocket graph' when turned upside down. Some of them wanted to know where the other half of the graph was. The teacher suggested they should count backwards to find the other half. (So these children, too, introduced themselves to negative numbers). The children, already familiar with the constant ratio relationship of straight lines ($y = 2x$, $y = 3x$, etc.), were able to suggest the relationship between y, the area, and x, the length of the side of the square, as $y = x \times x$ which they later wrote as $y = x^2$.

Reference has already been made to the second problem the teacher set the children: to make a graph of the relationship between the area and the diameter of circles. The children decided that they would find the area of circles of diameters 1 inch, 2 inches, 3 inches, up to 12 inches by drawing the circles on graph paper and counting the squares. They used $\frac{1}{4}$ inch graph paper for this. They drew this graph with the axes used for the 'square' graph, but in a different colour. They were able to appreciate the similarities between this graph, the 'squares' graph, and the 'yard of string graph'. In each of these two relationships the teacher discussed with the children the possibility of finding the areas of squares, and of circles, of sides and diameters which were not necessarily whole numbers of inches. They found the areas of a square of side $1\frac{3}{4}$ inches and of a circle of diameter $1\frac{3}{4}$ inches and verified that these came on the smooth curves which they had drawn through their points. They then used these graphs to find the areas of squares and of circles of various dimensions.

Now that the children had returned to consider the yard of string problem, the teacher persuaded them to try to find the area enclosed by a circle of circumference a yard, using the graphs they had drawn. This did not present them with much difficulty because they had already discovered the diameter of a circle of circumference 1 yard, from their circumference/diameter graph, to be nearly $11\frac{3}{4}$ inches. Now from their area/diameter graph they were able to read off the area of a circle with this diameter. This area can be seen to be substantially greater than the area of a square of perimeter 1 yard.

Another group of children (ten years old) after drawing the graph of the squares $y = x^2$, turned their attention to the problem of 'How cubes grow'. Some of them used real cubes to do this. The others drew up a table for themselves without the use of the cubes. They made a graph (which they called: 'How cubes grow') illustrating the relationship between the length of the edge of the cube and its volume. At first they drew this using the same scale as for the graph, 'How squares grow' but they found the cube graph sloped so steeply that it soon went off the page. The second attempt is shown in Figure 6.12.

Length of edge of cube in inches	Volume of cube in cubic inches
1	1
2	8
3	27
4	64
5	125

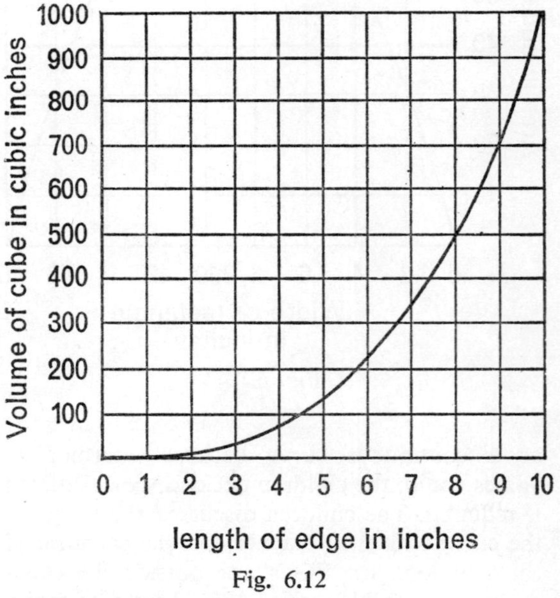

Fig. 6.12

They also drew a graph to show the relationship between the diameters of a set of balls and their volumes and compared this with the graph of the cubes. (The children decided to find the volume of the balls by putting the balls in a large measuring jug containing water and measuring the increase in volume when each ball was completely submerged.) One boy, who was an angler, produced figures from his angler's diary, showing the weight of various fish (trout, salmon, carp, etc.) at different lengths. He made a graph of the figures of weight/length and was surprised to find they gave a smooth curve resembling the curve of the cubes. He determined to check some of the figures given when he next went fishing. (In this case the figures used were probably obtained from 'the curve of best fit'.)

The constant product group

Reference has already been made to the class of 48 ten-year olds who became interested in geometrical shapes and who drew a graph showing the relationship between the number of sides a regular shape had, and its angles. Since, when the children began to investigate the problem the teacher was absent, ill, they were left on their own. They became so interested in the problem that they organised themselves into groups to cover the computation involved and worked for two days on end in an attempt to solve this problem. Here is an account of their effort in their own words.

'We drew the graph at your suggestion up to twelve sides. The graph turned out to be a curve so Michael and I decided to see if there was a turning point (Fig. 6.13.) The graph was of extra interest because if we could reach 180 degrees we should have come to a figure supposedly made by a straight line. We continued the graph to 240 sides and then discontinued because it looked as though it would go on for ever. (The children then turned their attention to the figure pattern.) We jumped in 10s, 50s, 100s, 1,000s and finally 1,000,000s in our efforts to reach 180 degrees. When we saw the pattern we realised that we never should reach 180 degrees or turn the graph. On May 11th at 10.15 a.m. we finally gave in.

We think this is the most exciting piece of mathematics we have ever done. It is just like research work'.

Number of sides	Angle of Polygon
3	60°
4	90°
5	108°
6	120°
8	
9	
10	
12	

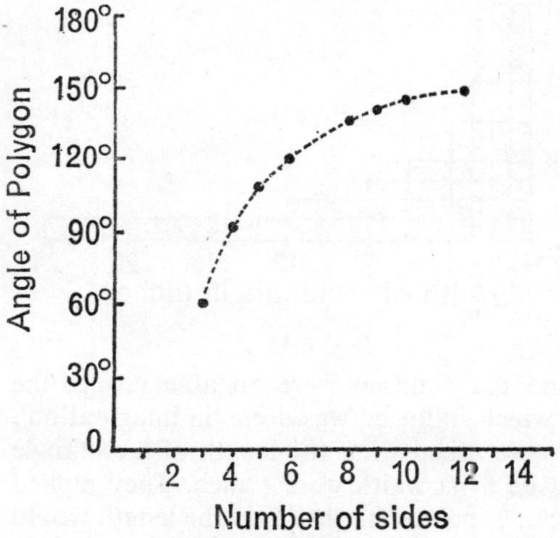

Fig. 6.13

In their own way these children had given themselves first-hand experience of a mathematical limit, an experience which is rare, unfortunately, even amongst mathematical scholars. The children were excited by their results and, on the teacher's return, bombarded her with questions in their efforts to understand the difference between the 'rocket' or squares graph, with its turning point, and this new graph which went on and on, never reaching 180 degrees. (In fact the graph the children drew was not a continuous one, because they were considering polygons.) An interesting question can be asked: What would be the angle of a closed two-sided figure? (Fig. 6.14) Does the point represented by this value appear to lie on the curve joining the other points?

Fig. 6.14

To give the children further experience of the second type of curved graph, they were each asked to cut 24 square inches and to make and sketch as many rectangles as they could, using all these square inches each time. They then formed groups of eight and made a graph of their results by sticking the rectangles on a sheet of paper as shown in Fig. 6.15.

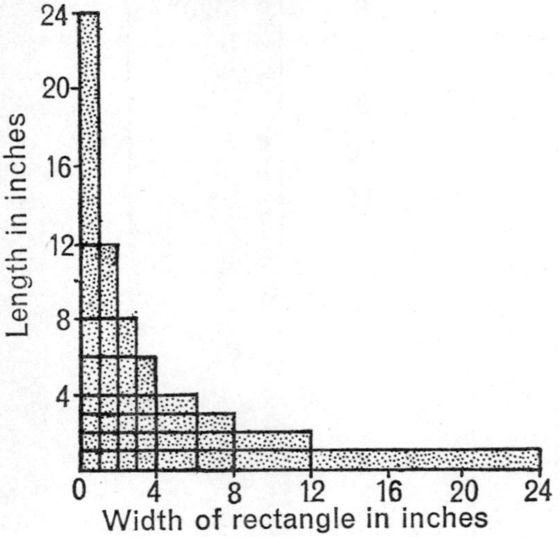

Fig. 6.15

Because the children were an able group, the work which followed was done 'in imagination'. They were asked what the length of a rectangle would be if its width were $\frac{1}{2}$ inch. They replied 4 feet; at $\frac{1}{4}$ inch width they said the length would be 8 feet; at $\frac{1}{8}$ inch width the length would be 16 feet. At this point a girl said, 'I see, the rectangles will go on and on, getting thinner and thinner, until they are paper thin, but they will never disappear altogether. This is just like the other graph!' This relationship was soon established as: length × width = 24. The children then drew a second graph showing how the length of these rectangles varied with their width when the width chosen was not a whole number of inches. They volunteered that this was a continuous graph and discovered that its algebraic relationship was xy = 24. (It would have been better to use 36 square inches as the constant area because the 6 inch square could then be included.) Another group of children drew a graph showing the relationship between the perimeter and width of these rectangles. The graph showed clearly that the square has the least perimeter.

Another group of ten-year-olds met this constant product relationship through their interest in regular geometrical shapes. They investigated the relationship between the angles subtended at the centre of a regular polygon by each of its sides, and the number of sides. This led to an investigation of the kaleidoscope (with its 'step' graph.)

Another exciting example of this constant product relationship was discovered by a group

12	24	36	48	60	72	84	96	108	120	132	144
11	22	33	44	55	66	77	88	99	110	121	132
10	20	30	40	50	60	70	80	90	100	110	120
9	18	27	36	45	54	63	72	81	90	99	108
8	16	24	32	40	48	56	64	72	80	88	96
7	14	21	28	35	42	49	56	63	70	77	84
6	12	18	24	30	36	42	48	54	60	66	72
5	10	15	20	25	30	35	40	45	50	55	60
4	8	12	16	20	24	28	32	36	40	44	48
3	6	9	12	15	18	21	24	27	30	33	36
2	4	6	8	10	12	14	16	18	20	22	24
1	2	3	4	5	6	7	8	9	10	11	12

Fig. 6.16

of ten-year-olds already familiar with the constant area example of this relationship. They made a multiplication square as follows: the bottom row was obtained by counting in 1s, the second by counting in 2s, the third by counting in 3s and so on. When this was finished they were asked to colour the squares containing the number 24 in black, the squares containing 12 in blue and the squares containing 36 in red. (Fig. 6.16). They dotted in the curves joining each set of numbers and compared them with the constant area graph. One group of children decided to make a table square of 24 units each way to see how this shape continued. They investigated the products of 12 and found that each was formed from an x number (bottom row) multiplied by a y number (left-hand column).

12 × 1	4 × 3	2 × 6
6 × 2	3 × 4	1 × 12

Teachers may be interested to encourage their children to make models in three dimensions of the multiplication square. If the square is placed horizontally on the table, balsa wood (of say $\frac{1}{8}$ inch thickness) or thick cardboard can be used to build vertically according to the number on the square. The balsa wood needs to be cut in squares to fit the squares of the multiplication square. Thus taking the bottom row there will be 1 layer on 1, 2 layers on 2, 3 layers on 3, 4 layers on 4 and so on. The resulting shape may well be recognised by children as the new shape used in architecture in schools, in churches, and even in garages; it is the hyperbolic paraboloid.

Another 'experiment' giving rise to this constant product relationship is the fraction family. Some nine-year-olds, using squared paper, drew columns to represent the following fractions 1, $\frac{1}{2}$, $\frac{1}{3}$, $\frac{1}{4}$, $\frac{1}{5}$, and so on. They recognised the resulting shape as one like that made by the constant product group.

Here is an account of an investigation, initiated by a boy of ten, which resulted in a detailed study of a number of graphs. The boy was one of a large class whose introduction to 'discovery' mathematics began only in their last year in the junior school. The teacher had planned a variety of interesting experiments for the class which they worked in pairs or small groups, but there were certain topics which she

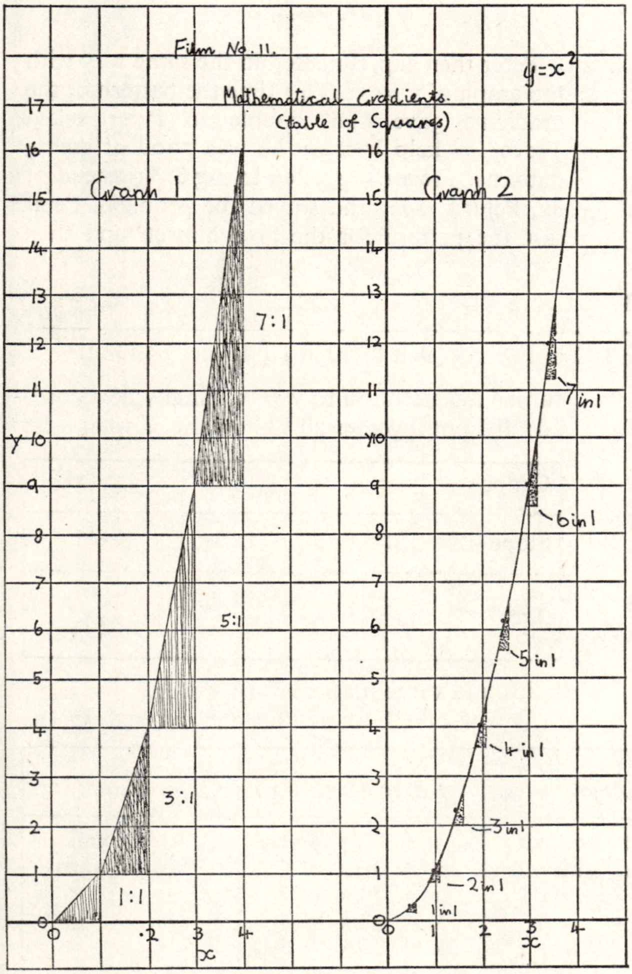

Fig. 6.17

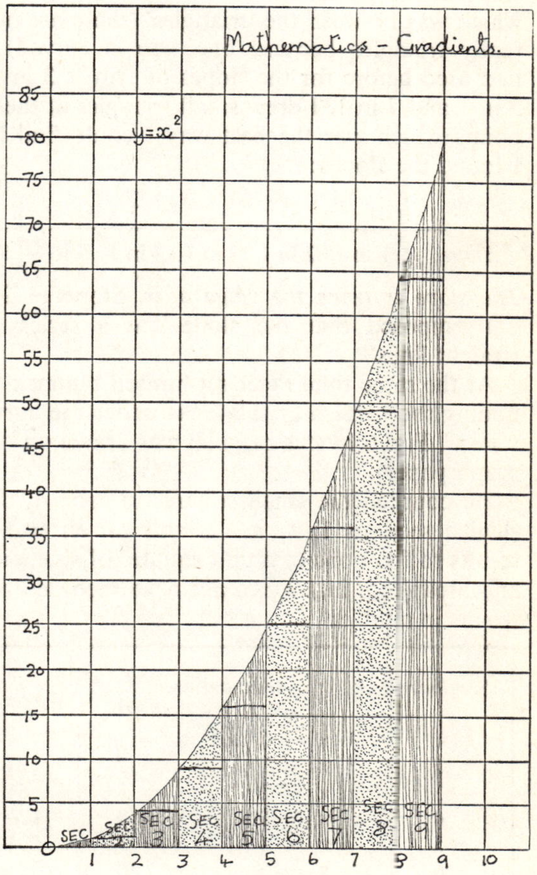

Fig. 6.18

gave to the class as a whole. These included an introduction to gradients through the graphs of the multiplication tables, and situations which led to the graph of the table of squares ($y = x^2$). Through this work Peter became intensely interested in patterns in mathematics and, of his own accord, set himself to discover the pattern of the changing gradients of the curve $y = x^2$ (Fig. 6.17, graphs 1 and 2).

Here is part of the 'facts and figures of graph 1' which Peter drew up as a table.

Section	*Piece of y*	*Piece of x*	*Gradient*
From 0, 0 to 1, 1	1	1	1 in 1
From 1, 1 to 2, 4	3	1	3 in 1
From 2, 4 to 3, 9	5	1	5 in 1
From 3, 9 to 4, 16	7	1	7 in 1

He continued: 'What I wanted to find was the slope at the points (1, 1), (2, 4), (3, 9), (4, 16) which was between the 'triangles' (these are not really triangles because one side is curved) I had used before for the slopes of 1 in 1, 3 in 1, 5 in 1 and 7 in 1. I drew small triangles at these points which was the best way I could find it. I found the slopes:

x		1		2		3		4		5		6
Slope	1 in 1	2 in 1	3 in 1	4 in 1	5 in 1	6 in 1	7 in 1	8 in 1	9 in 1	10 in 1	11 in 1	12 in 1

The slope is twice the value of x. Slope = 2x.

I supposed that the slope was a series of straight lines'.

At the same time Peter set himself the task of finding the pattern of the areas under the curve $y = x^2$, Fig. 6.18 (the original was drawn on $\frac{1}{10}''$ graph paper).

He counted the small squares in each of the shaded sections 1, 2, 3 . . . and converted his results to fractions of a unit square (of side $\frac{1}{2}$ in. and area $\frac{1}{4}$ sq. in.). Once again he recorded his results in a table:

Sections	*Area between*	*Area*	*Area between*	*Area*
1	x = 0 and x = 1	$\frac{1}{3}$ of a sq. unit	x = 0 x = 1	$\frac{1}{3}$ sq. unit
2	x = 1 x = 2	$2\frac{1}{3}$ sq. units	x = 0 x = 2	$2\frac{2}{3}$ sq. units
3	x = 2 x = 3	$6\frac{1}{3}$	x = 0 x = 3	9
4	x = 3 x = 4	$12\frac{1}{3}$	x = 0 x = 4	$21\frac{1}{3}$
5	x = 4 x = 5	$20\frac{1}{3}$	x = 0 x = 5	$41\frac{2}{3}$
6	x = 5 x = 6	$30\frac{1}{3}$	x = 0 x = 6	72
7	x = 6 x = 7	$42\frac{1}{3}$	x = 0 x = 7	$114\frac{1}{3}$

Although Peter could see, from the increases in the first column of areas, that there was a pattern, the pattern of areas in the last column was not at all obvious. Peter recorded: 'I could see no pattern in them and to make them whole numbers I multiplied by 3 as the numbers were in thirds'.

x	1	2	3	4	5
Area × 3	1	8	27	64	125

These are the cubes of the x numbers, so the area under the curve is the x number cubed then divided by three.

$$A = \frac{x^3}{3}$$

Peter then experimented in the same way with the graph of $y = x^3$. This time the pattern of the gradients gave him trouble so Peter asked Trevor to help because he was good at seeing patterns. Trevor suggested trying $3x^2$ (instead of 3x, Peter's idea) and solved the problem. Peter saw the pattern for the area himself and then turned his attention to y = x. Finally he recorded: 'If I put together all I know this is what it is:

Graphs	y = x	$y = x^2$	$y = x^3$
Slope	1*	2x*	$3x^2$**
Area	$\frac{x^2}{2}$*	$\frac{x^3}{3}$*	$\frac{x^4}{4}$

I found those marked *.

Trevor and I found the one marked ** (he

saw it from the pattern and we proved it with long length graph paper). I wrote down $\frac{x^4}{4}$ because it follows the pattern of the other areas'.

In just this intellectually honest way Archimedes might have recorded his work nearly 2,500 years earlier when he was studying the same problems or Sir Isaac Newton in the 17th century.

In consequence of these discoveries with $y = x^3$ Peter became interested in the area of the six faces of a cube. He wrote:

'After doing the cubes and squares graph I decided to do another graph using the volume and area of six faces on cubes. (Fig. 6.19.) It was interesting to see the two lines crossed at a cube on the side of six units. Has this got anything to do with the six faces of a cube?'

To solve this problem Peter drew two more graphs which he called

$\frac{V}{A}$ (six faces) $\qquad y = \frac{x}{6}$

and

$\frac{A \text{ (six faces)}}{V}$ $\qquad y = \frac{6}{x}$

The final graph, the last in this remarkable series, led Peter to discover the meaning of a mathematical limit for he considered both a side of 1,000,000 inches and a side as small as 1,000,000th of an inch and wrote: 'The line will never meet the y axis'.

So ended a piece of work which began in November 1963 with a problem of Peter's own invention and which so fired his imagination that his interest was sustained night after night for more than six months. The methods Peter used were those used by all great mathematicians and scientists: an intelligent guess (hypothesis), an experiment, trials and errors, and the careful ordering and recording of results. By these means Peter discovered the answer to his highly abstract problem in mathematics. He could not have done this if he had not approached the problem by experimental discovery methods which led him to say with complete conviction, when he was asked why he persevered so long 'In mathematics there is always a pattern if you look for it'.

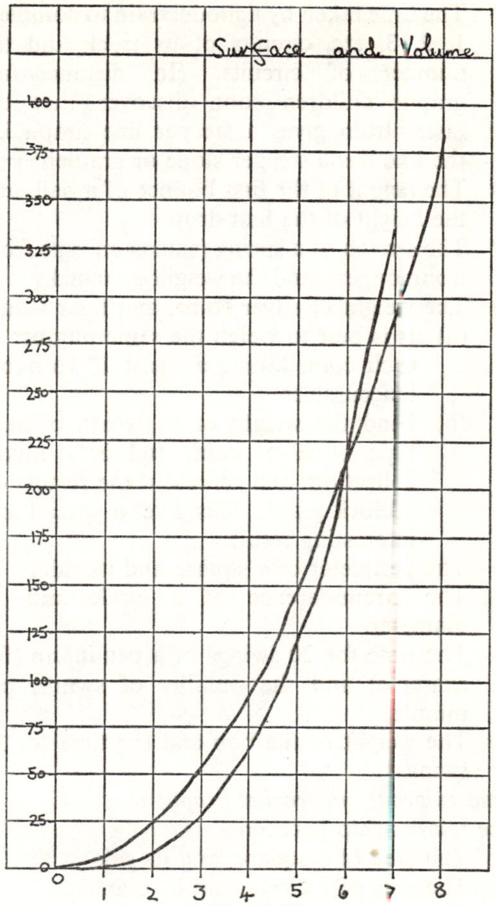

Fig. 6.19

Summary of experiments leading to relationships

Constant ratio or direct proportion relationship

The relationship between

1. The distance travelled on a railway journey (determined from a scale railway map or from a regional timetable), and the fares (also given in the regional timetable).
2. The volume (or weight) of water collected from a dripping tap, and the time.
3. The volume of water, and its weight.
4. The weight of a collection of stones of similar composition, and their volume.
5. The corresponding weights in ounces and in grams as given on tinned and bottled foods.
6. The number of flashes of a Belisha Beacon, and the time.

7 The time taken by a model train to complete 1, 2, 3, etc. circuits of its track and the number of circuits. (In distance/time graphs children soon discover that the faster train gives a steeper line graph i.e. the line has a steeper slope or gradient.)
8 The height of the first bounce of a ball, and the height of the first drop.
9 The stretch of a spring (extension type from ironmonger), and the weight attached.
10 The weight of silver coins, and their value:
 (a) It is best to weigh the same number of each coin, taking at least 10 to avoid inaccuracies.
 (b) Find the weight of £1 worth of each type of silver coin, and of a mixed collection, and represent the results on a block graph. This gives a special and interesting result.
11 The perimeter of a square and its side.
12 The circumference of a circle and its diameter.
13 The time for 20 swings of a pendulum (for example) and the number of swings per minute.
14 The weight of the bob and the time for 20 swings.

Squares group (the rocket graph)
The relationship between
1 The area of a square, and its side.
2 The area of a circle, and its diameter.
3 The surface area of a cube, and its edge.
4 The distance travelled by a toy car (or heavy ball-bearing) down a long slope, and the time.
5 The time taken by a pendulum to beat 20 times, and the length of the pendulum.
6 The braking distance of a car, and its speed (from the Highway Code).

Special Case. The area of a rectangle of constant perimeter, and its width.

Cubes
The relationship between
1 The volume of a cube, and its edge.
2 The volume of a ball, and its diameter.

Constant product group (inverse proportion)
The relationship between
1 The width of a rectangle of constant area, and its length.
2 The angle subtended at the centre of a regular polygon, and the number of sides.
3 The constant products in the multiplication square.
4 The fraction family.
5 The number of sides a regular polygon has, and its exterior angle.
6 The see-saw or lever.
 The number of equal weights and the distance from the fulcrum.

Special Case. The number of sides a regular polygon has, and its interior angle.

Summary of graphical relationships

Here are the main types of graphical relationships which have been considered in this chapter.

The constant ratio group:

$\frac{y}{x} = m$ (where m is any number) or, to take the simplest case of the 'one times table'.

	$y = x$
The squares	$y = x^2$
The cubes	$y = x^3$
The constant product: $xy = c$,	$xy = 24$ etc.
The simplest member of this group is	$xy = 1$ or $y = \frac{1}{x}$

The majority of the relationships obtained from the experimental work undertaken by children in primary schools belong to one or other of the types mentioned (although the algebraic relationships which exist between the variables in one or two of the examples quoted are not as straightforward as the types just given). An exciting feature of this aspect of the work is that these four relationships themselves belong to one family. If the relationships in their simplest forms are rearranged,

The cubes	$y = x^3$
The squares	$y = x^2$
The constant ratio ..	$y = x \quad (x^2 \div x)$
The next member of this family is	$y = 1 \quad (x \div x)$
The constant product ..	$y = \frac{1}{x} \quad (1 \div x)$

it can be seen that all these are members of the family $y = x^n$ (where n is a positive or negative whole number or zero).

It would seem from the above that one member of the family, $y = 1$, is missing. This is because this is rather a special member which appears less frequently. This member of the family has been discovered by junior children (although the graphical representation must be by a block graph because of the limited number of observations made). Some nine-year-olds were

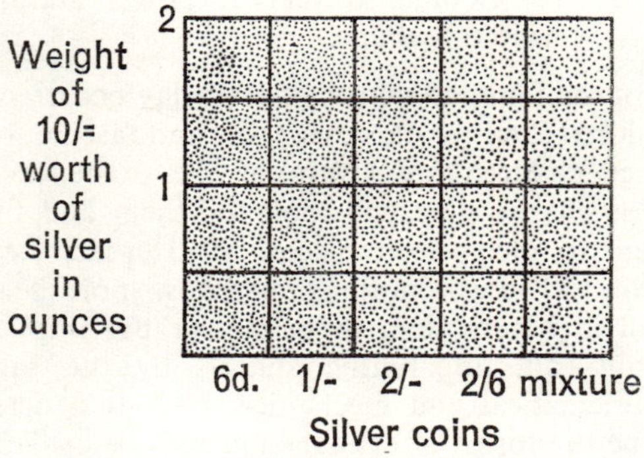

Fig. 6.20

finding the weight of silver coins. They decided that they would find the weight of ten shillingsworth of each of sixpences, shillings, florins, half-crowns and a mixture of coins. They found that in each instance ten shillingsworth of silver weighed 2 ounces. This is of course an example of the graph $y = c$ (where c is any number). (Fig. 6.20). This could, of course, now be tried with our decimal coinage.

There is one other important family of relationships which come within the experience of young children and which lead to a satisfying graphical representation. This is 'growth relationships'. The infants who made drawings of the growth of a tadpole, and those who made drawings of a sweet pea plant, were drawing 'growth curves' from experimental results. Two other examples of these relationships which have been discovered by children are (1) the graphical representations of a set of kitchen weights and (2) the graph of the chessboard problem which is the continuation of (1). Both of these should, of course, be represented by block graphs because they are not continuous relationships.

Summary

1 Children of very varied abilities can represent graphically the results of their own investigations and experiments. By this means they can see relationships between the variables concerned which they would not otherwise be able to appreciate.

2 Graphs, once drawn, should be discussed to ensure that children understand the implications of their investigations. They should also be used (forwards and backwards), and the children should be encouraged to write about their discoveries. 'Reading the graph' is as important as making the graph.

3 For juniors the 'zero' is essential and must be included on the axes. (When zero is not included the resulting representation may be a misleading statistical graph!). The significance of the zero value, when this occurs, should be discussed with the children. The possibility of extending the graph as far as possible is also a valuable mathematical idea.

4 Despite the variety of the activities and interests of children of primary age, the number of distinct relationships discovered is few. Moreover these relationships themselves belong to one family of relationships. The types of relationships which occur most frequently are:

(1) No simple relationship. Pictorial, block, column graphs made from a restricted number of observations. These are non-continuous relationships.

(2) Continuous relationships.

(a) The constant ratio relationship or ready reckoner graph (direct proportion); squares; cubes, constant product groups (inverse proportion).

(b) growth curves.

(3) The transition from pictorial to block graphs and from block graphs to relationship graphs needs to be slow. Children need a variety of experiences if they are to understand the implications of graphical representation. The salient features of each type of representation can come from the children by discussion with the teacher.

5 Relationship graphs can be seen and appreciated by the following means:

(1) A straight line appears on a razor shell.

(2) The squares (parabola) can be seen when a ball is thrown (projectile) or from a jet

of water. (A tall tin, with a column of holes in the side, when filled with water and held over a sink provides good indoor experience for children of this relationship.)

Curve stitching (with equal spacing), as shown by Fig. 6.21 also shows this relationship.

In the figure the spaces between the numbers are all equal. The axes can be drawn at any angle less than 2 right angles on a piece of thin card. If a pinhole is made at each numbered mark on the axes the pattern shown can be stitched with coloured silk. Start with the needle underneath at 1 on the upper axis (a knot at one end of the silk will prevent it being drawn through). The needle is pushed through to the upper side and down through 1 on the lower axis. The needle is then pushed up through 2 on the same axis and down through 2 on the upper axis and so on.

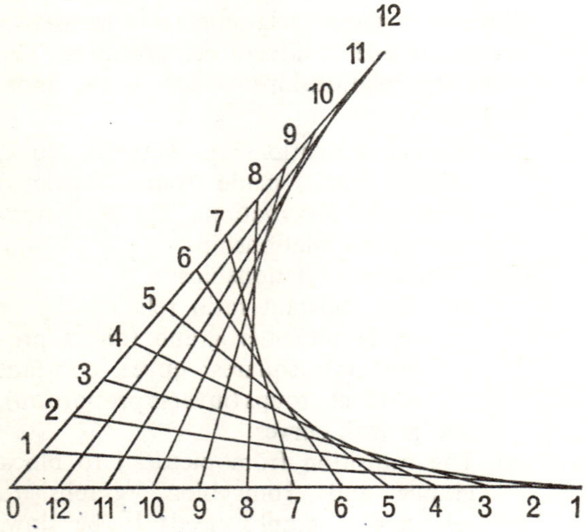

Fig. 6.21

For further exciting shapes which can be made in this way see the book list in Appendix 1.

(3) Constant product. This can be represented in two exciting ways:

(a) Two pieces of glass (the type used to cover coloured transparencies is suitable) are bound together using an elastic band and a small piece of elastic can be used to wedge apart the two pieces of glass at a vertical edge. If this apparatus is then dipped into a shallow tin containing coloured water, the constant product curve will be seen. It is essential that the surfaces of the glass should be thoroughly cleaned with detergent first.

(b) Cooling towers at power stations have this shape.

In the familiar shapes of everyday occurrence children (and we ourselves) can find fascination. Once children are aware of the existence of these shapes they will look for them and find them in unexpected places. Sir Herbert Read wrote: 'There is nothing, perhaps, more beautiful in nature than these regular but intricate forms—all, apparently, shaped by the same mathematical and mechanical laws that determine the forms of crystals and cells, snowflakes and beetles' eyes.' It is this sense of fascination and wonder at the shapes and relationships which result from investigations of the environment that we want all human beings to enjoy throughout their mathematical education.

In the last two chapters on the content of the work in the primary school the transition from traditional to modern mathematics in the particular field under consideration has been included. In graphical representation also, there are important applications in modern mathematics. An example will be included to show an extension in this field which might well be enjoyed by older, abler juniors.

Reference has already been made to the use of mathematicians in industry. The mathematician is given a set of conditions and asked to predict the most efficient order of operations or the proportions of the products which are to be made, in order that maximum profits may be derived. The understanding of this problem, and the preparation for the programming of the conditions by computer, comes most readily from the graphical representation of the conditions. The problems appropriate are those involving a large number of very simple conditions. The method (called linear programming) is usually concerned with making one of the quantities as large as possible (for example, the profit). A very simplified example is included in Appendix 6.

7 Classroom problems

'What you have been obliged to discover by yourself leaves a path in your mind which you can use again when the need arises.'

G. C. LICHTENBERG, Aphorism

In this chapter we shall consider various problems which arise in the classroom when the kind of approach envisaged in this book is introduced. These comprise:

I. Making a start.
II. Starting points.
 (a) The environment
 (b) Other subjects.
III. Planning a scheme of work.
IV. Assessment of children's progress.
V. Parents' attitude.
VI. Co-operation in mathematical education.

The classroom situation we want to create is best summarised by Professor George Polya, Professor of Mathematics at Stamford University[1]. He gives three principles of learning, which, he says, can equally well be three principles of teaching.

1 Active learning. The best way to learn anything is to discover it by yourself. This is the principle which underlies the Socratic method and which is almost as old as teaching itself.
2 Best motivation. For efficient learning, the learner shoud be interested in the material to be learnt and should find pleasure in the activity of learning.
3 Consecutive phases. Kant wrote: 'Learning begins with action and perception, proceeds from thence to words and concepts, and should end in desirable mental habits'. In other words, for efficient learning, an exploratory phase should precede the phase of verbalisation and concept formation, and eventually the material learnt should be merged in, and contribute to, the integral attitude of the learner.

With these principles in mind, the problems which arise in the classroom will be considered.

I. Making a start

There is a very wide variation between one school and another, and what is appropriate for one school will not necessarily be advisable for another. At one extreme there are schools in which the timetable is very flexible and the approach to most subjects is very informal; children in these schools are well used to planning their own work at times, and to going to fetch books without reference to their teacher. At the other extreme, there are some schools in which teachers adhere quite closely to a timetable and where the children do not normally leave their places to seek information without first consulting the teacher. Between these extremes come as many variations as schools. It is important, from the teacher's point of view and for the children's sense of security, that changes should not be made too suddenly. Children in schools where there is a good measure of informality will adjust themselves readily to working assignments in mathematics which demand working in pairs or in groups, and to the greater part which discussion will play in the work in mathematics. Children in schools where the organisation is more formal will need to become accustomed to taking more responsibility for their own work and to the greater measure of freedom.

It is important that a gradual beginning should be made for other reasons. It is essential that the teacher shall be able to convince herself, as she experiments with the different way of learning mathematics, that children do indeed learn by their own discoveries. If the approach to new methods is a gradual one, she can convince herself as she goes along. Suppose therefore, that, in the first instance, a teacher is willing to give one period a week to providing children with opportunities to learn mathematics for themselves. If, for example, there are 40 children in the class, this means that 8 children a day will be learning in this way, while the

[1] *American Mathematical Monthly*, Volume 70, No. 6. June/July 1963

others are doing the computation and problems which they would normally do from a text book. Another advantage of this gradual beginning will now be apparent. 'Discovery' material for 8, or at most 10 children, will not take as long to prepare, nor require as much space, as material and assignments for 40 children, although, of course, a fairly wide range of material will be required because of the spread of ability of 40 children (even in a streamed class).

One aspect on which the teacher will need reassurance is that the standard of computation does not fall as a result of the decreased time allocation. It is important, therefore, to ensure, either before making a start, or concurrently with it, that each individual child's basic number knowledge is sound. (A simple test of readiness for this has already been suggested: the ability to add two numbers such as 35 and 48 efficiently; that is, without counting on or counting back in ones. This demands a firm knowledge of numbers trios up to 20 as well as of place-value.) Once, then, the teacher has convinced herself that the children have learnt from their own discoveries and that the standard in computation has not fallen, she may be willing to give two periods a week to learning in this way. This will mean that 16 children a day will be working on assignments, while the rest are working on computation from text books. Eventually a teacher may feel confident enough to reduce the time spent on systematic computation still more. At this stage, she will probably prefer to plan the work so that most or all of the children tackle their practical assignments at the same time. The latter type of organisation has advantages; for systematic computation can then be based on, and arise from, the practical assignments. This kind of integration in which the systematic practice in computation is based on the practical assignments is an ideal which should be kept in mind. Of course, the practical assignments themselves will require some computation for their solutions but this, of itself, is not likely to be sufficiently systematic to maintain efficiency.

Many teachers may quite properly raise the difficulty of the extra space required for children to work on practical assignments. Where numbers in the class are large and the children are cramped for space, some restriction must be put on the selection of material. But some investigations can be undertaken outside the classroom, in the corridor or in the playground. (This applies particularly to those which arise in science.) On the other hand, many suitable assignments can be carried out on a desk, particularly if the lid can be propped to make it horizontal, or on a pair of desks if, as is hoped, two children are allowed to work together. Once a teacher is really convinced that the way to learn mathematics is through the children's own discoveries, this conviction will help her to overcome all the difficulties which confront her.

If a headmaster wants to introduce a different approach to mathematics in his school, in the first instance he, too, must convince himself (as well as his staff) that children can learn from their own discoveries and in response to the teacher's questions. His best plan is probably to work with his two most flexible or most interested members of staff. If he works in two classrooms with a group of children, the teachers can observe his method and his success with the children, and he can subsequently encourage the teachers to try for themselves. In this kind of work, an extra pair of hands, especially those of an enthusiast, is invaluable, particularly in the initial experimental stage. The advantage of working with two classes, so that the teachers concerned can discuss their problems with each other, will be readily appreciated. It cannot be over-stressed that a radical change of method cannot be effected without the full co-operation of the teachers concerned, and it can only take place gradually as the teachers become convinced themselves that the method is right and practicable for their children. Once they are convinced and once they enjoy mathematics for themselves, they will not look back and their enthusiasm will infect other teachers.

II. Starting points

The Environment

Sometimes topics arise in the classroom which have potentialities for mathematics. At other times interesting mathematical problems may be suggested by newspapers and magazines. Once the teacher, and from her the children, become aware of mathematics in the environment, more and more frequently will problems be found arising within this field of experience. But it takes time to acquire a mathematical eye and ear, a sensitive awareness to mathematical possibilities. In the first place, the teacher must set the stage herself, and must provide the children with problems based on interesting pictures and information which she has mounted on cards for the children to use. She will soon find that the children begin to suggest problems for themselves and to collect interesting information on which they can base these problems. Such material, prepared by the children themselves, can then be made available for other children to use.

Chapter 9 comprises the experience of teachers and heads who have made substantial changes in their school in the teaching of mathematics. From this it will be evident that, although in the initial stages the work is 'teacher guided', as the children develop a more independent attitude to their work, more of the responsibility for planning the work and for setting the problems is taken by the children themselves.

Contributions from All Other Aspects of the Curriculum

Not only is mathematics a unity in itself but it can also have a unifying effect upon the curriculum. All subjects of the curriculum have some contribution to make to mathematics and, conversely, mathematics has an important contribution to make to the various other aspects of the curriculum. Of course, far more opportunities will arise in some subjects as, for example, in geography and science, than in others. Once a teacher has become alive to the mathematical possibilities of her own strong subject, she will make the most of these as they occur, as the following examples will show.

In the numerous examples of children's work which have, so far, been quoted, the major part which language plays will be immediately apparent. The content of some of the work, particularly that of younger children, makes a greater contribution to English than to mathematics and yet each subject increases the contribution of the other. An understanding of mathematical concepts comes not only through first-hand experience but also through the child's attempts to put his experience and discoveries into words, at first orally and then in writing.

Some children who find imaginative writing difficult, have no difficulty in writing a simple, clear, and sometimes moving account of their discoveries. For these children this aspect of the work is creative writing and may well lead to imaginative expression in other media. The confidence engendered by success in this kind of recording may encourage children to succeed in fields where previously they felt inadequate.

This important contribution which mathematics makes to spoken and written English should be kept in mind when the question of an optimum time allocation for mathematics is raised.

Geography

Geography and mathematics have many important points of contact. Some of these have already been described as, for example, in the map making and the use of maps and scales to which reference was made in the previous chapter. A development of this is illustrated by the following example. Some eight- and nine-year-olds had found out that the equator was about 25,000 miles long. They were asked to find the distances, from London Airport, of Sydney, San Francisco, Athens, Rome and other large cities. They discussed the problem among themselves and solved it in the following way. They first measured the equator on the globe with string (and a tape measure) and found it to be 42 in. long. They found that Sydney was 20 in. from London by the 'shortest string route' they could discover by experiment. At first they were content to say this was less than 12,000 miles. Later, in discussing this problem with the teacher, they decided to make a ready reckoner graph and to read off corresponding distances.

It was interesting to notice that, without hesitation, the polar route was used if shorter, even though these children knew nothing about 'great circle navigation'. It is becoming usual to find an inflatable globe as a part of infant school equipment. Even these young children unhesitatingly use the polar route to find the quickest route from London to other parts of the world.

Mathematics is an essential part of any field studies undertaken in geography. These include direction finding and compass directions, surveying, weather observations; these are aspects of geography and of mathematics. These activities are essentially those of older juniors of the nine- and ten-year-olds. The making of a simple survey of a part of the school grounds involves the use of a mariner's compass (the Silva compass is the most efficient and relatively inexpensive for this work). It also involves direction finding and measuring. Most school grounds are either so simple in shape that the children lose interest or are so complicated that they lose heart. It is usually easier to begin with a 'prepared' shape, such as a triangle made with three bamboo sticks (its sides of length at least 10 yards). Children can be left to decide the measurements they need to take if they are to make a scale plan. Here is a list prepared by some ten-year-olds.

1 Pacing (or measuring using a surveyor's tape) the three sides. The direction of the base line must be fixed.
2 Using a surveyor's tape and a compass. Here the children discovered two distinct ways of doing this. One involved measuring a base line and siting the third vertex from each end of the base line; the other involved measuring two sides and the angle between these sides.

   Another exercise which interested the children was to set out by eye a square, to take the necessary measurements which would enable them to make an accurate plan of this square, and then to make the plan of the square to see how accurate they had been.

Many schools keep regular records of the weather. In one county at least a Meteorological Association (initiated by primary school teachers but also open to secondary schools) has been set up, and the careful records kept by a variety of schools are interchanged.

In one such school a ten-year-old boy measured the height of the river Trent every day for a year. He made a graph of his observations and superimposed a graph of the daily rainfall. He always commented on the interesting features of his graphs and related the rise and fall in the river to the rainfall.

Another topic of geographical and mathematical interest which is frequently studied by schools is the shadow stick. One school made a special study of the length of a shadow stick at noon each day over a period of two or three years. The results were represented graphically and the periodicity which was revealed was of great interest to the children. Normally, however, children are content to keep records for shorter periods; for example, for a month at hourly intervals during the day (when the sun shines).

Science

Science, like mathematics, has been described as a discovery of relationships. It is inevitable that science and mathematics should be very closely associated. During the past few years the nature of the science included in primary schools has been changing as rapidly as mathematics. Not only has the scope been increased to include physical science, but nature study is not being displaced, it is itself becoming a science rather than a collection of specimens. Science then is 'a discovery of relationships obtained by personal observation, by experiment, and by inference'. A question is asked, an experiment is devised, the experiment is carried out sometimes over and over again, observations are made and inferences are drawn from these observations.

Observation, however, is different from mere aimless looking. Observation is undertaken to discover something unknown; it is looking with a purpose, a purpose stimulated by a question. Very frequently the observation will involve measurement of some kind. In the recording of measurements, the arranging and ordering of results and their interpretation, children experience mathematics at work. They collect the results, assess their validity (neglecting those results which are obviously incorrect) and then interpret them. This may involve tabulating, drawing a graph, or finding the average of a series of experimental results. In all these activities, children are having first-hand experience of the relationship between mathematics and science.

Reference has already been made to many examples which might be termed scientific

PLATE XVI

Older juniors: Science and mathematics are closely related; girls and boys enjoy the same experiments. The girls are testing the hardness of ten samples of water from different parts of the country by adding soapflakes of the same size, one at a time. The boys have made a filter.

PLATE XVII

Older juniors: Finding the capacity of a container by various methods.

PLATE XVIII

The boys are using pulleys to find the relationship between the load lifted and their effort (measured on a spring balance).

PLATE XIX

In-service courses in mathematics for teachers of primary schools. Teachers, too, enjoy learning mathematics by discovery.

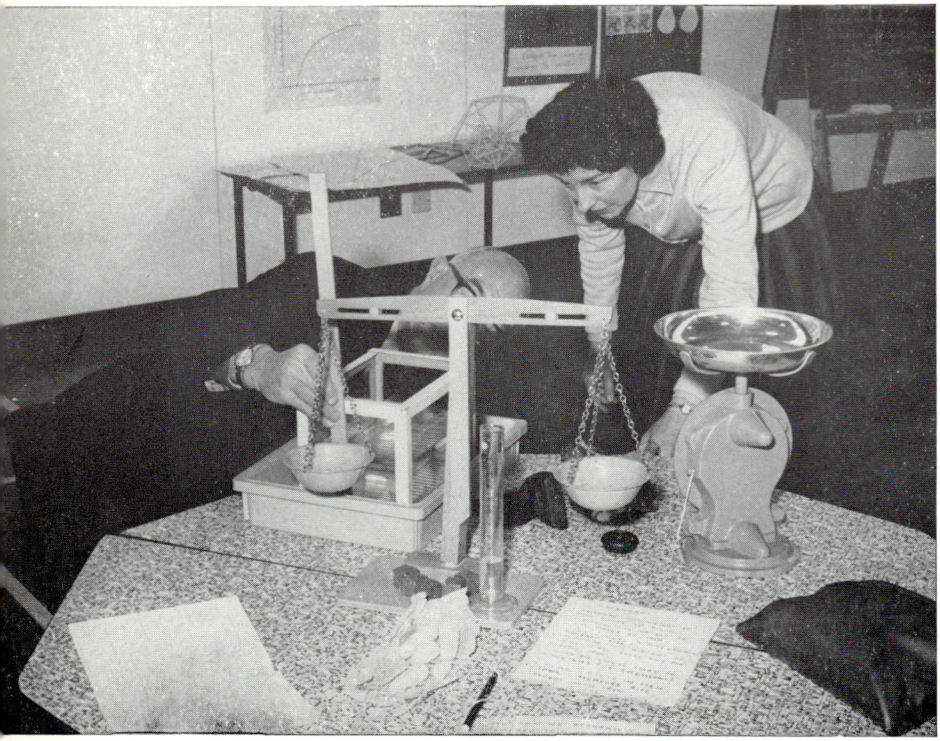

PLATE XX

Finding the weight of water in a fish tank.

PLATE XXI

Finding why some shapes fit together and others do not and why bees use hexagonal cells.

in origin. If we consider that science is concerned with the properties of materials, these include:

1 The strength of materials (the girder bridge made of balsa wood and the train).

2 The stretching of springs and elastic; the relationship between the stretched length and the weight added.

3 The speed of various objects. The relationship between the distance covered and the time.

The majority of the examples included in the 'summary of relationships' table in the previous chapters were scientific in origin. All of these have been undertaken by children from primary schools, some of them very young. For example, the 'bouncing ball experiment' was undertaken by some children of eight who subsequently made a block graph recording the height of the first bounce of the ball dropped from various heights. The majority, however, are examples from the work of ten-year-olds. An example is taken from the work of some children who found the relationship between the weight of a collection of stones and their volume. It was their own idea to find the volume of the stones by completely filling the bucket of water, which they stood in a basin. They then carefully lowered each large stone in turn in the water, catching the overflowing water in the basin. This they measured in a measuring jug.

The same group of children were asked if they could find how many times as heavy as water a large stone was. It was their own idea to weigh the water which overflowed when the stone was carefully lowered into the water. They compared the weight of the stone with the weight of the water which overflowed when the stone was lowered into the water and found the stone was about three times as heavy as water.

Some examples of investigations undertaken by young children of various ages from six to eleven have already been discussed in previous chapters, and particularly in Chapter IV (in the statistics section) it is evident that mathema-atics and science must frequently overlap and reinforce each other. Sometimes it is difficult to distinguish between these two aspects of the curriculum, and at the primary school stage there is no reason why these two should be separated.

Other subjects

From time to time opportunities will arise in other subjects for giving a mathematical slant to the work in hand. We do not suggest that mathematics be introduced for its own sake but that sometimes it can be used to illuminate or give greater significance to the solution of a problem the children have posed or to a topic under discussion. We give a few examples from children's work.

(a) A teacher of older juniors, an enthusiast for history, suggested that the children should take different periods and illustrate the lengths of reigns of Kings and Queens in block graph form. The whole class took part and the different historical periods were made attractive with pictures of the reigning monarchs and of important incidents. A 'time line', a horizontal one, was then made and fixed to the walls of the room. Here ample space was given to each period and the children entered illustrated details of incidents occurring in the different periods as they discovered these from their reading and from sound and television programmes.

(b) The nine-year-olds in another school were encouraged to seek, from their mathematics library, the answers to such mathematical historical questions as: Why is a hundredweight not 100 lb? When a boy discovered the answer for himself he added several subsidiary questions for the others in the class, such as 'In which country is a hundredweight a 100 lb?' 'When and why did the hundredweight in England change from 100 lb?'

(c) A life-size model of Goliath was made by some ten-year-olds. The model included his sword, shield and helmet made to scale. Various details which interested the children, such as the weight of Goliath and David, were calculated. Another class of older juniors made a scale model of the Temple. They worked out the equivalents in the British system of weights and measures.

We began this section with a subject which makes a major contribution to all aspects of learning: communication by means of spoken and written language. It is appropriate to end with another, more basic, language which has, or should have, a powerful and integrating effect on the whole of learning; the communication through the materials of art and craft. In the visual and tactile arts, as in mathematics, children are engaged in the first-hand exploration of the inter-relationships of shapes and spaces. Many mathematical shapes will appear, particularly in models and later, in patterns and abstract designs in three and two dimensions. Art and craft and mathematics have a common vocabulary: for example shape, form, pattern, proportion, symmetry, structure are words frequently used in both aspects of communication. The emotional satisfaction of handling and perceiving these forms, textures and rhythms is not to be underestimated as a factor in learning. In yet another art form, in movement, mathematical shapes are also of importance.

It was surely no accident that, in the Renaissance period, the greatest artists were also great mathematicians and engineers. Two examples immediately spring to mind: Michelangelo, sculptor and painter, who built the fortifications for Florence which are still standing today, and Leonardo da Vinci, painter, the first man to attempt to make a flying machine.

Each of these aspects of education, art and mathematics, has much to contribute to the other. We, as teachers, need to be aware of inter-relationships and of the common vocabulary so that we can be quick to seize opportunities as these arise.

We finish this section with two quotations each of which pays tribute to the contribution of mathematics to beauty.

On Beauty, by Sir Christopher Wren. Published in Tract I of Parentalia, 1750.

There are natural causes of Beauty. Beauty is a Harmony of Objects, begetting Pleasure by the Eye. There are two Causes of Beauty, natural and customary. Natural is from *Geometry* consisting in Uniformity (that is Equality) and Proportion. Customary Beauty is begotten by the Use of our Senses to those Objects which are usually pleasing to us from other Causes, as Familiarity or particular Inclination breeds a Love of things not in themselves lovely. Here lies the greatest Occasion of Errors: here is tried the Architect's judgement: but always the true Test is natural or geometrical Beauty.

Geometrical Figures are naturally more beautiful than other irregular; in this all consent as to a Law of Nature. Of geometrical Figures, the Square and the Circle are most beautiful; next, the Parallelogram and the Oval. Strait Lines are more beautiful than curve; next to strait Lines, equal and geometrical Flexures; an Object elevated in the Middle is more beautiful than depressed . . .

Sir Herbert Read, in *Education through Art* writes: When we call such things beautiful (the bee's cell and the microscopic animals and plants of the sea) we are really admitting that certain mathematical proportions give rise to that emotion in us which we normally associate with works of art.

III. Planning a scheme of work

During the period when a school is changing from a traditional to a discovery approach to mathematics, teachers in different parts of a school may well be giving children of very different ages experience designed to give rise to the same mathematical concept. This is inevitable for two reasons. First because teachers experimenting with material new to them and a new approach will probably choose those topics for which the necessary practical experience is easy to organise, or those topics which appeal to them and in which they therefore have most confidence. Secondly, in a transition period, there will be children of, say, ten-years-old who have not previously had first-hand experience of concepts such as perimeter, area, symmetry and so on. This does not mean that children of nine will tackle a problem in the same way as a child of six, for the older child usually passes quickly through the elementary stage and so will go much farther.

This preliminary period may well last for two or three years and during this time the teacher's record of the ground covered, of children's responses, of successes and failures will be invaluable to the headmaster as a basis for his future planning. When teachers begin to feel more confident in working in this way, there have been a number of instances to show that the need for a scheme of work makes itself felt. We shall now turn our attention to the planning of a scheme of work, but it must be emphasised that such a scheme must be a broad framework within which teachers must feel free to experiment. Such a scheme should be revised and improved from time to time.

In drawing up a scheme for mathematics, as for science (see *Science in the Primary School*) two important factors should be kept in mind: the characteristics of the children concerned and the nature of mathematics itself. By the former we do not only mean the lively curiosity of young children which makes them able and eager to devise experiments and to make discoveries for themselves, but also the way in which individuals learn (children acquire mathematical concepts in very different ways).

Reference has already been made to the abstract and analytic nature of mathematics. It is through his own first-hand experiences that a child is ultimately able to abstract mathematical concepts. As Montaigne said: 'The truth is such a great thing that we should not disdain any means that could lead to it'. Professor Polya's comment on this, with reference to the learning of mathematics, was: 'Abstractions are important; use all means to make them more tangible. Nothing is too good or too bad, too poetical or too trivial to clarify your abstractions'. Ultimately mathematics is concerned with abstract relationships, although, in the beginning, the learning of all concepts must come from experiencing particular instances of them. But once a child has abstracted the concept, the concrete experience which led him to this abstraction is no longer important except as an association to help him to recognise the concept in an unfamiliar situation.

Throughout the previous chapters insistence has been laid on the necessity for the teacher to know the mathematics she wants the children to learn. Reference has also been made to the importance of associating mathematics and language, particularly, but not exclusively, during the exploration stages. The practice required to fix the concept is the last stage in the learning process. In planning a scheme of work, therefore, the following factors need to be considered, although not necessarily in this order. We should always begin with the child's environment:

1 Concepts
2 Experience
3 Materials required
4 The associated language
5 Practice required (mechanical skill) and applications.

Before we outline the possible content of a scheme for primary schools certain points need to be made. These points comprise a statement of aims and general principles which need to be observed in the learning of mathematics by young children.

1 Emphasis needs to be laid on real discovery by the children. The experiences which are planned will depend on the ability and response of each individual child. A range of experience will be required even for a small group of children.
2 Discussion between teacher and children is an essential part of the learning process: occasionally with the class, frequently with a group, occasionally with an individual.
3 The experiences devised for the children need to be progressive. And the child must be aware that he is making progress.
4 The child's recording of his work whether oral, written, expressed by a diagram or by a graph, must be his own. Considerable flexibility must therefore be allowed. Flexibility of method must similarly be allowed in problems. The first attempt must always be the child's own.
5 Computational processes. Even in this field first-hand experience can lead a child to devise his own methods of written computation in the first place. These can be refined later.
6 Records of the child's progress. Such records are perhaps even more important than the teacher's forecast. This important aspect of the work will be discussed in detail in the next section.

7 Books. In mathematics, as in English, a reference library of attractive books can be a very valuable asset and source of ideas for children (and for staff). During the past few years many publishers have produced attractive and readable text-books. These would form an admirable basis for a library. In Appendix 1 is a list of books which teachers and children will find both attractive and useful.

8 The teachers. For the sake of continuity it is essential that every teacher should have a copy of the entire scheme of work. It is also important that teachers should have considerable latitude within the framework of the scheme. Frequent meetings, both informal and more formal, of members of staff will be found invaluable both as an aid to spreading new ideas and to ensure continuity. Teachers would also find it valuable to have access to a complete range of materials such as graph paper of all sizes, weights and measures of all kinds, and structural materials.

The mathematical concepts which are included in the list which follows have all been successfully acquired, through their own discoveries, by children of varying abilities, of primary school age. They may therefore be assumed to be within the capabilities of young children. It must be emphasised, however, that this list has been drawn up on the assumption that all children can discover these mathematical concepts for themselves. Conversely, if a child finds difficulty with abstraction of an idea, then it means either that he is not ready for it, or that the experiences provided by the teacher have not been graded finely enough for the child's ability. Some children require far more intermediate steps than others, and questions which will give them a clearer lead. On the other hand it is of greatest importance that able children should not be given more frequent experience and more help than they need.

Each one of the concepts included should be introduced at recurring intervals, at least once a year and many of them far more often, but each time in a new guise, with the idea of progression in mind. Suggestions for such progressive experience in *length* have already been made in Chapter 4. Similar progressive experience for the concepts of *weight* will be found in *The Teaching of Mathematics in the Primary School* prepared by the Mathematical Association, 1955. Headmasters will also find that a study of the examples described of the work of children of various ages in Chapters 3, 4, 5 and 6 will give them ideas for planning their schemes of work. In general, the mathematical concepts covered include:

1 Number systems: whole numbers, fractions directed numbers.

2 Application of number to measurement.

3 A study of the properties of shapes met in everyday life.

4 A study of functions or of the relationships between pairs of variables expressed in graphical form.

1. *Number systems*

(i) Sets of objects: sorting, classifying, ordering, matching by one-to-one correspondence.

(ii) Cardinal or counting numbers, counting: one-to-one correspondence of object and number name. Conservation of number. Written numerals.

(iii) The number line. Numbers in order (ordinal); combining numbers up to 20.

(iv) Place-value. Other ways of representing numbers (Roman numerals, Egyptian numerals, etc.).

(v) Extension of the number line to 100. Ability to add and subtract, without counting on in ones, two figure numbers.

(vi) Use of bases other than 10 for written numerals.

(vii) Extension of the idea of numbers: fractions and decimal fractions based on concrete experience. The four operations using these numbers based on first-hand experience.

(viii) The operations of addition, subtraction, multiplication and division based on varied concrete experience. Recording at first in the child's own words; symbols then used as shorthand; finally practice.

(ix) Patterns of numbers obtained by cumulative addition using the same number and successive subtraction of the same number from one of its multiples; multiplication and division tables. (Automatic response.)

(x) The operations applied to larger numbers. Discovery of written computational processes: addition, subtraction, multiplication and division; a variety of methods used. Practice in one efficient method.

(xi) Number patterns: remainder or modulus arithmetic.

2. *Measurement*

(i) Concrete experience of all kinds of measurement and use of money, length, weight, capacity, time, temperature, speed.

(ii) First-hand experience in the four operations with standard units of measurement.

3. *A study of the properties of geometric shapes (see summary at the end of Chapter* 5)

(i) Properties of the common solid shapes and regular flat shapes.

(ii) Direction, angles and compass directions. Parallel lines.

(iii) Dimensions: perimeter, area, volume; conservation of length, area, volume; perimeter, area, volume of irregular shapes.

(iv) Symmetry.

(v) Similarity.

(vi) Marking position.[1]

4. *A study of functions. Graphical representation.*

(i) Collecting data and recording these by real objects or by symbols, or by pictures.

(ii) Collecting data and recording by block and column graph.

(iii) Relationships between two variables. Data collected and recorded by graphs.

(iv) Types.

(a) Constant ratio or ready reckoner graph, straight line.

(b) Constant product (hyperbola).

(c) Squares (parabola).

(d) Cubes.

(e) Growth curves.

(v) Positive numbers and negative numbers. Directed numbers.

Teachers may be interested to know that a pamphlet has been drawn up by Essex teachers entitled *Suggested Outline of Primary Mathematics.*

IV. Assessment of children's progress

One of the features of the work described which will give teachers most cause for anxiety is the difficulty, at least in the early stages, of assessing each individual's progress. It has always been easy to give children a test in mechanical arithmetic or even in problem arithmetic, and to assess their apparent progress from this. It is only when teachers make a close study of each individual's number knowledge and the method by which he does even simple written computation, that real discrepancies and basic weaknesses are revealed. It is by no means unusual to find that at least one half of a class, at any stage in the primary or secondary field, are combining numbers (by addition, subtraction, multiplication or division) by counting on or back in ones. Yet such children may achieve full marks on a mechanical test if time is not taken into account. A written test on mechanical computation may be an invalid indication of mathematical attainment. How then is a child's progress to be assessed? It must be admitted that learning by discovery is a slower (although surer) process than apparent learning by instruction, followed by mechanical practice. Therefore if a child's progress is measured by achievement in mechanical tests alone this will not be a true measure of his progress in mathematics. Moreover, if the results of mechanical tests done by a child taught by traditional methods are compared with those of a child brought up to make his own discoveries, the performance of the former child would probably be superior to that of the latter at the ages of seven and eight. By the age of nine, however, the latter child would have caught up with the written computational processes so that his performance in this respect would equal, if not surpass, that of the other child.

[1] See (a) The Mathematical Association's *The Teaching of Mathematics in the Primary School*, chapter on spatial aspects; (b) geography section in this chapter.

But there is one aspect in which teachers would have no doubt about the superiority of new methods: the child's ability to think for himself and his confidence in problem solving, real or imaginary (from a text book). When a child is accustomed to using real materials to solve problems, when he is used to making his own discoveries, he becomes self-reliant in this respect and often shows considerable initiative and invariably makes an attempt at any problem with which he is faced. The method he evolves may not be the most efficient, but it is most likely that it will lead to a possible solution.

Although, therefore, it may not be easy for a teacher to assess a child's progress during the transitional stages, when a school has revised its methods and schemes throughout, the problem of assessment will not be so great. As will be seen from the content of the previous section, there are certain definite mathematical concepts, the acquisition of which will be a landmark in the child's progress. (One aspect of this will be the ability to perform traditional written computational processes.) These concepts will cover a field far more extensive than that of traditional arithmetic: geometry, functionality (leading to graphical representation and hence to algebra). An important aspect which should therefore be taken into account in assessment is not only the child's ability to think for himself (and hence to discover relationships) but also his ability to communicate or to record his discovery in symbolic form: in words, in numerals and other mathematical symbols, in tabular form, by a diagram or by a graph.

It cannot be over-emphasised that, in all assessment, the teacher's personal record of a child's progress is of paramount importance. This should be kept to pass on from teacher to teacher and from school to school. If the change from one school to another is to be effected smoothly, continuity must be maintained. It is essential therefore that there should be exchange visits of teachers between contributory infant and junior schools and between contributory junior and secondary schools. These visits need to be long enough for teachers to spend a few days in the classrooms of other schools, not only to meet and to get to know the children, but also to study and understand the methods used. Such exchanges need to be two-way. By this means also, receiving teachers can come to understand and interpret the individual records they receive of children's progress.

V. Parents' attitudes and anxieties

Naturally enough, parents are apt to judge their children's progress entirely by their achievement in mechanical sums. The question: 'How many sums did you get right today?' is probably more frequently put to a child than any other. Once parents have evidence that their child can read, their next concern is that he should become proficient at arithmetic. For many, this anxiety is based on their hopes for their child in the selection test, and since the majority of the tests still consist largely of mechanical sums, parents use efficiency in mechanical processes (the so-called four rules in number and quantity) as their criterion of progress.

Now it has been stressed, throughout this pamphlet, that although discovery methods are slower in the early stages ultimately there is no loss of efficiency in computation and far less practice will be required to maintain efficiency. Many teachers have reduced the time spent on computational practice to one or at most two periods a week; some teachers already base this practice on the children's concrete experience. But it is necessary for heads of schools to take the parents into their confidence when changes of method are proposed. A large majority of parents will be aware, through radio and television programmes, and through the national press, that many primary schools are introducing 'new' methods in order to give children opportunities for discovering mathematical ideas for themselves. Provided it is explained to them that the newer methods are slow, if achievement is measured in computational processes alone, they will accept this, especially if it is pointed out that by the time they are nine, children brought up by newer methods will be able to perform computational processes very efficiently.

In one county the parents requested a county inspector to give them a series of lectures on new methods of learning mathematics. In one primary school the parents asked the headmaster to give them a series of talks on mathematics. One headmaster invited the parents to his school where he had set out, in each classroom, the practical assignments planned for the children to enable them to acquire various concepts. The parents were asked to try the assignments; they found these difficult and volunteered that there must be something in the new methods if children could solve such difficult problems. The most usual way of informing the parents of changes in the approach to mathematics is for the headmaster to discuss the changes and possible consequences at a Parent-Teachers' association or a special meeting. One headmaster sent a letter to all parents explaining the change of policy.

But the first changes may be introduced by a teacher herself and if, in the first instance, it is not possible to call a meeting of the parents, other steps must be taken to prevent children from giving the wrong impression at home. In this case the teacher needs to be careful in her references to the change of method. She might, for example, place stress on the excitement of the new subject: mathematics, which the children are to learn. She can, with care, prevent the wrong story going home by referring to the concrete experience as 'a mathematical investigation or experiment' (which it is) and by referring to the child's recording of the investigation as a 'sum' if necessary. Children undoubtedly enjoy their practical investigations and may easily give the wrong impression as the following example indicates. When a boy was asked by his mother: 'What did you do in arithmetic today?' He replied, 'Oh, I didn't do any sums today. I weighed some stones'. The mother was amused the first time but when, on the second day, in response to her enquiry the boy replied 'I didn't do any sums today either. I weighed some water', the mother began to be alarmed. If, instead, the boy had explained to his mother that he was solving an exciting mathematical problem: that he was finding out how many times as heavy as water stones are, the impression created at home might have been a very different one.

To sum up, discovery methods of learning mathematics represent a major change of policy. In justice to parents, therefore, an explanation of such methods and their implications, as far as assessing a child's progress is concerned. needs to be given.

VI. Co-operation between schools

Reference has already been made to the importance of ensuring the continuous mathematical development of children as they pass from one school to another; from infant to junior schools and from junior to secondary schools. In-service courses have often provided initial contacts between teachers from all types of schools, which some have been quick to develop. Local Education Authorities for their part are encouraging visits between teachers from infant, junior and secondary schools so that different approaches and difficulties encountered are appreciated from first-hand experience.

What would be the effect of discovery methods on children when they transfer to the secondary school? It is rare now to hear the complaint that the primary schools are taking the excitement from new topics by providing wider mathematical opportunities. On the contrary, there is now an appreciation of the change in children's attitudes towards mathematics, and a readiness to make the most of this. In primary schools, the approach to mathematical topics is, in the main, of an exploratory nature rather than of an ordered adult kind. This approach is frequently referred to by mathematicians as Stage A, the intuitive approach which will, for the large majority of children, form the basis for a more ordered and more abstract development at the secondary stage. But it is important to remember that at all stages of education from the five-year-old to the university student, the principles of sound learning are the same; the young child or student must be given opportunity to take the next step for himself. In the words of an American professor of mathematics: 'If I want my students to learn mathematics, they must create it for themselves'.

The co-operation which is now taking place between infant and junior schools, and which is beginning to take place between junior and secondary schools, is reflected in the wider contacts which have been initiated between teachers of mathematics in schools and universities and mathematicians in industry. In 1963, for the first time, a co-ordinating Joint

Mathematical Council was set up to bring together teachers of mathematics in schools of all kinds and in universities, and representatives from industry. Nor is the joint responsibility for mathematical education which this development implies confined to Great Britain. The following statement is taken from an American Report on curriculum reform[1].

'Mathematical education, to fulfil the needs of an advanced and advancing community, must be under continual scrutiny and undergo constant change, and it is the responsibility of all mathematicians working in university, school or industry, to concern themselves with the problem of keeping mathematical education vital and up-to-date.'

The changes which are taking place in this country in the content and presentation of mathematics in primary and secondary schools are also part of a world-wide movement: to assess, to experiment and to prepare new syllabuses in the light of classroom experience. This movement, in general, has been concerned with reforms in secondary school mathematics. The chief aim has been to revise the content, partly to bring it up-to-date and partly to ensure that the revolutionary developments initiated by the use of the computer for calculations were reflected in the new syllabuses. These changes were foreshadowed by the mathematics report of the O.E.C.D.,[2] which was drawn up as a result of discussions involving representatives of teachers of mathematics from all over the world.

In Great Britain, experiments are in progress at the secondary stage in which a variety of schools is taking part: the Schools Mathematics Project, the Midlands Mathematical Experiment, a project initiated by St. Dunstan's College[3] and other projects introduced more recently.

Some similarity of aims of the reforms in the learning of mathematics at the secondary stage and at the primary stage will be evident from the following excerpts taken from the American Report to which reference has already been made:

'The discovery approach, in which the student is asked to explore a situation in his own way, is invaluable in developing creative and independent thinking in the individual. In this system memorizing a mechanical response does not help the student to advance. His innate interest and competitive nature force him to concentrate on the creative problem at hand'.

It is clear, however, that at a later stage, the discovery approach is not expected to predominate:

'This development of independent and creative habits of thought does not require the complete devotion of the curriculum to the discovery method. Discovery directed by a dialogue between teacher and class, and the direct teacher-presentation of material, will be required to attain a reasonable rate of advancement'.

The lack of definite knowledge about children's mathematical capabilities when they are given opportunities to discover mathematical truths for themselves is illustrated in the following paragraph:

'We do not propose to teach by drill. At every level we propose to present mathematics as a pursuit of the truth by a process of enquiry: we propose to elicit all the insight and all the creative responses that the student is capable of. Just how much they will turn out to be capable of we do not know: but the experience of a few bold experimenters amply proves that the present apparent limits on the insight and creativity of children are being set by the materials presented to them, and not by the native talent of the children'.

But there is no uncertainty about the advisability of the creative learning of mathematics in the following statement:

'Mathematics is something which people do: it is not something they receive in the passive sense. We believe that this principle holds even at higher maturity levels'.

In this chapter we have considered the changes which are being made in the teaching of mathematics in primary schools as these affect teachers, children and parents. In the next chapter we shall turn our attention to

[1] *Goals for School Mathematics*. Report of the Cambridge Conference on School Mathematics. Educational Services Incorporated, 1963.

[2] *Mathematics Today: a Guide for Teachers* ed. H. F. Fehr, New Thinking in School Science Series (O.E.C.D., 1964).

[3] Each of these projects has published material. Full references to this material will be found in Appendix 1.

another section of the educational community which is concerned in these changes: the training colleges, in the wider setting of the general problem of training. We shall therefore consider courses for teachers in service as well as for teachers in training.

8 The teacher and mathematics: present and future developments

In this chapter two major topics will be considered: the mathematical training both of prospective teachers and of those already in service, and present research on the formulation of mathematical concepts.

1. Teachers in service

Teachers in primary schools have been subject to many pressures during the past few years, all of which have tended to increase and not decrease the scope of the curriculum: for example, in mathematics, in science, and in modern languages. In the large majority of countries there is a programme of regular in-service training to keep teachers aware of such educational developments. In this country such training by means of courses is entirely voluntary, and the demand normally far exceeds the provision. A summary of the provision of such courses up to the time of publication follows.

Reference has already been made to the publication, in 1955, of the Mathematical Association's Report on the *Teaching of Mathematics in Primary Schools* which stimulated discussions on mathematics among groups of teachers in various parts of the country. In 1958 the Ministry of Education organised the first national mathematics short course for teachers in primary schools. There was an overwhelming demand and one or two such courses have followed in each of the succeeding years. In 1960 a more concentrated series of in-service courses was initiated by the Ministry of Education in response to the ever increasing demand by teachers, through local education authorities, institutes of education and teachers associations. These local courses are normally organised by H.M. Inspectors and staffed by H.M. Inspectors and training college lecturers. By the spring of 1965 nearly 200 in-service courses had taken place in which more than 16,000 teachers were concerned (including some 2,000 mathematics teachers from secondary modern and grammar schools). Some 400 training college lecturers (in mathematics or education) have given assistance with both local and national courses. No demand has been refused.

The duration of these short courses is normally 3 days; some 60 primary school teachers (20 infant, 40 junior) and up to 20 mathematics teachers from secondary schools attended each course. The emphasis throughout is on mathematics as the discovery of relationships followed by the expression of the relationship in symbolic form (in words, in numbers, by a diagram, in letters or by a graph). The programme normally comprised 4 or 5 practical sessions, 2 or 3 lectures and two group discussions. During the practical sessions teachers worked in pairs on assignments based on work done by primary school children, (An exhibition of such work collected from schools in many parts of the country illustrates this). The assignments are, however, written in language appropriate to adults. The purposes of the practical sessions are:

1 To give teachers opportunities for the discovery of mathematical relationships at their own and at children's level.

2 To give them insight into the structure of the number system and of the operations of addition, subtraction, multiplication and division.

3 To show them the mathematical possibilities of the environment.

4 To provide them with some starting points in their own work with children.

5 To give them opportunities for discussion.

Wherever possible teachers are encouraged to express graphically the result or relationships they are investigating.

The practical sessions include:

Structure

1 Discovery of the meaning of the operations of addition, subtraction, multiplication and division using environmental materials, as these apply to numerical situations, and to weights, measures and money.

2 Increased understanding of the implications of place value (using structural apparatus and the abacus. Use of structural apparatus for number relationships and to clarify the meaning of the four operations. 'New Look' mathematics for the secondary school teachers and those interested among the primary school teachers.

Applications of mathematics

3 The use of the environment in all aspects of measuring and money; contributions of all other subjects of the curriculum to mathematics, particularly science and geography.

4 Spatial Aspects. These cover a very wide range, for example; perimeter, area, volume; symmetry; similarity; the study of various mathematical shapes, man-made and natural, solid and two-dimensional.

Throughout the course teachers have opportunities of seeing and discussing work done by children and, on some occasions, have seen children at work in the classrooms. A number of teachers, both head and assistant, and of training college lecturers have talked of the work they have done with primary school children.

In the final lecture, which is based on the graphs drawn by teachers on the course as well as those done by children, the teachers are shown the mathematics underlying the assignments and in particular that the large majority of these lead to various members of one family or relationships: $y = ax^n$.

As a result of these and many other courses a new approach to mathematics is beginning to develop in some primary schools in many parts of the country. But, although some teachers may be encouraged by these courses to make a start, most of them recognise the need for more systematic help once they have taken the plunge. At every course this problem is raised and teachers are encouraged to form local study groups composed of primary and secondary school teachers. Some of these study groups are supported by the local education authorities, others have been sponsored and financed by institutes of education. Once again the staffing is often drawn from the Colleges of Education, or from local education authority organisers. It has been very fortunate for this campaign that since 1956 some of the mathematicians among Her Majesty's Inspectors of Schools and members of the mathematical section of the Association of Teachers in Colleges and Departments of Education have met annually for a conference lasting several days. For three years the conference has devoted a good deal of its attention to ways and means of improving the teaching of mathematics in primary schools; some mathematics lecturers new to College of Education work, education lecturers and local education authority organisers have been invited to these conferences. A pamphlet has been written as a result: *Primary Mathematics for Schools and Colleges.*[1] A close unanimity of purpose has developed in the campaign to help teachers in primary schools to improve the teaching of mathematics, and College of Education lecturers are giving very valuable assistance at in-service courses, and in the ensuing study groups.

Some College of Education lecturers have initiated courses for teachers in the schools in their own areas and they have sometimes followed these by 'day release' courses for teachers which have taken place while students are in the schools on school practice. Others have initiated experiments within schools or groups of schools which entail regular meetings of teachers for discussion. In more than one area the parents have become interested and have enthusiastically attended practical mathematics sessions.

In a few counties a Mathematics Adviser has been appointed by the Local Education Authority; in such areas the ready response of the teachers has had a marked effect on the work in the schools.

There is no doubt about the progress made in schools in those areas where, for a period regular opportunities are provided for teachers to meet, discuss and work. But it must be admitted that, in those areas where an initial course has not been followed up, there has been

[1] ATCDE, 1963.

little lasting effect despite the goodwill of the teachers concerned. Problems of classroom organisation and of convincing colleagues of the value of the work have often proved too much for a teacher deciding to make a start herself.

There are various ways, however, in which teachers can help themselves to learn more mathematics.

1 By reading. A list of books which will be helpful in this respect will be found in Appendix 1. To help the teacher who has, as yet done little or no such reading, an asterisk has been placed by a few books which are particularly easy to read as a beginning. Reference has already been made to a number of attractively produced text books which have appeared on the market during the past few years. Most of these books would be valuable as a source of ideas for teachers.

2 By forming a study group of the kind to which reference has already been made. Teachers attend these to continue their own first-hand discoveries of mathematics. In more than one instance the groups are enthusiastically supported by mathematicians from grammar schools and secondary modern schools. The groups meet for various purposes.

(i) to give teachers, and especially those who have not already attended a course, opportunities for discovering mathematics at their own level and at children's level.

(ii) to bring work teachers have tried with children (often following a practical study session on a specific topic) to compare results with other teachers and discuss difficulties.

(iii) to learn more mathematics by discovery methods closely related to the work done with children. The groups in some areas are affiliated to a branch of the Mathematical Association or the Association of Teachers of Mathematics.

(iv) to experiment with different methods of teaching to try to discover those methods which are most successful with children of different characteristics.

(v) to learn some of the 'Modern' or 'New Look' Mathematics which is being introduced in secondary schools.

3 By taking a one-term supplementary course in mathematics (by secondment) at one of the Colleges of Education. These courses were instituted in 1962 and details may be obtained from the Department of Education and Science. The object of these one-term mathematics courses is not to turn out mathematical specialists in the sense in which this is understood in secondary schools. It is hoped that these teachers will go back to give a lead, perhaps, in study groups in their own area and also, of course, in their own schools. In some cases it may be possible to arrange for this 'specialist' to work with a teacher with a group of children in her class and to give help with the organisation.

II. Students in training

Reference has already been made to the annual conferences of the A.T.C.D.E. mathematics section and mathematicians among Her Majesty's Inspectors of Schools. An important consequence of these conferences has been the wide interchange of ideas between one college and another, and between H.M.I. and College of Education lecturers. As a result, great changes have taken place in professional courses for intending primary school teachers during the past few years. It is rare, in these days, to find a college without a mathematics lecturer, and some have four or more lecturers. It is also rare to find a mathematics professional course limited to a term's lectures on method. In many colleges students are given opportunities to discover mathematical truths for themselves from the beginning of the course. This has brought about a marked change in students' attitudes to mathematics and its teaching. In general, too, the time allowance for these professional courses is substantial; often two periods a week for two years. (See the last contribution of chapter 9 for an example of a good professional course.)

Moreover, before students on teaching practice are faced with the problems of organising mathematical experience for a whole class, it is becoming usual to give them the opportunity of working with a small group of children (maximum six); in this way the students are able to convince themselves that children can learn by their own discoveries. One college sent the students out for a week towards the end of their first term; six or eight students were allocated to a class to experiment with a small group of children, using a discovery approach to mathematics. The students returned confident and stimulated saying, 'It works! Children *can* find out for themselves if you don't tell them'. The exhibition of children's work resulting from this week's experiment was most impressive.

Several lecturers also testify that, if students are thrown on their own resources from the beginning of the course (by means of practical assignments through which they discover mathematical truths for themselves), they quickly become aware of their own mathematical deficiencies and overcome these for themselves, so that remedial classes are no longer necessary.

FILMS

The following 16mm. films show primary children learning mathematics and science. These would prove useful at in-service courses, for parents, and at Colleges of Education.

Decimalisation and Metrication 30 min black & white

A film in the BBC *Expanding Classroom* series. Age range of children 7 to 11 years. Available for purchase or on hire from BBC Television Enterprises, Film Hire, 25 The Burroughs, London NW4 4AR.

Maths is a Monster 30 min black & white 16mm

A film from the *Discovery and Experience* series. Age range 5 to 11 years. Available for purchase or on hire from BBC Television Enterprises, Film Hire, 25 The Burroughs, London NW4 4AR. Also available on hire from NAVA Library, Paxton Place, Gipsy Road, London SE27 95R or Concord Films Council, Nacton. Ipswich IP10 0JZ.

Children and Mathematics

A series of five 30-minute black and white 16mm films of the Nuffield Mathematics Teaching Project designed to help teachers in infant, junior and the early years of secondary school.

Available on hire from NAVA Library, Paxton Place, Gipsy Road, London SE27 95R or can be purchased from BBC Television Enterprises, 25 The Burroughs, London NW4 4AR.

Maths Alive 30 min colour 16mm

Primary children at work. Age range 5 to 11 years. Made by John Howard for DES and Schools Council. Available for purchase or on hire from EFVA, 33 Queen Anne Street. London W1.

I Do and I Understand 15 min black & white 16mm

Shows mathematics in a third year junior class.

Available on hire from Petroleum Films Bureau, 4 Brook Street, London W1 or can be purchased from Sound Services Ltd, Wilton Crescent, Merton Park, London SW19.

Into the Secondary School 20 min black & white 16mm

Shows 'Nuffield type' mathematics in the first year of two secondary schools.

Produced by BP.

Available on hire from Petroleum Films Bureau, 4 Brook Street, London W1 or can be purchased from Sound Services Ltd, Wilton Crescent, Merton Park, London SW19.

Maths with Everything 20 min black & white or colour 16mm

Shows mathematics in the infant school.

Available on hire from Concord Films Council Ltd, Nacton, Ipswich IP10 0JZ or can be purchased from Graphic Films Ltd, 1 Soho Square, London W1.

The above three films were made for the Nuffield Mathematics Teaching Project.

Dance Squared 3 min 30 sec colour 16mm

Made by National Film Board of Canada.

Available on hire from NAVA Library, Paxton Place, Gipsy Road, London SE27 95R, 95R, British Film Institute, 43 Lower Marsh, London SE1, or Sound Services Ltd, Wilton Crescent, Merton Park, London SW19.

Can be purchased from Canadian National Film Board, 1 Grosvenor Square, London W1X OAD.

Notes on a Triangle 4 min 56 sec colour 16mm

Made by National Film Board of Canada.

Available on hire from NAVA Library, Paxton Place, Gipsy Road, London SE27 95R, or British Film Institute, 43 Lower Marsh, London SE1.

Can be purchased from Canadian National Film Board, 1 Grosvenor Square, London W1X OAD.

Donald Duck in Mathmagicland 26 min colour 16mm

Available on hire to LEAs from Walt Disney Productions, 68 Pall Mall, London SW1.

Into Tomorrow 28 min black and white 16mm sound

Produced by Nuffield Junior Science Project. A film about a class of children in a junior school who began a study by a visit to the local street.

Available for purchase or on hire from the Rank Film Laboratory, Greenford, Middlesex.

Children Observed 20 min colour 16mm sound

Nuffield Junior Science/Schools Council film. A film about infant and junior children responding to a variety of situations and materials without the interference of adults. Two versions of this film are available with the same visuals but separate commentaries—one by Miss M. Brearley, the other by Professor E. Lunzer.

Available for purchase or on hire from NAVA library, Paxton Place, Gipsy Road, London SE27 95R.

The Explorers 20 min colour 16mm sound.

Nuffield Junior Science/Schools Council film. A film about three classes in a junior school at work on their 'scientific' activities. It shows not only how they pose and tackle problems but also reveals the increasing sophistication and rigour which comes from continued experience.

Available for purchase or on hire from NAVA Library, Paxton Place, Gipsy Road, London SE27 95R.

III. Research

The emphasis of research projects has shifted from instruction to learning; no longer is research centred on the comparison of one computational method with another. During the past few years many research projects have been carried out concerning the way in which children acquire mathematical concepts and, as we have seen in Chapter 2, many of these have been based on experiments carried out by Piaget in Switzerland. Research projects have also been carried out, chiefly under the auspices of the National Foundation for Educational Research, into the relative merits, as teaching aids, of the various types of commercial structural apparatus on the market. In addition, there have been valuable pieces of research work such as Dr. Biggs's *Anxiety, Motivation and Primary School Mathematics* (NFER, 1962). All these have lent support to and made their own contributions to the changes which are in progress in mathematical education in primary schools.

Of all the research undertaken during the past 20 years into the learning of mathematics by young children, by far the most important to the individual teacher is that done with her own children in the classroom. Devising experiences, with a definite aim in view, observing the children in the process of learning through first-hand experience, asking questions and recording answers, this is the class teacher's part, and a most rewarding and vital part it is. In the beginning, the demand for changes in the teaching of mathematics came from the teachers themselves. In the end it is they who carry out their independent researches in their own classrooms and it is they who should discover, for themselves, the answer to their question about the best way for the children in their class to learn mathematics.

NUFFIELD FOUNDATION PRIMARY MATHEMATICS TEACHING PROJECT

From 1965 the Nuffield Foundation sponsored separate primary mathematics (5–13) and primary science projects. In each project an organiser was appointed to lead a team whose purpose was to assess the needs of children and teachers and to experiment in schools to discover the mathematical potentialities of primary school children. Many schools in different areas were concerned in the preliminary stage.

The declared object of the mathematics project was 'to produce a contemporary course for children from five to thirteen'. This was designed to help them to connect together many aspects of the world around them, to introduce them gradually to the processes of abstract thinking, and to foster in them a critical and logical, but also creative turn of mind.

The work of the project was set against the present background of new thinking concerning mathematics itself. But there was no novelty for its own sake: any topical aspect of the subject introduced had to be more intelligible and purposeful (and so, easier to teach) than that which it replaced. Perhaps the most important message of 'modern' mathematics at this level is its ubiquity, the fact that doing sums is only a fraction of the programme envisaged.

The organiser and his team were able to seek guidance from a consultative committee. A range of teaching resources was prepared, including ample teachers' guides, pupils' materials and visual and other aids. These materials were subjected to testing with pupils of various ages and levels of ability and were revised in the light of experience. Finally the resulting range of resources was published (by John Murray and W. & R. Chambers).

Programmed Learning

Another field in which considerable research has taken place is in programmed learning. Small groups of teachers in various parts of the country, usually sponsored by an institute of education, have experimented in making programmes for teaching machines.

The majority of the programmes so far have been concerned with the learning of mathematics at secondary level. The programmes intended for primary school children have been concerned mainly with revision of the processes of addition, subtraction, multiplication and division. Such programmes have, therefore, afforded no opportunities for discovery by the children themselves.

It is difficult to envisage the part programmed learning could play at primary school level because children do not learn by the same logical methods used by adults to codify mathematical concepts. There is no doubt, however, that teachers themselves benefit from having to devise programmes. There is also no doubt that programmes subsequently tried on children have to be modified. Whether programmes can be devised which will afford children opportunity for individual discovery is open to question. It may turn out that branching programmes, in which children are given multiple choice answers, are superior to linear programmes of which the criticism is sometimes made that there is little opportunity for real discovery.

It has been found that programmed learning has a use in a more limited field, as for example, to help a child who, through absence, has missed the acquisition of a new concept. It also affords an opportunity for meeting a concept, already learnt, in a new context. The superiority of programmed learning over a good text book affording opportunity for discovery has yet to be firmly established. Teaching machines enable a child to follow his own progress step by step but if the steps are too small the child may lose interest. In any event, a teaching machine at best can never be an effective substitute for a teacher's quick response to a child's needs. In brief, teaching machines have yet to prove their worth in learning by discovery

9 Straight from the classroom

In this chapter teachers, head teachers, and College of Education lecturers write of their personal experiences of the introduction of mathematics (considered as the discovery of relationships) to the children in their classes and schools and to students in colleges. All of these are the records of work done during the past five years; all are part of the concentrated national effort to improve the teaching of mathematics in primary schools. A variety of experiences has been included since the problems of an infant school differ from those of a junior school and those of a rural school from those of a town school. It is hoped that some of the experiences included in this section will be of help to those teachers about to make a start for themselves. The sections have been contributed by

1 The headmistress of a city infant school.
2 The headmistress of a rural infant school who is also a class teacher.
3 The headmistress of a rural primary school who is also a class teacher.
4 The headmaster of a large junior school in an urban area
5 A former class teacher who is now employed as a part-time specialist in an urban school and who works with various class teachers in their mathematics lessons.
6 A College of Education lecturer in science who has worked with young children.
7 A team of College of Education lecturers at a college which offers a one term supplementary course in mathematics to teachers from primary schools.
8 An administrative officer of a Local Education Authority.

1. The Headmistress of a City Infant School

The first example is from a city school containing children of ages five to eight; the classes are large, each containing between 35 and 40 children of the same age group but of very varying abilities. In this school a wide range of opportunities for numerical and spatial discoveries are provided simultaneously. The headmistress writes:

Once a teacher herself is aware of the possibilities children begin to make quite enlightening discoveries. What we, as adults, take for granted, children produce as astonishing discoveries. Here are some examples from the field of number relationships:

'If you cut one piece of paper in half you have two pieces.
In 300 are 3 hundreds.
Twenty is the same as 10 and 10.
Two is made from 2 ones.
2 is an even number. You can put even numbers in pairs.
There is 0 at the end of every figure when you count in tens.
When you count in 5s it goes like a pattern'.

We encourage children to count up the scissors etc., and to tally them with the labels on the tins and to seek the lost when one or two are missing. They distribute paint brushes four to a pot. We number the pages in our writing books and in our homemade reading books. At school prayers children go out in many different collections. It may be red jumpers, classes, children in a certain district, those who are five years old. One day a boy said: 'Why don't you ask those who are five and a half years?' An interest in structural material grew last year and this seems to have helped to fill a gap in understanding.

The spatial work is a very valuable source of mathematical experience although the wonderful opportunities are not always fully exploited and explored by the teachers. Our models are made from waste materials. (In this school model making by the children themselves is developed as a serious creative activity.) These we cover with newspaper. At the beginning children tend to wrapup the box. like a parcel. Teachers train the children to estimate the amount of material required to cover a box Estimation at first is haphazard. The paper chosen is mostly too small. Eventually children draw round the box and finally measure in order to make allowance for overlap.

The youngest children usually begin by making a house from a box which they stand upright. They cut the roof from the corner of a box (often suggested by the teacher when the children consult her) (Fig. 9.1). The windows are stuck on in an haphazard fashion and in no particular pattern. Although the door is usually at the bottom it is

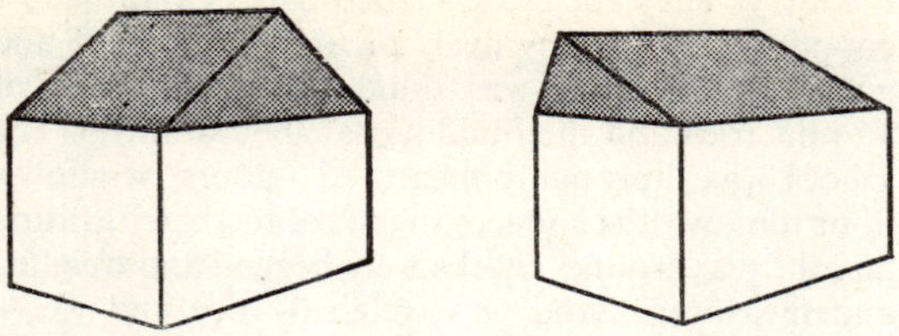

Fig. 9.1

not in proportion. When a teacher suggested that Christopher's house needed a bigger door he made it taller as in Fig. 9.2.

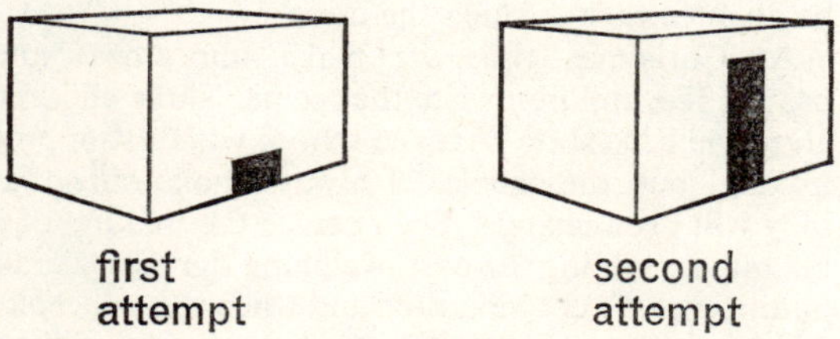

Fig. 9.2

Cars and buses are made sometimes with one box or perhaps with a smaller box attached in front (Fig. 9.3). Many wheels are added and not usually

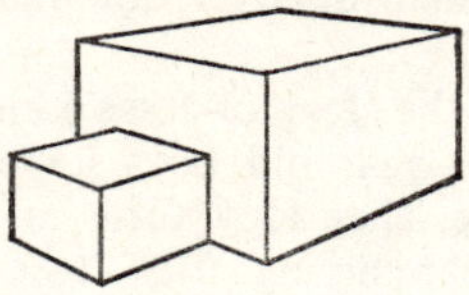

Fig. 9.3

in matched pairs. Ships are made from a box on a box and sometimes a funnel is added.

We make all manner of dolls. The first attempt is often a flat doll cut out in cardboard. Some are made from tins or a toilet roll or a roll of material. Round tins cause surprise when measured, as do fat dolls. As the children develop they become more self critical and models, of whatever kind, become more detailed. The dolls develop limbs and, at this stage, making a pattern for a doll becomes a necessity. By eight a child may realise that he can fold the paper in two in order to cut a symmetrical pattern. Dolls' clothes call for mathematical estimation and many are the setbacks. 'It's too little'. Children are often unable to believe the need for increasing the size and go back to smaller sizes repeatedly.

Models, when finished, can be set up for display. For example, in a room of five-year-olds was a row of houses, all numbered, and with spaces left for intervening houses: 10, 17, 21. This was followed up by a consideration of even and odd numbers.

At six to seven years most children become more inventive, branching out on group models of some intricacy in which a great deal of looking up goes on. For example, a large doll's house produced a wealth of experience. It comprised six rooms each containing specialized furniture made to size. Bathroom and kitchen have all modern equipment including washing machine and refrigerator. Windows are given real curtains made of material. The children's recordings contain the following information: 'The doll's house is 1 ft. 6 ins. across and 1 ft. 6 ins. long. A bath in the bathroom is 8 ins. long. The coffee table is 9 inches in circumference. The basin in the bathroom is $4\frac{1}{2}$ ins. The sink measures $2\frac{1}{2}$ ins. The pot with fruit is $3\frac{1}{2}$ ins. round.'

At the same stage rails are made for trains which are made to run under bridges. Often the bridge has to be raised because the train will not go underneath. Harbours are made for ships and roads are made for the cars. Plan making, too, begins at this stage.

(The plans made by a six-year-old of the house he had made have been described in Chapter 5.)

This account illustrates the variety of mathematical activities which can arise in an infant school from the ordinary creative work of the classroom when the headmistress and her staff are aware of the mathematical potentialities of the work they are doing. There is no one in this school specially qualified in mathematics but the headmistress herself has sought to make the most of any numerical and spatial opportunities which arise. From the outset language and mathematics are closely associated. Formal written computation is normally begun towards the end of the year in which the children reach the age of seven.

2. The Headmistress of a Rural Infant School Who is also a Class Teacher

In the next account, written by the teaching headmistress of a three-class infant school, the underlying philosophy is the same as in the previous account. This headmistress takes the class containing the oldest children: in the description of her work it is interesting to note that she has a strong sense of progression (from the youngest children to the oldest).

In this school the mathematics is interwoven with practically everything we do and so the children are 'mathematics minded'.

We try to provide our children with a rich and stimulating environment so that they enjoy a wealth of purposeful experiences. In these the children find not only sheer pleasure and the joy that comes from discovery, but power in their own ability to think.

Much of the teaching is incidental, for real situations crop up throughout the day, and we try to grasp opportunities and use them to advantage. We use the children's interest and questions and often what began as a simple question goes on to become an interesting piece of work. After a story about David and Goliath told to six-and-a-half year old children, I was asked, 'How tall was Goliath?' I read in the Bible that he was 6 cubits and a span. 'How long is a cubit and a span?' the children asked. They looked through our book shelves and we found what we wanted in 'The Story of Measurement'. Christopher and John made a cubit measure with cardboard and somebody discovered that two cubits equalled a yard. Then the giant's length was marked out on the hall floor. Several children lay down to compare their height with the giant's. The next step was to cut a length of coloured braid 9 feet 4½ inches long and I climbed on the tallest step-ladder we had and fastened it on the hall wall; it was much too long to be pinned up in a classroom. Lengths of braid of different colours for the tallest and shortest boys in the class were pinned beside the giant. Interesting drawing, painting and written work developed.

Children delight in measuring and recording their height and growth. They found that the teacher's height was always the same. 'Why?' they asked. They measured the kitchen staff and on one occasion requested H.M.I. to remove her shoes and be measured!

Another group of five-and-a-half year-olds recorded their heights with inch squares of coloured paper stuck on a chart. It was easy to see which child had grown the most and which the least when the next recording was made.

The reception class teacher measured her children against a large piece of pegboard. First they stood in a line and moved about until the shortest child headed the line with the tallest at the far end. Then each child's peg was marked with its name. Coloured laces were looped round the pegs and it showed in simple graph form the varying heights of the children.

A new road and a housing estate begun near the school sparked off a tremendous enthusiasm for counting, weighing and measuring. The youngest children watched the bulldozer with large scoops and a smaller earth remover with smaller scoops. They recorded with their teacher's help that it took three times as many small scoops as large ones to fill the lorry. They cut brick shaped papers and made a counting book. Many lively pictures were made and good written work was done about the surveyor and his rods and the buildings as they went up. The school was thoroughly measured—doors, windows, floor tiles, widths and lengths of rooms, the furniture and the playground. Bricks were begged and weighed and measured. Sand was weighed—dry and wet—and the differences in weight were recorded.

Another interesting piece of work resulted from a piece of elephant's skin which had been given to me. The children marvelled at its thickness and then proceeded to discover many interesting facts about elephants. The height of an elephant was recorded on a wall in the hall with a comment that 'It wouldn't be able to walk through the door'.

At Christmas time we make mincemeat and pastry. The children write the recipe. Three children go to the little shop near the school with a shopping list and buy the articles. I always make sure that they will need change. Then comes the making of a bill and reckoning the cost, weighing the ingredients, finding out the cooking time and when the mincepies will be done and, very important, how many mince-pies do we need?

I have just been asked how much orange squash we shall need for the party and how much it will cost. This gives an opportunity of finding out that three teacupfuls can be poured from a pint. Eventually we shall discover how many gallons of squash we need.

Arising from the story of Jesus's birth, a number of six-and-a-half-year old boys joined to make a Christmas stable. They took turns at sawing, sand-papering and hammering after Roy, Michael and Alan had measured the lengths and used a set square to get their lines straight. The stable was covered with paper, crayoned to look like stones and was most effective.

Michael, a five year old, looked for the longest and then the shortest pieces of straw in the manger used at the Carol Service. He measured these and with his teacher's help mounted them and recorded the lengths.

This year the reception class are making a frieze about 'The Twelve Days of Christmas'. This entails drawing, painting, the use of scrap materials, different shapes and the counting and grouping of numbers.

Nature Study and gardening provided many opportunities for using mathematics. Bird tables have been made by boys of five-and-a-half years, six to six-and-a-half-years. The very young boys chose pieces of wood of the same length, the older boys measured and sawed their wood. Counts were made of the birds that visited the tables. Birds' footprints in the snow were measured and compared. Children measured their own feet, too.

They measured and recorded the growth of roots, of leaves, of bulbs grown in water; they measured the bulbs and plants grown in various classrooms, discovering which grew faster. They noted the different shapes of leaves and the precise order of leaves on the stems found in plants. The area of leaves was found by using the squared backing paper from Fablon. The children were encouraged to notice the strong legs of elephants and rhinos and the slender legs of deer. There is a constant question, Why? We always try to find the answer.

When gardening, children exclaim at the long roots of weeds, especially 'twitch grass'. Kevin found the longest piece and measured and mounted it: $14\frac{1}{2}''$ was the record.

At Assembly we were talking about the moon and the children were telling me the shape of the crescent moon. Suddenly, Nicholas (five years old) said it was only a quarter of a moon.

Telling the time is important. We keep time at school, we know what time we have to be at school, when it is playtime, dinner time, etc. Birthdays are celebrated at school. After Assembly we sing a Birthday Song which tells how old the child is and we clap five, six or seven times, depending on his age.

The children like to make booklets about different times in their day, using a clock stamp to make the clock face. An old clock with the fingers still working is a great help in showing children that if it is say half past ten, the hour hand is also half way past ten.

The five-and-a-half to six-year olds were interested in shadows and this developed into measuring their own shadows and the discovery that the length varied at different times of the day. 'Why?' they asked. Then a shadow clock was made with a jumping stick and pebbles and again some interesting work developed. The whole school watched the shadow clock and the interest aroused in the older children (six-and-half to seven years) developed into experiments with magnets and compasses. They made their own compass with wood, paper and a bar magnet. Their home-made compass was as correct as the bought one.

This term, a group of children was deeply interested in the time differences in other parts of the world after I had returned from a holiday in Canada. We have a globe on which it is possible to find out the time all over the world. These children would set the time in England, for example, 10 a.m. and find that people in Montreal were still fast asleep at 5 o'clock in the morning. Or, when the children were going home for tea in England, children in Vancouver were just getting up for breakfast. A booklet was made and their records set down.

The children also wanted to find out how long it took to go to Canada by ship, how long by air, and how long to cross Canada by train and by air.

We have interested our children in the Old People's home near the school and when an old lady was ninety-eight this month we sent her a letter and the children worked out in various ways the difference in their ages. One child used Cuisenaire rods, another squared paper, another spots, another an abacus, another a pegboard. One child wrote that Miss Brealey was nearly a hundred, another that she would be a hundred in two years time, another that she was ninety-two-years older than he was.

Each room is equipped with scales and the older children have balances and a spring balance too. Shells, pebbles, sand, conkers and bottle tops are kept in large tins and in the autumn real apples and pears, too, are weighed. With spring balances children weighed large stones and then suspended them in a bucket of water and at first were astonished at the result. Renate wrote about how light her legs felt in the bath and how heavy they felt when she lifted them out.

Real money is used whenever it is possible. Children count the dinner money, the young ones learn to distinguish the coins, sort them and know their value. They help to count any collection we make, e.g. our collection for Dr. Barnardo's Homes, the Carol Service. In the reception room the teacher always uses real money when the children play at shops or sell train or bus tickets. Children handle real money when they buy National Savings Stamps at school, bring their dinner money, go shopping, or spend their pocket money. We have found, without doubt, that children can reckon more easily with real money.

The children are encouraged and helped to find the names of different shapes. The toys and models they make from junk materials help. An empty cocoa tin for an engine is a cylinder, so is the electric water heater. They look for other shapes. Which is a strong shape? We have a Meccano set from which triangles and other shapes are constructed. We use set squares. We look for symmetry and beauty of shape.

3. The Headmistress of a Rural Primary School Who is also a Class Teacher

For some years many infant schools have given careful thought to the environment in which children begin their education. In a relaxed and informal atmosphere teachers provide stimulating, varied material using children's interests wherever possible. Activities of high educational potentiality are deliberately planned and by skilful questioning, teachers interest the children and guide their learning. Nearly all children thrive in these conditions and seem to make maximum progress.

The transfer from an informal infant school to a junior school was, until a few years ago, difficult for children because the aims and teaching methods presented such a marked contrast in the two schools. But, during the past few years, many junior schools, too, have become more informal in method. Reference was made in the first chapter to the changes which have taken place in subjects such as Art, Physical Education and English. Here is an account, written by the teaching head, of the change in approach to mathematics in a small rural primary school.

My school is a primary school of 150 children in 5 classes, 2 infant and 3 junior. I am a teaching head responsible for the third and fourth year juniors. Some of the children spend 2 years in this class as every child must spend 2 years in one class. There is a wide range of ability in the school and the whole background varies. With the exception of one assistant mistress who joined the school in January 1963 the staff has been at the school for several years.

Although we have tried to keep abreast with modern methods our teaching methods in mathematics tended to be rather formal. After I had attended a Ministry of Education course in mathematics as a representative of a group of island teachers interested in the teaching of mathematics, I introduced a new approach in the teaching of that subject. The children were given material to solve mathematical problems in a practical way; they normally work in pairs. I started with my own class and their response was so encouraging that I had no hesitation in planning to extend this approach to all classes. The members of staff spent some time with my class watching them at work. This was followed by a staff meeting at which, after discussion, a basic collection of cards was drawn up for each class of juniors. I have found the initial work in compiling and grading the mathematical problems amply repaid by results. The teacher of the top infants was very interested and planned her teaching to give the children a foundation upon which we can build.

When introducing this new approach to the class of second year juniors I spent some time with the class myself, using at first a group of 8 children working in pairs and gradually extending the group until all the children were taking part. The children were most enthusiastic and were soon working well with the class teacher who was as keen as they were. The same method of introduction was tried with the youngest juniors with similar results.

At first the recording worried the teachers a little. Was it really necessary? Did it take up too much time? But they quickly realised its value and now it presents little difficulty.

The parents are keenly interested. We had a display of cards, material and children's work at our last open evening and I could not get the fathers away from it. We had to extend the time by one hour! We have had many visitors from overseas as well to see the children at work. All have remarked upon the quiet application of the children to the job in hand. They are really interested and not easily distracted. They have all been impressed by the concentration of the children, their mathematical vocabulary, their willingness and ability to discuss what they are doing and their wide mathematical knowledge.

I have been surprised at the interest shown by mathematics teachers from secondary modern schools who have all said how well they could use this method with their own children. The children who have gone on to both grammar and modern secondary schools are doing very well in their mathematics. One rather below average boy said to me, when returning to visit us and looking at our 'mathematics shelf', 'You know, that way of teaching mathematics helped me a lot. It's paying off now'.

Here are some of the beneficial effects of this method which has now been working for four years. The children are more alert and ready to think for themselves. Their powers of reasoning are more developed and this shows in other subjects too. They have learnt to work together quietly, each contributing his share either in the discovery or in applying the technique. Children of all levels of ability can successfully solve the problems set if these are carefully selected. The more intelligent will often take the discovery far beyond that which was asked for. The less intelligent find satisfaction in the practical aspect itself and in the mastery of the technique required. The reasoning power required in solving the problem has helped to raise the standard of performance in the selection test; in English and the verbal test as well as in mathematics.

The new methods of teaching mathematics have also had some more unexpected results. The recording of their results by the children has widened their vocabulary and raised the standard of their English. The initiative required in solving the mathematics problems has been carried over into other aspects of school life. The children in all the junior classes have organised and presented concerts in aid of various charities.

Finally there is no doubt about the children's attitude to this way of learning mathematics. The headmistress asked them one day to write down the reasons for their enjoyment of the lessons. Here are some replies of the eight-year-olds: '*After the work we find we know new things which we did not know before. I feel important*'. (By a child of I.Q. 75:)

'*With every card I discover new things to talk about when I get home*'.

'*I learn more by using things instead of just figures*'.

'*We learn things in a pleasant way, there are so many different things to do, the lesson goes too quickly.*

The nines and tens write:

'*It is fun working out problems and finding out things from the graphs we make*'. '*We find out things for ourselves instead of the teacher telling us what to do. We learnt to be independent* (*and that is a good thing.*). *We have to do the actual experiment instead of reading from a book how it is done. It gives us the full responsibility to find the answer ourselves*'. '*I feel that I am working with and learning about real things not just doing sums on paper. I like to find out if my results are true by my graphs. It would be better if we had it more often*'.

There follows some advice by this headmistress on the 'experiences in mathematics' which she provides for her children.

I have gathered these mathematical experiences from various sources and have kept the language as simple as possible for each age group. The apparatus required needs some careful preparation and should be easily accessible to the children. Much of the apparatus required by the younger children can be homemade; the older children need accurate weights and measures in good variety.

The cards are graded in each group according to difficulty and, as no child can work through every card, these are selected by the teacher so that there is some definite progression. I have put first what the child has to collect and then what he has to do.

The children usually work in pairs of about the same ability. Recording is done roughly at first, then checked, then copied into the record book. It is kept as simple as possible but to my mind it is an essential part of the experience.

4. THE HEADMASTER OF A LARGE JUNIOR SCHOOL IN AN URBAN AREA

The problems of an informal infant school, even those of a large one, and those of a small rural school (where there are opportunities for a good deal of staff discussion) differ from those of a large junior school. The headmaster of the next school asked a pertinent question at the end of a four-day residential mathematics course. 'How long would it take me to introduce new methods and material into the teaching of mathematics in my large school with its 20 staff?' The answer he received was a cautious one. It was suggested that he should go slowly at first and not tell his staff too much at once and that if he had three classes working in this way at the end of the first term he would have done well.

One term later the work of this school was put on exhibition for a local primary mathematics course. The children's work and teachers' assignments filled two classrooms. Every one of the classes had contributed something. Here, in his own words, is an account of how the headmaster and his staff achieved this.

Our school is a new one and serves a large housing estate with an industrial background. We have over five hundred boys and girls, representing a reasonable cross-section of urban life and enjoy excellent co-operation from the parents.

As a staff we have long been aware of the acute shortage of teachers of mathematics and all we have read and heard has pointed to the need for a change of attitude towards the subject. We came to realise that often our work was too narrow, with over emphasis on computation, so we tried in a number of ways to correct this fault. Apparatus was introduced, all kinds of situations were demonstrated to the children, and we tried to make problems and situations real and connected with the children's own experience and environment. But somehow, with one or two exceptions, we did not quite achieve our aim. The trouble was that we did too much for the children—we showed them what would happen, drew conclusions for them and showed them how to tackle problems in such a way that no problems remained. In short, we did not allow the children to find out for themselves. We deprived them of the joy of discovery.

Two years ago, I attended one of the early vacation courses organised by the Ministry of Education, where I heard lectures, took part in discussions and worked through a good number of practical sessions. I came away from that course both humble and enthusiastic—humble because some of the experiments made me realise my own limitations, but enthusiastic to apply what I had learned to our children. The experiments gave me opportunity perhaps, of thinking about mathematics in a new way and from the course I believe I got the very things I hoped our school course would give the children.

When the new term commenced I invited members of my staff to hear about the course and see some of the equipment I had made. Two or three friendly, informal meetings produced a good deal of sensible discussion and much genuine interest. I suggested that consideration might be given to trying out one or two ideas but gave no definite direction. About a fortnight later we met again in year groups and discussed our plans. In each class there was a wish to make graphs about a variety of everyday situations and topics suggested included mathematics and science, mathematics around us, the story of numbers, shapes and sizes. Most important, all agreed to use any suitable opportunity to give the children chances of experimenting, observing and recording, thus making their own discoveries of mathematical ideas. I found the staff very co-operative and ready to help one another and through frequent informal talks, enthusiasm and interest were maintained and ideas exchanged.

As far as the children were concerned, they soon became interested in this new work—especially in making graphs. They obviously discussed their work at home, for all sorts of information was supplied by parents—mothers as well as fathers. Some children bought their own graph paper for weekend use, and within three months, almost everything connected with private and public life in the district had been investigated and graphed. (There was no secret left in this district!) In the classrooms too, interesting pieces of work began to appear on both walls and tables and it was soon apparent that mathematics had come to life.

Up to this time we had used an Arithmetic Syllabus which followed much the usual pattern—a statement of the general principles underlying our approach, a list of topics which might reasonably be covered by each year group and notes about number bonds, backward children and practical and oral work. I wanted to change it, but was anxious at this stage to avoid over-direction. I felt that new ideas must develop naturally. Therefore I contented myself with writing a new introduction and added one or two illustrations to suit different age groups. Each class was given an additional collection of mathematics books and about fifty reference books were placed in the school library.

I should like now to mention in detail some of the work which has been attempted during the past year, beginning with a third year class where all the children were of ability far below average. Most of them could do little beyond very simple computation, they understood little of what they were doing and disliked mathematics. The teacher realised the need for oral work and discussion to build up a good mathematical background, so he spent quite a long time each day chatting with the children informally, getting to know their interest and unobtrusively introduced number bonds, table facts, everyday problems, mathematical vocabulary and various forms of measurement. He arranged his room informally, allowing the children to work with whom they wished. This immediately created a better relationship amongst the children and with the teacher. Work cards and apparatus were prepared and the children had easy access to them. Even the most simple of these cards presented language difficulties and for the least able children another solution had to be found. This was partly solved by the preparation of work boxes, each designed to contain all the material required for acquiring a thorough background for each aspect of number work. Much of this apparatus was self-explanatory, but oral directions were also given. Simultaneously, two or three mathematical topics were developed, arising from interests and suggestions about the Service Station, the Docks and the Railway Station. The children in this class now rate mathematics as one of their favourite lessons and can work happily and profitably for an hour at a time. Their reading and written work has improved and they discuss their doings freely. We are naturally concerned with their progress to secondary education and it is interesting to observe that teachers of remedial groups from our secondary school have spent some time visiting the classes and talking to the children.

A mistress in charge of a fourth year class of below average ability first tried to develop interest in money through shopping. She too, met with apathy, then she spent a long time in discussion with the children. As a result, they created the Mitchell Family. It started in a small way, but after a year is still flourishing. It differs from any other project I have experienced for it started with mathematics and mathematical situations have persisted as its main focal points. Each child has a folder called 'Mathematics and the Mitchells' which contains work connected with the Mitchell household, the young twins, father's work at the local oil refinery, Auntie Jean's wedding, plans of an imaginary neighbourhood, many graphs, including one of Brian's 'bob a job week' efforts and scale models. Work cards covering a wide range of mathematical tasks suited to these children's abilities were prepared and the children soon began to add problems of their own.

A number of the staff are very interested in mathematics and science and have improvised simple apparatus for making discoveries about such topics as friction, levers and pulleys, plant growth and soils. This gave the children practice in accurate observing and recording and they often represented their findings graphically, sometimes using these to draw simple conclusions. Making geometrical models arose after a visit to the Natural History Museum. The children bought postcards about minerals and crystals and noticed various geometrical shapes. They learnt how to use instruments for constructing plane figures and tried to visualise what solid figures would look like when flat, and eventually constructed the figures. Many of these children, boys as well as girls, have taken great interest in curve stitching. We found however that before this work could look effective and serve any useful purpose a considerable amount of skill in geometrical construction and accurate measuring was necessary.

Recording numerical facts pictorially is always enjoyed by the youngest children and we used this interest in the study and interpretation of simple graphs. It was very easy to find opportunities for graph making and much time and thought was spent in collecting information about such topics as names, birthdays, heights, pets and holidays, deciding on suitable scales and recording neatly and accurately. Most of these graphs also involved a surprisingly large number of calculations and were often supplemented by written work. 'All About Two', 'Dozens and Dozens', 'All About Me' and 'How Do We Measure It', were among a number of delightful books produced by seven and eight-year olds.

We have now been working along these lines for about two years and are beginning to feel ready to review and systematise our work. We wish to ensure progression and avoid overlapping so together are now producing a syllabus based on our combined experience, which we hope will suit our school. Within this framework, of course, there will still be much scope for the individual teacher and for using the children's ideas. We are all agreed that this flexibility must persist if the work is to retain its spontaneity, and exchange of ideas will continue.

One of the most pleasing features arising from our work has been the increased co-operation between our school and others in the district. Colleagues from Modern, Grammar and Technical Schools have visited our classes and discussed the extent to which our work might be continued at any rate in their first forms, and we have been stimulated by their ideas.

Ours is an ordinary school and we make no lavish claims but there is no doubt that the children and their teachers now enjoy mathematics more than ever before. There is ample evidence that the children discuss their work at home and it is most refreshing to learn that parents ask 'What are you doing in mathematics?' instead of 'How many sums did you get right'? Attainment as measured by standardised tests shows progress, but more important to us is the hope that the children may be developing real mathematical understanding on a basis far wider than can be measured in any examination.

5. A Former Class Teacher Now a Part-Time Specialist in an Urban School Working with Class Teachers in Their Mathematics Lessons

A class teacher faces problems of a more personal nature than a headmaster; she has to plan the work for the children in her class, collect the materials required for their discoveries and record individual progress. The teacher who is responsible for the description which follows had the unusual experience of first being a mathematics specialist in secondary schools and then a class teacher in a primary school. She is now attached to a primary school where she teaches mathematics throughout the school, working with the class teachers in turn. In this way she has gained experience of the way children of all ages learn mathematics.

I have been fortunate in the varied experiences I have enjoyed during my teaching career. These have enabled me to regard the present new approach from many different angles. It has taken time to form a definite opinion but I now feel strongly that the new approach is right, because it accords so naturally with the needs of the modern child.

This approach required a basic change of attitude on my part and, as such, demanded considerable thought. An account follows of this change and the methods used to meet the many problems which arose. The problems were mine, as a teacher, rather than the children's; a change which proved so natural to them, was not acceptable to me with my preconceived ideas of methods and standards.

I made the initial step in this new approach by deciding to base all my teaching on the premise that no child should be asked to accept a mathematical truth purely on my authority. At that time I could not be sure that this was a practical proposition but several years of application of the principle have proved that it is so. With its acceptance my major worries, such as children's dislike and fear of the subject, their reliance on memorising, and their guesswork, have disappeared, Admittedly the action was akin to 'jumping in at the deep end', and quite understandably others may prefer to edge in cautiously.

A natural progression, after such a decision, was to decide that if truths were to be realized by a child, then situations must be provided in which those truths could be discovered. A most disconcerting and unexpected problem then presented itself. I found that my own understanding of fundamentals lacked the necessary depth for planning situations which could assist the child towards full understanding. It will be appreciated that, after twenty years of teaching mathematics, such an admission was not an easy one to make. An analysis of my own mathematical understanding revealed that, while I had appreciated the difficulties inherent in more complex situations, I had not fathomed those in apparently simple ones. To uncover what had been cloaked for so long by conventional patter required a review of mathematical concepts and long established methods.

My next concern was to plan the forms that experiment could take so that children could gain understanding. I have tried many kinds of apparatus and have come to the conclusion that it is preferable to use environmental material wherever possible, e.g. finding halves, quarters and eighths through experimenting with the common measures of capacity, or thirds through the use of school milk bottles. On the whole, the simpler the material, the more useful it has proved to be. Leaves, for example, provided apparatus that gave a fuller understanding of perimeter and area than the customary approach using rectangles. The physical actions of fitting string along the edge of a leaf prior to measuring it, and placing the surface of a leaf flat on paper marked in square units prior to counting the squares covered, contained in themselves the real meaning of the terms. Similarly the close winding of threads to cover a width of one inch, and the consequent finding of the width of one thread as a fraction of an inch, led to an awareness that there can be no limit to the minuteness of fractional parts. These are but two examples of many which could be given, to illustrate the valuable contribution made by very ordinary materials.

In the early stages of discovering number relationships, some form of structural apparatus is essential. I have found that sets of text books of the same size can be used to great advantage for this purpose. A dozen books, for example, can be piled in different ways so that children can realize that 12 is 2×6 or 6×2 or 3×4 or 4×3; or two books at a time can be taken six times from twelve, to give a realisation of the measuring aspect of division; or twelve books can be halved into two sets of six, so that the sharing aspect can also be appreciated. The advantage of such apparatus is that ample material is readily available. A plentiful supply of one inch squared paper, cardboard square inches and cubic inches in a number of colours have also proved most useful at different stages.

My strong personal preference is for apparatus made by children themselves. An example which shows the value of this was concerned with children planning and making a 1,000 cubic centimetre container so that they could find the equivalence of a litre in pints and a kilogram in pounds. Not only were mathematical concepts learnt during the process of making but the experience helped to make a more marked impression than if manufactured measures had been used. If children are encouraged to devise their own apparatus, they remain alive to possibilities inherent in situations. Indeed, some of my most useful and attractive apparatus has been planned and made by children.

I have found that there must be careful supervision when children are experimenting, if the maximum benefit is to be derived from it. With large classes much oral questioning is not possible, however ideal this may be. Where children can read and write with reasonable ease, I have found that the answering of questionnaires has been good for them and helpful to me. They have had to order their thoughts to answer the questions and give clear conclusions, and I have been able to judge the extent of their understanding. I found, at first, that I had to steel myself to accept their unconventional expressions; for example, 'The straight graph ascends in equal steps', knowing that too early an imposition of conventional terms could harm growing understanding. When I have had time to listen to discussions by children engaged in experimenting, these have proved most enlightening. I have been as surprised to find difficulties where I had least expected them as to note aptitudes where I had no previous reasons for suspecting they existed. A valuable by-product of hearing such discussions has been the further studies which I have been able to encourage. What a pity that inevitably, with large classes, so many such opportunities are lost!

I had long considered discussions of paramount importance in furthering interests and establishing conclusions, but not until recently did I appreciate their value in promoting an interest in, and understanding of, number relationships and processes. I have found that through discussion relationships have emerged and flexibility of methods been encouraged. One of the many instances of this occurred when children were filling in a multiplication chart. The following chart shows how they used their understanding of the composition of numbers. They filled in the rows for 4, 6, 8, 9, 10 and 12 times a number as shown; the remaining rows were first completed by repeated addition, a further discussion led to the use of the associations shown in the brackets.

Numbers up to 12 *multiplied by numbers up to* 12

(a) 1 2 3 4 5 6 7 8 9 10 11 12
(b) 2 4 6 8 10 12 14 16 18 20 22 24
(c) 3 Add rows (a) and (b)
(d) 4 Twice row (b)
(e) 5 Add rows (a) and (d)
(f) 6 Twice rows (c) or three times row (b)
(g) 7 Add rows (a) and (f)
(h) 8 Double twice row (b) or twice row (d)
(i) 9 Three times row (c)
(j) 10 Twice row (e)
(k) 11 Add rows (a) and (j)
(l) 12 Twice row (f) or six times row (b)
Three times row (d) or four times row (c)

This was a most rewarding experience for me. It confirmed the value of practical work designed to encourage an appreciation of number relationships. A similar experience was encountered with a class of older children, when they analysed the graphs produced by perimeters and areas of squares on sides increasing by one unit at a time and also of the volumes of cubes based on the same pattern. (See Figure 9.4.)

It may be of interest to give an idea of the proportion of time given to each aspect of this approach to mathematics. Only a rough estimate is possible, but basing it on a fairly wide age and ability range, I would estimate that roughly one third of my time has been given to discussion and another third to experiments. The remaining one third has been used for the practice of skills. This reduction in the proportion of time given to computation may occasion some surprise. Initially I experienced a sense of personal guilt; this was not helped by the fact that the reduction in the number of pages of repetitive exercises in children's books left me denuded of the conventional proof of our sustained efforts. I should now feel an equal sense of guilt at having children over-practise what is known and understood. There is no longer the need for this monotonous practice because the need to establish a meaningless order of procedure has ceased to exist. Enough practice must be given, however, so that the reliability of essential skills can be established, and as a teacher I regard this as being of the utmost importance. However profound and extensive the understanding may be, what satisfactory use can be made of it if weaknesses in computation lead to a wrong conclusion? Incidentally, children so trained enjoy tremendously a lengthy calculation when they are bent on making a discovery.

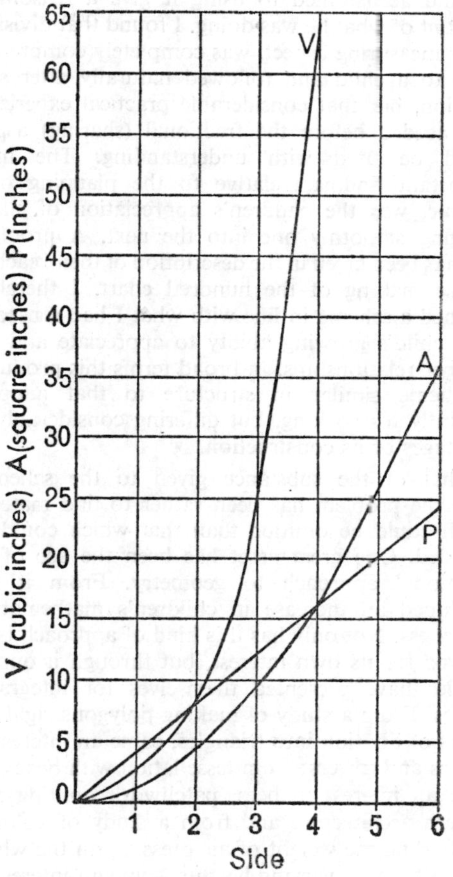

Fig. 9.4 Cubes—Graphs of Perimeter of one face, Area of one face and Volume plotted against Side

The Perimeter graph is different because it ascends in equal numbers. The others ascend in a pattern, but not in equal numbers. (Ten-year-old girl)

Having come to a conclusion about the parts to be played by experiment, discussion and computation I was confronted by another pressing problem. Experiments had proved to be most educative but, as a practising teacher, I felt that an overall scheme was necessary to ensure full and natural mathematical growth. I was in the fortunate position of being able to question children, over a four-year age range, in order to evaluate those lines of thought which were natural to them and which unacceptable. From my own experience, for instance, no child discovered equal additions as a means of subtraction, nor could a child accustomed to using it give a reasonable account of what he was doing. I found that division, in its measuring aspect, was completely comprehensible to a child and followed naturally after subtraction, but that considerable practical experience was needed before the fractional (sharing) aspect could be used with understanding. The most important finding, relative to the planning of a scheme, was the children's appreciation of stages merging smoothly one into the next. A proof of this has been given in the description of their reaction to the making of the hundred chart. I therefore planned a scheme in line with what I had sensed to be a child's growing ability to appreciate and use number relationships. In broad terms this produced a scheme similar in structure to that adopted generally for so long, but differing considerably in the stages of its construction.

What of the substance given to the scheme? Here the problem has been rather to find material which could be omitted than that which could be included. One great asset has been the use of an intuitional approach to geometry. From it has developed an increase in children's mathematical awareness. Not only has this kind of approach been enjoyed for its own interest, but through it opportunities have presented themselves for integrated studies. From a study of making polygons rigid, by means of division into triangles, came an interest in bridges and towers; from tessellation with hexagons came an interest in bees, patchwork quilting and modern architecture and from a study of volume, and finding the weight of air pressing on the whole human body at varying heights, came an interest in mountaineering. Indeed by the time children have reached the upper part of the school they are able to use their understanding of mathematics in ways which would not have seemed possible when the subject was more rigidly confined. The most comprehensive example of this came through a practical approach to the metric system. Through the understanding thus gained, children were able to plan a tour abroad, find the distances to be travelled and the cost, construct useful conversion graphs and find, not only the cost of staying in the country of their choice, but the cost of the whole holiday. Mathematics here played the useful role it would play if such a holiday were really contemplated. Other subjects entered quite naturally into the scheme, for children found out all they could about interests for the tourist and so delved into the history, art, customs and language of the country of their choice. To watch a large class confidently and competently coping with all the problems involved, gave me an assurance, if such was needed, that all the thought and planning behind their studies had been, not only worthwhile, but most generously repaid.

6. A College of Education Lecturer in Science Who Has Worked With Young Children

Reference has already been made in a previous chapter to the pioneer work undertaken by some college of education lecturers and lecturers from university departments of education in the teaching of mathematics in primary schools. The teaching experience of the majority of mathematics lecturers has been in secondary schools. During the past few years a number of them have spent considerable periods in primary schools working regularly with a class of children. In this way they have gained experience of teaching young children and have also sought to discover the potentiality of young children in the wider field of mathematics. The two accounts which follow are based on the personal experiences of lecturers with classes in a primary school. The first is by a science lecturer who worked with a class of infants and also with juniors of various ages.

If we believe that young children see the world around them as a whole, and that they learn most successfully through the solution of practical problems related to the real world, it follows that it is impossible to divorce mathematics from science. Indeed, any attempt to do so would force the child into an unnatural pattern of development.

The examples which follow illustrate the range of scientific studies which have been undertaken in primary schools and the mathematics which arose directly and naturally from these studies, many of which occurred in nature study.

The mathematical ideas which can be derived from science fall into three main groups: computation, graphical representation and statistics.

A simple pendulum made from a metal washer tied at one end of a length of cotton passing through a cork was taken into a class of six-year-olds. Immediately the children began counting. The cotton was steadily pulled up above the cork (so shortening the length of the pendulum). The children continued counting and one child wrote: 'When the pendulum is large it swings slow, and when it is short it swings fast' so that a scientific principle was emerging as a result of the children's observations.

The pendulum soon became the class timing device. For example, when a pet rat was brought to school the children wanted to count its heartbeats and compare this result with a count of their own heartbeats. The latter task presented great difficulties for a young child does not find it easy to detect a pulse in the wrist. This was overcome by putting a short length of drinking straw on to the point of a drawing pin, and then standing the head of the drawing pin on the artery in the wrist. By this means, the pulsing of the blood could be *seen* as a movement of the straw. The children counted the number of pulses while the pendulum swung thirty times.

Many other problems arose. Do all our hearts beat at the same rate? Do grown-ups' hearts beat more slowly or faster than children's hearts? Do our hearts beat the same when we are sitting, standing, and when we have run once round the playground? If we run twice round the playground do our hearts beat twice as fast as if we have only run round once? All these questions were answered by counting the number of pulses while the pendulum swung thirty times. With older children this heartbeat study would probably involve the drawing of graphs, but otherwise little more would be done than had been done by the infants.

The same group of six-year-olds became involved in more counting through an examination of leaf litter which contained the leaves of sycamore, beech and horse chestnut. After sorting the leaves into separate heaps, they were asked to estimate the relative numbers of the three different types of leaf—a difficult but valuable exercise. The leaf litter also contained a collection of animals, the most attractive of which proved to be snails. These provoked a lively study of shapes, especially of the spiral, which went on intermittently for several weeks.

Another topic which is often considered in the primary school is the loss of water from plants, but the quantitative aspects of the subject are usually thought to be suitable only for advanced biology classes. Fortunately, expensive apparatus is not essential, provided that it is possible to weigh things, in which case there are a number of problems which can be solved by older juniors. Two such problems began when the children observed that a heavy mist often hung over a nearby wood and field. The children were first asked how much water was lost from the grass in a field. The solutions of these apparently difficult problems were reached in the following manner. The suggestions for the experiments came from the children; the teacher had been careful to have suitable material at hand. Attention was first turned to an elder sapling whose leafy shoots were few enough to be counted. One of the shoots was taken from the tree and placed in a jar of water. Oil on the water surface prevented loss by evaporation. The jar and its contents were weighed at intervals and the loss in weight in twenty-four hours was calculated. A quick multiplication gave a value for the weight of water lost from the entire sapling.

Meanwhile, a turf from the field had been cut to such a size that it fitted snugly into a pie dish with a little water in the bottom. Again, the dish and its contents were weighed at intervals and the rate of water loss in twenty-four hours was calculated. This time a variety of problems was asked which involved different calculations. These included: the weight of water, in grammes, which was lost from the turf in the dish; the number of pounds of water which would be lost from a square yard of turf in a day; the number of tons, and gallons, lost from an acre in a year; what was this when expressed as inches of rainfall?

Areas come easily from leaf studies. Some of the six-year-olds who examined the leaf litter were confronted with leaves of different shapes and asked if they could say which was the larger of the two. This started an argument about whether the length or the width would be the thing to measure, but when they were given a sheet of squared paper, they recognised that the problem could be solved by drawing round the leaves and, as one child said, '... counting the boxes'. Parts of squares were happily ignored.

In addition to providing many opportunities for counting, estimating, and computation, science also offers a chance to represent findings graphically. In particular, there is great scope for studying the relationships between variable quantities. The simplest form of graphical representation is the recording of varying quantities or numbers.

A class of six-year-olds were asked to keep a day-to-day record of the number of male and female visitors to their classroom. This they did by piling up blue and green plastic cubes to represent males and females. Eventually, this was interpreted in terms of columns of squares on squared paper, and finally a book of weekly records was compiled. An interesting weekly pattern was revealed. Monday was the day with most visitors, presumably people delivering messages, collecting dinner numbers, and so on.

The children became so enthusiastic that they began to collect information about themselves, drawing a chart which showed how many boys and girls came to school in jeans during the cold spell, and another to show the numbers of boys and girls who had blue, green or brown eyes.

Sometimes, from this type of graph there *can* come a picture of relationships. It is surprising how even very young children can appreciate relationships when these are demonstrated graphically. For example, some six-year-olds began to make and to study musical sounds. This they did with tuning forks, water in test tubes, wires stretched across boards, and indeed with any means which presented itself. They soon noticed that small tuning forks gave higher notes than large ones, that short wires gave higher notes than long wires, and so on. Ultimately, they presented their findings graphically.

The tubes of water were held up against a sheet of paper fastened to the wall so that the children could draw round them, and the water levels were marked. There resulted a graph showing the relationship between length of air column and notes of the musical scale.

Similarly, gummed paper was cut to the lengths of the strings stretched on the boards and then fixed on to paper to show the relationship between the length of the strings and the musical notes. The children even opened the front of an old piano and tried to measure the strings, but this proved to be too difficult, although they were sure that it could be done if they had a table grand!

But they did measure the size of their chime bars, and the bars on their dulcimer, and represented them in the same way. It is interesting to notice that the children were disturbed by the 'kinks' between 'me' and 'fah', and between 'te' and 'doh', in what was otherwise a straight line along the tops of their coloured strips of paper. But when they looked at the notes of the piano keyboard, they saw where the half notes came. They then made new graphs spacing the strips of paper so that the tops of the strips were in a straight line.

Another type of graph which showed a relationship is illustrated by a piece of work which was done by a class of nine-year-old girls. They had been observing some young rats which were being kept in the classroom, and attention was drawn to the way in which the animals reacted to sudden movement towards them. The discussion which followed became centred on how quickly the girls themselves could react. Three of them were asked to stand hand in hand. The first girl squeezed the hand of the second girl who then squeezed the hand of the third girl as quickly as she could. The rest of the class tried to measure how quickly she could do this, but found that it was far too difficult. Eventually, it was decided that the whole class should sit in a large circle, holding hands, that the time taken for the squeeze to be passed all round the circle would be measured, and that the result would be divided by the number of girls in the class, so as to get an average value.

The teacher completed the circle and held a stop watch, which she started at the same moment as she squeezed the hand of the child on her left, and stopped as she felt her own wrist squeezed by the child on her right. The time was noted, and the experiment was repeated a number of times. The results were then represented graphically. The number of times the experiment was tried was marked along the base line, and the various times measured were shown as a series of vertical straight lines. The pattern which emerged is shown in Fig. 9.5. It should be noted that there is no justification for

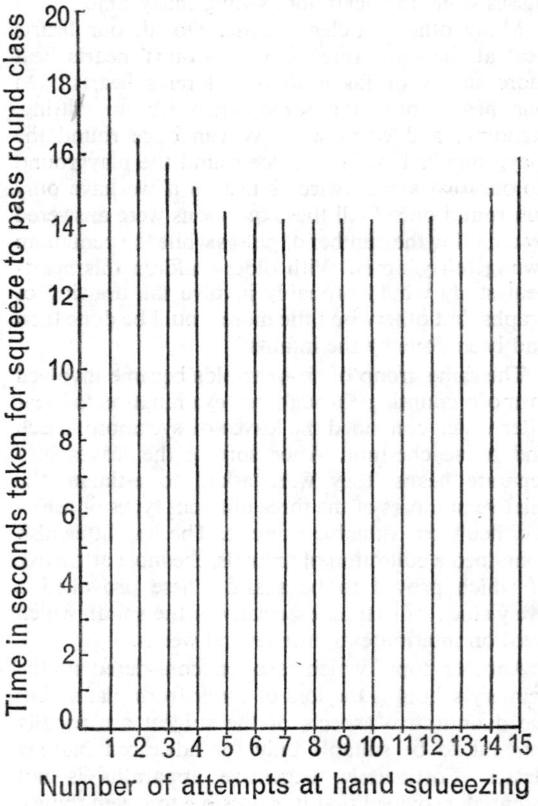

Fig. 9.5

joining the tops of the lines in a graph such as this. The lines represented a series of discrete measurements and should be treated as such.

It was most interesting to see that this class, whose only previous experience of graphs had been the temperature chart, was able to devise the experiment, suggest how the graph should be drawn, and was also able to interpret it. They found it easy to explain that their performance had improved with practice; that they reached a stage where they could improve no further; and that their performance then fell off because, they said, their brains were tired. One girl went so far as to say, 'This is like when we do arithmetic. As we practise we can do the sums faster. Then we can't do them any faster. And then if we go on too long, we start to get them wrong because our brains are tired'. (True insight from a girl who had never looked at a graph before).

Graphs which show relationships are well illustrated by growth processes for in them is to be found change in size in relation to passage of time. Once again it was found possible to carry out these studies with six-year-old infants. They were asked to find how fast their young rat grew during succeeding weeks. After a good deal of discussion the following system was devised. The animal was weighed not against standard weights but against metal washers. In this way, standard units of weight, with all their attendant difficulties, were avoided. As one child wrote after three days: 'Snowy now weighs nine washers. He has gained one and a half washers'.

The method of recording was rather different from usual. The class was given a long piece of balsa wood in which were stuck a number of steel knitting pins. Each time that the rat was weighed, the washers were heaped round the appropriate knitting pin, successive heaps becoming steadily higher. After two weeks, the piles of washers 'made a graph' which showed the change in weight of the animal as time went by. The children had, of course, built a model of a growth curve.

The children then asked their teacher if they could measure the rat's tail whenever they did a weighing, and this they did with a piece of string. The string was held against the animal's tail, and then transferred to a piece of squared paper, the length being marked off. The appropriate number of squares was coloured in, and a growth curve resulted.

This approach was a particularly satisfactory one, for in both cases the transfer of information to the graph had been done directly, in the first case by piling up the washers which just balanced the animal's weight, and in the second by holding the string first against the tail and then against the paper. In this way there was no difficulty in representing real weights and lengths in terms of symbols on paper.

An interesting approach to graphs, which revealed a remarkable degree of insight on the part of six-year-olds, came through a study of beech leaves. The study became concentrated around the numbers of veins on the leaves. Did all leaves have the same number of veins? No, they did not, the children decided. Did small leaves, then, have fewer veins than large leaves? The whole class was involved in order that sufficient data might be collected, and each child counted the veins on the smallest and largest leaves he could find. The figures left no doubt that the smaller the leaf the fewer the veins. Neither were the children in any doubt about this aspect of growth. One boy actually volunteered the information that as a leaf grows older it grows more veins.

From that point the investigation followed various lines, certain children arranging a series of leaves along a base line on a sheet of paper, in order to show the steady growth of a leaf. The vein numbers were written in over all the leaves. One child made the growth curve permanent by doing rubbings of the leaves, another by making leaf prints with paint and a roller.

Another example of graphs illustrating mathematical relationships came from a class of ten-year-old girls who were learning about Italy. The story of Galileo in the cathedral at Pisa resulted in the construction of simple pendulums from a split cork, cotton and washers. The time of swing was investigated in relation to the length of the cotton. In this case, the horizontal axis was marked with the number of swings which the pendulum made in one minute. The vertical axis showed the length of the pendulum. The transfer of length to paper was made directly by holding the cotton against the paper at the right point along the X axis. The girls, who had never drawn a graph before, were able to decide from their graph how long the cotton would need to be if it were to swing once a second, and they tested the accuracy of their interpretation by trying it with their own pendulums.

There are, of course, some problems in science which cannot be solved by straightforward counting and measuring, and a new mathematical technique has to be employed. Such a case arose when a teacher decided that it was desirable to extend the study of plants and animals to find out something about 'populations'.

It would be quite impossible, as well as meaningless, to count the number of a particular insect in a pond, worms in a lawn or weeds in a field. In cases such as these it is necessary to employ sampling methods. Sampling and statistical methods are important scientific techniques which are increasingly employed, and it is gratifying to find that young children will accept and use such methods. (Reference was made in Chapter 6 to the more sophisticated treatment of 'sampling' undertaken by a class of ten-year-olds and also to the first attempt by some six-year-olds).

A problem of this nature was attempted by a class of eight-year-olds who were interested in weeds in general as a part of a study of farming. At their teacher's suggestion they drew a list of plants to be found in a lawn, and in a field nearby. Eventually, they decided that they would like to compare the numbers of different weeds which were growing in the two habitats, and the method of sampling was used.

Each pair of children was supplied with a loop of string four yards long, and a few beads of four different colours. The string was thrown at random on to the grass, and was spread out, where it fell, into a rough square. On each dandelion in the square was put a white bead, on each daisy a red bead, blue beads on plantains, and green beads on buttercups. The various beads from all the groups were then collected and strung into four lengths, and the process was repeated in the field. When the strings of beads were fastened side by side on a sheet of card, it was obvious to all which plant was most plentiful. As one girl wrote 'We could easily see how many weeds there were from the length of the beads'. This technique involved one to one marking, so that even very young and not so able children knew that one bead was equivalent to one plant. (This particular class was in the lower stream of a two-stream school).

Similar methods can be employed in sampling a pond or stream, and such an investigation was attempted with a class of ten-year-olds. This time the samples were taken by pushing the net (for one yard) along the bed of the stream and washing the contents into a pie dish of water. The presence of any creature was recorded by a tick against its name in a list. Results were shown as a block graph.

A small group of ten-year-olds were discussing the way in which weeds thrive whilst garden flowers do not. It was suggested that the weeds must produce large numbers of seeds in order to be so prolific, and an investigation of seed potential was started. The weed chosen was white dead nettle, since there were several convenient clumps nearby. A square yard was staked out with string, and the number of stems of the plant within the square were counted. Then a sample of twenty stems was taken from the patch, and the number of flowers, fallen flowers, and flower buds on each stem was counted. From this sampling it was possible to find the average number of flowers produced by a dead nettle stem. Examination of several flowers revealed that any one flower yields four seeds, and simple multiplication gave the children an estimate of the number of seeds likely to come from the whole weed patch. One group found that their square yard had a seed potential of 24,000 seeds. The problem now took on a new look. No longer did the children wonder why there were so many weeds, but why there were not more of them.

Not only was this a valuable exercise in mathematics, but it was also the very beginning of the children's thinking on natural selection and, therefore, on evolution. There followed experiments on percentage germination, and discussions on survival.

The use of measurement in science in the hands of a good teacher is a two-edged weapon. On the one hand the science provides a means of introducing mathematics; on the other hand measurement extends the scope of science, makes it more exact and satisfying as a subject, and in the case of nature study can only serve to make it more exciting and to give it a long needed 'shot in the arm'.

7. A Team of Lecturers at a College of Education Offering a One-Term Supplementary Mathematics Course for Primary School Teachers

The next contribution is from a college of education, outstanding, yet representative of a growing number of colleges, for the range of its contacts with schools and with teachers in-service, as well as for its professional and main courses in mathematics for intending primary and secondary teachers.

Within the college the courses include:

(i) A two-year professional course, of two hours a week for all intending primary and junior/secondary teachers.

(ii) A one-term supplementary course for serving teachers in primary schools.

Outside the college the lecturers have substantial personal contact with some schools. An account of the experience of one lecturer, who took a group of nine-year-olds for geometry on one afternoon a week for a term, follows this section.

Courses for teachers include one evening a week for primary school teachers in a neighbouring county as well as a course for similar teachers within the county. The contacts with secondary schools are equally varied since this college has sponsored a mathematical experiment in secondary schools and runs a one-year supplementary mathematics course for secondary teachers.

Here are a lecturer's comments on teaching geometry to a class of primary children.

Going into a primary school to teach geometry to a class of children one afternoon a week for a term taught me a great deal about both geometry and children.

The class concerned had been brought up on arithmetic only and had no experience of practical work. We started very gently with a discussion on the different shapes that they could see around them and then progressed to an investigation of these shapes by paper-folding and measuring.

The children showed themselves to be very versatile in finding different things to measure on an ordinary sheet of paper. Some found, for example, that the longest measurement that could be made across the paper was from corner to corner. Others found that opposite edges were the same distance apart wherever the measurement was made—this was an obvious introduction to parallels.

Once the children found that everything they discovered was important, they became much more venturesome and we soon established all the metric properties of rectangles and squares. On the basis of this pattern of investigation, other shapes were treated in much the same way.

Measurement of angles brought in simple navigation in the playground, and the children had plenty of practice in work with fractions and ratio in the course of drawing maps and analysing and measuring the routes they had drawn.

In writing about what they were doing the children were, at first, very brief, but they soon found there was much more they wanted to say. The result was that they wrote freely, as they thought, and this told me a great deal about how the children were thinking about the task in hand.

Because they were working in groups, ideas spread quite quickly and the children were able to explain to each other what they had done and how they arrived at their conclusion.

Here are the lecturer's comments on running a teacher's study group.

The group consisted of 32 teachers from a variety of primary schools ranging from small two-teacher schools to large 'streamed' primary schools. The age and ability ranges of the children they taught were equally wide, so many of our discussions were enriched by a great variety of experiences.

The group functioned for two terms and met every Saturday morning for about two and a half hours. During the first term the teachers concentrated on learning as much as they could about mathematics and its presentation in schools. Each session consisted of a period of practical work followed by discussion and a lecture on the mathematical implications of the work done.

In the discussions the teachers brought out what they had discovered and talked about how the work could be organised with a class of children. Every problem was tackled with the enthusiasm of mountaineers determined to reach the top of Everest! Not once did I ever hear the words, 'My children couldn't do this'.

In effect, the first term amounted to a very concentrated course on primary mathematics.

In the second term, though they were conscious of needing a much wider grasp of mathematics, the teachers started new work with their own classes. At this stage the study group became subdivided into six smaller groups, according to what they were doing in the classroom. Once a week we met to discuss the children's work during the previous week and to put together our ideas for further development. During each session the various sub-groups discussed independently at first, while I spent some time with each. After this we all came together as a complete group to pool ideas and discuss the development of the work as a whole.

As the term progressed, so did the enthusiasm of the teachers in the light of what their children were doing.

Now that the group has ceased to work under my guidance they still meet occasionally to discuss their work and, where possible, visit each others' schools.

The lecturers at this college have not hesitated to put into practice, in their various courses for students and serving teachers, the same principles of learning which were exemplified in the account just given of the work of a class of nine-year-olds. From the outset the groups were placed in the position of making their own discoveries in mathematics whether they were solving a problem using real materials or meeting a topic in mathematics entirely new to them. The declared aims of the primary supplementary course were:

(i) to extend the student's knowledge and background of the principles and content of courses for children of ages 5 to 13.

(ii) to give the student an opportunity of undertaking mathematical activity in a manner closely approximating to classroom conditions.

(iii) to put primary mathematics into the perspectives of the school curriculum and of the educational philosophies of the schools.

(iv) to give students the opportunity to discuss briefly aims, difficulties and trends in as many aspects as possible.

The course itself covered the ground included in the summaries in Chapters 3, 4, 5 and 6 and also statistics. In the development of these topics the emphasis was on structure and modern aspects of mathematics. Concept development and the associated learning theory were studied. Current ideas in primary education were discussed and attention was focussed on the mathematical possibilities of other aspects of the curriculum by asking heads of subject departments to discuss their own subject with teachers on the course. The integration of subjects was further encouraged because one room in the college was allocated solely to this group of teachers. The records demanded by the various subject lecturers were those which would be of use in classrooms: charts, models and visually arresting forms which would excite children's interests. The materials produced were displayed on the walls and ceiling of the room so that successive lecturers were able to see how various topics were developing. In this way the students were able to construct their own mathematical environment.

The lecturers wrote: The work of the students was highly individual and often reflected the needs of the children in the classes the teachers had left behind. In consequence the same topic was treated at various levels of child development. Such contributions formed a good basis for the discussion of the placement of different aspects of a topic in the school programme.

No specific exercises were set and marked. Practical work was possible at all hours of the day and the students, without exception, took full advantage of the possibilities. It was unusual to find the room empty at any time between 9.00 a.m. and 10.00 p.m. All discussion on mathematical development was based on the students' practical activities. In short, we taught them at their level by the methods we had used with primary children.

The teachers on the supplementary course had an interesting and perhaps unexpected influence on the work of the normal 3-year students. Sometimes the same topic was studied in both groups so that experienced teachers and students in training met for discussion and drew comparisons. The classroom awareness of the former was soon reflected, to a lesser degree, in the work of the 3-year students and this, in turn, had a stimulating effect on the way the lecturers developed these courses.

Reports from former students of the supplementary courses have been encouraging. Whilst it is probably true that we only hear from those we have influenced, these are so numerous that we are sure that our first objective of developing an enthusiasm for mathematics and a more catholic approach to its teaching has been very satisfactorily achieved. Some old students have organised courses for teachers in their neighbourhood; others have helped to reorganise the work in their schools and still others, now head teachers, are organising their schools in accordance with what we try to convey on the course.

Here, in the lecturers' own words, are the conclusions the team of lecturers put forward at the end of their second course.

Conclusions

(a) We feel that students must be challenged to the full and then be given ample time to respond each in his own way to the challenge.

(b) The students must feel that they have a status as trained teachers which allows them freedom and individuality.

(c) A mathematics room is a first essential; it is necessary as home, as a stimulus to the students, as an integrating influence on different aspects of the course.

(d) The college courses gain considerably from the presence of the teachers. Their experience guarantees that the methods being used in college will work in the classroom. They add to the enthusiasm of the 3-year course; by their discussions with 3-year students the teachers underline the fact that the training received at college is a first stage in the development of a teacher.

The final conclusion contains promise of the benefits which derive from the presence of the group of experienced teachers studying mathematics within the college. Already such groups have made their mark on the teachers of the future with whom they had come in contact.

8. An Administrative Officer of a Local Education Authority

The problem of in-service training, of keeping teachers up-to-date with the latest developments of various aspects of the curriculum is one which concerns the teaching profession itself, Area Training Organisations, Local Education Authorities and the Department of Education and Science. Here is an account of one Authority's lively effort to solve this problem.

The Dorset Mathematics Workshop

The word 'workshop' has so many different educational connotations in these days, not only in Britain but elsewhere, that it seems to have lost some of its original meaning. It might be helpful therefore if some description were attempted of a lively experiment being conducted in a number of primary schools in Dorset, an experiment in the teaching of mathematics in which 'workshop' does seem to recover some of its earlier significance. This experiment is having a revolutionary effect in the county's schools, not only in the impact it has on the presentation of mathematics and on the imaginative involvement of the children concerned, but also because the workshops already set up have become efficient centres of in-service training for teachers in surrounding areas.

These workshops have emerged out of close and friendly co-operation between the Dorset Local Education Authority and the county's primary teachers, as part of a campaign designed to change and modernise the whole approach to the teaching of mathematics, giving the subject a new significance for children. Briefly, before the workshop was invented, Dorset had already developed two phases of its mathematics campaign: an exploration of the application and significance of structural apparatus (in particular Cuisenaire), and an enquiry into the use of new and livelier text-books. This was brought about by means of a series of county-wide courses, conferences and discussion groups at which there was a very high percentage of attendance by primary teachers. The degree of co-operation by teachers in this intensive application to the study of the teaching of mathematics is perhaps the most significant single feature of the whole county campaign.

It was at this stage, with a lively corporate enthusiasm already aroused, that the third and most important phase of mathematical exploration began, an entry into the field of what is variously called 'discovery', 'practical', 'experimental' or 'activity' mathematics. Whatever it is called, this creative field of mathematical activity begins, so far as Dorset is concerned, in the approach initiated at a two-day county course in November, 1962, sponsored by the Ministry of Education.

A type of mathematics which will bring children into closer contact with the physical world around them, which will give them something more significant to do than repetitive calculation, and which will lead them to the formation and expression of personal judgements—this is the sort of mathematics which has completely caught the imagination of Dorset teachers.

The introduction of practical mathematics has taken many forms in different types of schools, but it generally follows the pattern of problem assignments, using familiar materials and situations from the child's own environment and employing measuring apparatus of all kinds. Depending on circumstances, this kind of activity is based on the mathematics corner, the mathematics table, or the mathematics trolley. In one particularly enthusiastic school, mathematics has become the central subject in the imaginative life of the school, having relationships with all other subjects. Mathematics appears in every corner. The effects of this on English, art, poetry, pottery and the general attitude to work have been far-reaching; and since geometrical shape and form, and the simple algebraic equation have invaded even the infant room, the subject is properly called mathematics.

In certain schools where accommodation permits, the novel idea of the mathematics workshop has been developed. Let the first of these schools, in Bridport, serve as an example, though it is worth noting that in every instance the workshop has taken on a different character, influenced by the personalities and interests of the headmaster and the staff.

At Bridport, the school is fortunate in possessing an annexe with spare rooms. The workshop itself has been allowed to take its own shape and gradually acquire its own furniture and equipment. It has large formica-topped tables and stools, a sink, racks and cupboards for equipment, tools, materials, paper, etc., and for the great variety of mathematical apparatus which has accumulated on shelves and on the walls (scales, clocks, stopwatches, micrometers, measuring-glasses, thermometers, rulers, inch-tapes, chains, click-wheels and so on). An adjoining room is gradually developing as an overflow work-room, with bench and tools for the manufacture of apparatus, a display area, a mathematics library and museum, and a home for the adding machine.

This is clearly a contrived and concentrated environment, designed to stimulate mathematical interest. But even if the environment can be called artificial, there is no doubt about the genuineness of its appeal to the exploring fingers and immediate interests of the children around whom it has developed.

A special word should be said about one of the most interesting aspects of the workshop situation, the collection of materials 'out of which', as a child said, 'to make mathematics'. This collection began in the school and in the children's homes and gardens, but it has now drawn upon local industry (fishing, rope-making, car-servicing) and includes such assorted articles as cork-floats, bicycle wheels and broken drain-pipes. A drip from the workshop tap provided some fascinating mathematics.

The control in the workshop situation lies in a central set of attractive assignment cards designed to cover problems in all the different aspects of mathematics (volume, time, weight, number series, length, etc.). This set is continually being amended and developed, often in ways suggested by the activities and difficulties of the children and it can also be adapted to the needs of particular children, able or less able. The children work in ability-matched pairs and are encouraged to discuss their problem and the best way of recording the results of their enquiry, in the form of a calculation, a block or line graph, or in words. Advice is not immediately offered by the teacher, but is readily available. It is in the discussion stage following the achievement of an answer that the greatest value lies. Here, a close relationship between practical and computational mathematics is achieved in the children's minds. They now feel they *need* to know the table of length or weight so that they can solve a problem which engrosses them. There is a fascination and compulsion in this kind of mathematics.

The impact of the workshop within the school is evident. A block graph shows mathematics as the favourite school subject. The children have voluntarily formed a mathematics club which meets after school hours in order to extend their own time and experience in the workshop. Their attitude shows a willing involvement and a readiness to think for themselves—a rare achievement. The latest product of the workshop is a very complex graphical census of all the traffic passing through Bridport, in all directions, in a 24-hour period, a census found to be of immediate value by local planning and road-safety committees.

There are new teaching problems involved in a creative situation of this kind, but the staff have found the same compulsion and the same stimulus to intellectual curiosity in this experimental work as the children have done. Colleagues from H.M. Inspectorate, the Universities, Colleges of Education, and from other Local Education Authorities have been impressed by the vigour of the experiment and have contributed ideas extending the range of work.

The Dorset authority are not only convinced of the value of the workshop in making an impact on the mathematical enthusiasm of junior children. They also see the workshop as a vital factor in the process of in-service training. Teachers from the area around the workshops have enjoyed taking the places of the children, working on assignments and problems and discussing the discovery approach to mathematics within the framework of the workshop.

One of the important results is that the Local Education Authority have been convinced by experience that the workshop technique has applications in other subjects. It has become clear that the practical approach has a similar value in science and to some extent in social studies. A parallel campaign in primary science was being mounted in September 1964, and at least two of the workshops were preparing to develop a mathematics/science programme, having already found how shadowy the division between these two subjects is and how much common ground they share. Finally, it may well be that the future development of the workshop approach will exert some influence on the design of new schools and the modernisation of old ones.

CONCLUSION

This book began on an optimistic note and it is fitting that it should be brought to a conclusion on the same note. Stress has been laid throughout on the necessity for close contact between the infant and junior and between the junior and secondary stages. We have looked forward to the impending changes at the secondary stage and have tried to show the essential unity throughout. Mathematics is a unity in itself and should have a unifying influence on the different stages of education.

It is necessary to emphasise once more that those of us who work with children frequently modify our views in the light of children's reactions to the mathematical experiences we give them. We do not expect that everything we have written will stand up indefinitely to the test of time and experience. But there is one characteristic of the changing pattern which has permanent validity. It transcends all others and it will compensate teachers for the extra work entailed at the initial stages.

Professor Whitehead said 'Every child should experience the joy of discovery.' We can say, with complete assurance, every teacher who embarks on a programme which will enable children to make their own discoveries in mathematics will share to the utmost their children's enjoyment of mathematics and their increasing confidence in their own powers.

Appendix 1 BOOK LIST

This list consists of mathematics books which teachers (and, in some cases, children) will find useful as a source of ideas, as background material, for the purpose of learning more mathematics and for enjoyment.

To help those who have not yet made a start on the reading of mathematics books a small collection of books which would be useful as a beginning has been marked B.

Those books which are suitable as reference books for children are marked C.

GENERAL BOOKS ON TEACHING IN THE PRIMARY SCHOOL

Blackie, J. *Inside the Primary School.* HMSO, 1967.

Hollamby, L. *Young Children Living and Learning.* Longmans, 1962.

Ministry of Education. *Primary Education: Suggestions for the Consideration of Teachers and Others.* HMSO, 1959.

Schools Council/Ford Foundation Anglo-American Primary Education Project. *British Primary Schools Today* (series of booklets). Macmillan Education, 1971 and 1972 (published in the US by Citation Press, Scholastic Magazines, New York under the title *Informal Schools in Britain Today*).

Sealey, L. G. W. and Gibbon, V. *Communication and Learning in the Primary School.* Blackwell, 1963.

University of London Institute of Education. *First Years in School: Aspects of Children's Development from the Ages of 4 to 7* (Studies in Education). Evans for University of London Institute of Education, 1963.

BOOKS ON THE TEACHING OF MATHEMATICS

Adams, L. D. *Background to Primary School Mathematics.* O.U.P., 1953.

Association of Teachers in Colleges and Departments of Education. *Teaching Mathematics: Main Courses in Colleges of Education.* A.T.C.D.E., 1967.

Association of Teachers in Colleges and Departments of Education. *Primary Mathematics for Schools and Training Colleges.* A.T.C.D.E., 1963.

Association of Teachers of Mathematics. *Notes on the Teaching of Mathematics in Primary Schools.* C.U.P., 1967.

Association of Teachers of Mathematics. *Some Mathematical Reflections.* C.U.P., 1970.

B. Barnett, N. M., Faithful, M. G. and Theakston, T. R. *Juniors Learning Mathematics.* Ward Lock Educational, 1964.

Beard, Ruth. *An Outline of Piaget's Developmental Psychology.* Routledge & Kegan Paul, 1969.

Churchill, E. M. *Counting and Measuring: an Approach to Number Education in the Infants School.* Routledge & Kegan Paul, 1961.

Combridge, J. T. (ed.) *Count Me In: Numeracy in Education* (A BP Progress Book). Queen Anne Press, 1968.

Fletcher, Harold (ed.) *Mathematics for Schools* (Books 1–7). Addison-Wesley, 1970.

Gale, D. H. *The Teaching of Number.* Hulton Educational, 1963.

Ironside, M. and Roberts, S. *Mathematics in the Primary School.* National Froebel Foundation, 1965.

Land, F. W. (ed.) *New Approaches to Mathematics Teaching*. Macmillan, 1963.

Lovell, K. *The Growth of Basic Mathematical and Scientific Concepts in Children*. University of London Press, 1968.

Marsh, L. G. *Approach to Mathematics*. A. & C. Black, 1970.

Mathematical Association. *Mathematics in Secondary Modern Schools*. Bell, 1959.

Mathematical Association. *Primary Mathematics: a Further Report*. Bell, 1970.

Mathematical Association. *Mathematics Projects in British Secondary Schools*. Bell, 1968.

Mathematical Association. *The Teaching of Mathematics in Primary Schools*. Bell, 1956.

Ministry of Education. *Teaching Mathematics in Secondary Schools* (Pamphlet No. 36). HMSO, 1958.

Nuffield Mathematics (series). Chambers/Murray, 1967–.

B. Sealey, L. G. W. *The Creative Use of Mathematics in the Junior School*. Blackwell, rev. edn, 1965.

Shuard, H. and Williams, E. M. *Primary Mathematics Today*. Longman, 1970.

STRUCTURAL MATERIAL (and of general interest also)

Dienes, Z. P. *Building up Mathematics*. Hutchinson Educational, 2nd edn, 1964.

Goutard, M. *Mathematics and Children*. Educational Explorers, 1964.

Goutard, M. *Talks for Primary School Teachers*. Educational Explorers, 1963.

Pollock, S. *Colour-factor Mathematics: a General Introduction*. Heinemann Educational, 1962.

Stern, C. *Children Discover Arithmetic: an Introduction to Structural Arithmetic*. Harrap, 1953.

METRICATION

Schools Council. *Change for a Pound: a Teaching Guide for the Introduction of Decimal Currency and the Adoption of Metric Measures*. HMSO, 1968; 2nd edn, 1970.

Schools Council. *Measure for Measure: a Guide to Metrication for Workshop Crafts and Technical Studies*. Evans/Methuen Educational, 1970.

Schools Council. *Metres, Litres and Grams: Introducing Metrication in the Primary School*. Evans/Methuen Educational, 1971.

HISTORY OF MATHEMATICS

C. Adler I. *Mathematics* (Learning with Colour Series). Hamlyn, new edn., 1966 (originally published as *The Giant Colour Book of Mathematics*).

C. Adler, I. *Mathematics: the Story of Numbers, Symbols and Space*. Golden Press, New York, 1958.

C. Adler I. *Time in Your Life*. Dobson, 1957.

B.C. Bowman, M. E. *Romance in Arithmetic: a History of Our Currency, Weights and Measures and Calendar*. University of London Press. 4th new edn. 1969.

C. Hogben, L. *Mathematics*. (Wonderful World Series) Macdonald, 1968 (originally published as *Man Must Measure*).

C. Hood, P. *How Time is Measured*. O.U.P., 1955.

Kline, M. *Mathematics in Western Culture*. O.U.P., 1965.

Midonick, H. *Treasury of Mathematics* (2 vols). Penguin Books, 1968.

C. Ruchlis, H. and Engelhardt, J. *The Story of Mathematics*. Harvey House/Bailey Bros, 1958.

C. Smith, D. E. *Number Stories of Long Ago*. Ginn, 1948.

C. Smith, T. *The Story of Numbers*. Blackwell, 1959.

C. Williams, S. E. *Stories of Mathematics*. Evans, 1953.

Geometry of Shapes

Cundy, H. M. and Rollett, A. P. *Mathematical Models*. O.U.P., 2nd edn, 1961.

James, E. J. *Mathematical Topics for Modern Schools*. O.U.P., 1960. (Book 2: Curve Stitching)

C. Ravielli, A. *Adventures with Shapes*. Phoenix House, Dent, 1960.

Rowland, K. *Looking and Seeing* (3 parts). Ginn, 1964.

Weyl, H. *Symmetry*. Princeton/O.U.P., 1952.

C. Weyl, P. K. *Men, Ants and Elephants*. Phoenix House, Dent, 1961.

General Mathematics (Background)

C. Bergamini, D. *Mathematics* (Life Science Library). Time-Life International, 1965.

Fielker, D. *Cubes*, 1969; *Statistics*, 1967; *Computers*, 1967; *Towards Probability*, 1971 (Topics from Mathematics series). C.U.P.

Hogben, L. *The Wonderful World of Mathematics*. Macdonald Educational, 1968.

B. Land, F. W. *The Language of Mathematics*. Murray, 1960.

Mold, J. *Circles*, 1967; *Tessellations*, 1969; *Triangles*, 1971; *Solid Models*, 1967 (Topics from Mathematics series). C.U.P.

Peter, R. *Playing with Infinity*. Bell, 1961.

Sawyer, W. W. *Mathematician's Delight*. Penguin Books, 1943.
A Path to Modern Mathematics. Penguin Books, 1966.
Prelude to Mathematics. Penguin Books, 1965.
Vision in Elementary Mathematics. Penguin Books, 1964.

Recreation and Puzzles

Adler, I. *Magic House of Numbers*. Dobson, 1958.

De Grazia, J. *Maths is Fun*. Allen & Unwin, 1958.

Dudeney, H. E. *Amusements in Mathematics*. Dover/Constable, 1961.

Gardner, M. *Mathematical Puzzles and Diversions*. Penguin Books, 1965.

Hunter, J. A. H. *Figures for Fun*. Phoenix House, Dent, 1957.

McWhirter, Norris and Ross. (eds and comps) *The Guinness Book of Records*. Guinness Superlatives, Enfield, Middlesex.

Northrop, E. P. *Riddles in Mathematics*. English Universities Press, 2nd edn, 1958; Penguin Books, 1960.

Applications of Mathematics

C. Deverson, H. J. *The Map that Came to Life*. O.U.P., 1967.

French, P. *Exploring Mathematics* (series). McGrew-Hill, 1965-9.

C. Hogben, L. *Energy* (Wonderful World Series). Macdonald, 1968 (originally published as *Men, Missiles and Machines*).

C. Lee, L. and Lambert, D. *Transport* (Wonderful World Series). Macdonald, 1969 (originally published as *Man Must Move*).

C. Lester, R. M. *The Observer's Book of Weather*. Warne, 1955.

Lockwood, E. *Statistics: the How and the Why*. Murray, 1969.

C. Longley-Cook, L. H. *Work This One Out*. Benn, 1960.

Nuffield Junior Science. *Teacher's Guides*, 1 and 2; *Animals and Plants*; *Apparatus*; Background information booklets; *Junior Science Source Book*. Collins, 1967.

C. Razzell, A. G. and Watts, K. G. O. *Mathematical Topics* (Series 1 and 2). Hart-Davis, 1964 and 1971.

Waters, D. *Forestry*. Pergamon Press, 1966.

C. Whitney, T. H. *Young Scientist's Approach to the Weather*. Warne, 1962.

New Look Mathematics (for interest and information)

Adler, I. *The New Mathematics*. Dobson, 3rd edn, 1964.

Fletcher, T. J. (ed.) *Some Lessons in Mathematics*. C.U.P. for Association of Teachers of Mathematics, 1964.

Heritage, R. S. and Lewis, W. I. *Learning Mathematics*, Books 1–4 (Pelican). Penguin Books, 1966–1970. (Metric edition: 1970-71).

Hope, C. (ed.) *The Midlands Mathematical Experiment* (Books 1–3 and two reports). Harrap, 1963. (Book 1, 2nd rev. edn. (metric), 1970).

Kaner, P. *Modern World Mathematics*, Books 1–5. Longman, 1968–.

Manchester Mathematics Group. *A Structural Approach to Mathematics*. Hart-Davis Educational, 1969.

Matthews, G. and others. *Contemporary School Mathematics* (St Dunstan's College Booklets). Edward Arnold, 1964–1966.

Moakes, A. J., Croome, P. D. and Phillips, T. C. *Pattern and Power of Mathematics* (series). Macmillan, 1968.

Paling, D. and Fox, J. *Elementary Mathematics: a Modern Approach*, Part 1, 1965, Part 2, 1969. O.U.P.

Paling, D. Banwell, C. S. and Saunders, K. D. *Making Mathematics*, Books 1–3 and workbooks. O.U.P., 1968 and 1969. (Books 1 and 2, 2nd rev. edn., 1971).

School Mathematics Project, Books 1–5, T and T4 (1964–1969) and Books A–G (1968–). C.U.P.

Scottish Mathematics Group. *Modern Mathematics for Schools* (nine books in all). Blackie/Chambers, 1965–.

Skemp, R. R. and Friis, J. S. *Understanding Mathematics*, Books 1–5. University of London Press, 1964-.

Textbooks

Attractive books of textbook type have been produced during the past few years by many publishers. These can play an important part as source books if one of each is included in each class library and in the staff library.

The teachers' books of the various series will be found particularly helpful.

Teachers will find it worthwhile to look at each new textbook published as most modern textbooks are attractive in appearance and contain some interesting material.

Appendix 2 MATERIALS USEFUL FOR EXPLORATION OF MATHEMATICAL RELATIONSHIPS

In primary schools, particularly in infants' schools, the normal environment possesses many mathematical possibilities. If these are to be used for the discovery of relationships in number, quantity and space, the following materials will be found valuable (not of course to be set out at the same time but to be available at the school so that they can be brought into use when required).

Pre-counting stage (language all-important)
Sets (collections) of attractive objects for sorting and matching (one to one correspondence) e.g. cups and saucers, knives and forks, spoons, plates in the home corner. Children (boys, girls in small groups), chairs, paint brushes, pencils, books, bottles of milk. Balls, hoops, etc. for physical education.

Counting, conservation of number, number relationships
At pre-counting stage—collections made by the children, for example, conkers, acorns, shells, building bricks, match boxes, marbles etc. Trays with written numerals 1, 2, 3, etc. (according to the children's development) in which children can set out the appropriate number from their collections.

Sets of objects made by the children bearing numerals for putting in order, for example, match box or toy houses, chairs for a concert.

Commodities for shops of various kinds, made by the children themselves. The number of each commodity varied to suit the abilities of small groups of children, and recorded in the shop's 'stock book'. Real money, also controlled in amount, to suit the group's ability. Purses containing real money in varied supply to count each day. As the till, cash box (contents suitably limited in amount) containing real money.

Structural material
(a) Commercial (b) Homemade
A 100 square made by each child when he is able. A 100 unit strip affixed to the wall horizontally, rigid strips 1 to 10 units long. Large number line in playground.

Abacus and counters.

METRIC MEASURES

Length
Ribbon, lace, wool, string, drinking straws. A number of metre sticks (slatting 2 mm thick, 2 cm wide, cut to length). Some unmarked, some marked in $\frac{1}{2}$, $\frac{1}{4}$ units, some marked in decimetre lengths, some marked in centimetres and decimetres in alternate colours. Useful measures can be improvised with centimetre graph paper e.g. metre measures made from a one (or two) centimetre wide strip. These can be numbered by the children, covered with Sellotape and used to measure perimeters and lengths on curved surfaces.

A 200 centimetre tape measure numbered in centimetres and fixed vertically to the wall as a height scale (alternate decimetres could be coloured). 30- and 25-centimetre rulers with alternate centimetre lengths coloured for easy reading, and no ends. ($\frac{1}{2}$ centimetres could be marked for guidance, but not labelled.) Rulers in centimetres and millimetres. Tape measures: 150 cm and 200 cm marked in cm, $\frac{1}{2}$ cm. Surveyor's tapes. Rulers in centimetres and millimetres 25 cm long.

An efficient map measurer, ungraded, such as the Curvex (from Spaldings, Sidney Street, Cambridge, price about 40p post free). Micrometer if children are interested in 'thin things' and can discover for themselves what the graduations mean; feeler gauges (from cycle shops).

Weight
Material for weighing: conkers, peas, rice, beans, sand, nails. Parcels made up in easy weights, clay or plasticine. Large stones.

Scales of all types (1) balance type with brass or iron weights, one-gram weights in plastic, 5 gram, 10 gram, 20 gram, 50 gram, 100 gram, 200 gram, 500 gram, kilogram weights. Brass weights are more accurate when practicable. (2) Compression scales in wide variety. Letter scale to 250 grams, 2 kilogram scale, bathroom scales to 125 or 130 kilograms, (3) Spring balances—extension type—a wide range.

Capacity and volume

Useful measures: empty fruit tins of varying sizes, milk bottles of different capacities, flat sandwich tins. Plastic containers and bottles, cups, jugs. Measuring jugs and cylinders in litres and millilitres. Plastic pails and basins, plastic tubing and funnels.

A large number of centimetre cubes in different colours. Sets of cubes of edges 1, 2, 3 to 10 centimetres (wood and hollow plastic). Plasticine or clay for making different shapes of equal volume. Rectangular, cylindrical, conical and other containers. Litre containers in various shapes.

Area

Centimetre squares, 5 and 10 centimetre squares, in plastic and in gummed paper in various colours. Square metre in square decimetre and square centimetre paper. Square centimetre paper in assorted sizes. Leaves, leaf patterns, patterned fabric for comparing areas.

Time

Mechanical clock with clear figures and movable hands.

Cardboard clock with clear figures and movable hands.

Egg timers, pulsimeters (15, 30, 60 seconds) from chemists. 'Photographic' clock with stopping device and a large second hand. Metronome. Pocket metronome from large music shops. Homemade pendulums (with bobs made of balls of plasticine or lead fish weights) for measuring short intervals of time with an arbitrary unit. Homemade water clocks (tins with holes of varying sizes). Stop watches, reconditioned, measuring in fifths of a second, can be obtained from Charles Frank, 67 to 75, Salt Market, Glasgow, C.1. Price about £3.

Bamboo cane as shadow stick (1 metre, $1\frac{1}{2}$ metres, 2 metres high). Calendar with large figures (Pages can be arranged with months in sequence, side by side, as completed). Radio and T.V. Times. Simple bus and train timetables.

Temperature

Thermometers. The most satisfactory are those with uncovered bulbs but these need careful handling. 'Fruit bottling' type from chemists or gardening thermometers from ironmongers' shops are best. It is useful to have one calibrated in Celsius (Centigrade) scale.

Shapes

For constructional work: waste material of as wide a variety as possible, for example, newspapers, glossy magazines, coloured paper, silver paper, cardboard of different colours, corrugated paper, textile pieces of differing textures, ribbons, straw, twigs, pebbles, paste, paint, clay, sand. Tins, boxes of all shapes and sizes.

Cardboard strips of varying sizes (for example 2 cm wide and of lengths of 10 cm and 20 cm. If these have one hole punched one cm from each end they can be fastened together with push-through paper fasteners. When putting in diagonals of polygons, (by joining one corner) keeping the shape regular, it will be found useful to have the larger strips with a series of holes punched at 1 cm intervals as far as the middle of the strip.

Drinking straws, pipe cleaners, elastic bands, shirring and roll elastic. Folding boxes in variety.

Mosaic puzzles, table mats of mathematical shape, rubbings or drawings of tile patterns, textiles with mathematical patterns, coloured plastic shapes of triangles, squares, rectangles, etc. One set of templates of regular shapes with sides 3, 4, 5, 6, 8, 9, 10, 12 for quick reproduction will be found valuable for occasional use when making solid shapes.

Circular tins of varying sizes (one collection of diameters 5 cm, 6 cm, 8 cm, 10 cm, 12 cm would be extremely valuable). Set of hardboard or cardboard circles of uniform thickness in in diameters 10, 15, 20, 25, 30, 40, 50 cm. Balls of varying sizes, wheels, hoops, calipers, tape measures and string. Set of polystyrene balls (various diameters) and cubes. Coloured ink. Housebricks. Sets of objects (usually toys) mathematically similar in shape. Sets of objects for children to determine whether these are mathematically similar or not (for example, soaps of the same brand, in different sizes). Match boxes of the same brand, in different sizes. Nests of toys.

Short lengths of dowel rod 10 cm, 15 cm, 20 cm, 25 cm with screw eyes at each end; push-through paper fasteners for making 3-D models. Metre lengths of string. Strips of sugar paper 2 cm wide for enclosing various shapes. Geoboards can be made from wood with nails at 2 cm intervals or 5 cm intervals from softboard

22 cm square (or smaller), covered with centimetre (or 2 cm) square graph paper, using ordinary pins and elastic bands or loops of shirr elastic in different colours.

Skeleton shapes made by the children with strips of cardboard and paper fasteners, (or with Meccano), for example, squares, rectangles, kites with diagonals of roll elastic. Some shapes can be made by fastening two diagonals at their centres and fixing a length of shirring elastic round all four extremities; the two diagonals can be of the same length or of different lengths.

Compasses, circular protractor or paper circular protractor. Kaleidoscope. Handbag mirrors.

Highway Code, diaries e.g. Angler's Diary. Photographs of interesting buildings, collected by children.

Plastic scale models; aeroplanes, etc.

Surveying

Circular protractor. Clinometer made from a protractor with a perspex pen holder as a sighting tube and a plumb line fastened at the centre. Right angled isosceles triangular framework with short sides $\frac{1}{2}$ metre or 1 metre in length. Bamboo canes for sighting rods or for marking position 1 metre in length. Marked lengths of string or surveyor's tapes. A trundle wheel one metre in circumference. Spirit level, plumb lines, Silva compass. (This may be obtained, scout variety, 80p. from good sports shops or from B. J. Ward, Ltd., 130 Westminster Bridge Road, London, S.E.1. Pamphlets with suggestions for its use are also available.)

Maps of varied scales and a map of England with the counties coloured. Regional railway timetable with scale map. Inter-City time map. plastic inflatable globe.

Other applications

Newspapers, magazines, timetables, advertisements, holiday brochures, Fordson's cloud chart (from Dagenham, Essex), Post Office leaflets, labels from tins.

For experiments with elastic bands and springs (extension) and for friction experiments:

Fifty cm length of wood about 1 cm thick, 10 cm wide, with a hook fixed at one end of one of the largest faces and a pulley attached to two metal supports at the other. Scale pans can be made from tin lids 10 cm in diameter with three small holes equally spaced round the rims through which pass short lengths of string. Clockwork trains and rails. Model cars, large ball bearings. Physical Education form can be used as a ramp for finding speed. (Rails to cover the length of the slope and a truck to fit will prevent toys from running off the track). A plastic watercan will serve as a displacement can for finding volume. Tins of 10 cm in diameter and about 15 cm tall are useful as a homemade rain gauge, with plastic funnel to fit, or as a sunshine recorder (with small hole 2 mm in diameter punched at the centre of the upright edge). 'Sunshine paper' (i.e. ferropaper) medium fast can be obtained from Haldens, 37 Brazennose Street, Manchester, 2. (40p will buy a roll of good size.) The tin can be lined with paper, leaving the hole free, and set outside (with lid on) for investigation. Ferropaper can be developed by washing with water. Mariner's compass.

Important

By far the most valuable material is graph paper, of varying qualities (some very inexpensive) cut in different sizes from small to large, with squares 5 cm, 2 cm, 1 cm, $\frac{1}{2}$ cm and no other markings; also cm and 2 mm markings. Small pieces can be cut for finding areas, and larger pieces, in a wide variety of sizes can be used for making special graphs. Isometric paper (equilateral triangular grid of edges 3 cm, 2 cm, 1 cm). Felt-tipped pens in a variety of colours are very useful for labelling and drawing the graphs. Plain paper of varying sizes, colours and qualities is also useful.

Appendix 3 NOTES FOR GUIDANCE OF LEADERS OF MATHEMATICS COURSES

A selection of assignments issued to teachers at in-service courses (age range 5–16)

The programme for an initial 3-day (12 session) course is described here. This can be adapted as required for sessional courses held at teachers' centres (frequently during the school day). These courses are only initial courses. It is essential for teachers to be given regular opportunities subsequently to meet at a centre where they can work at mathematics at their own level, prepare topics for children and bring and discuss the children's work resulting.

It is important that, for the greater part of the course, teachers should work in groups containing infant, junior and secondary (mathematics) teachers—for example, two infant, four junior and two secondary. Within these groups teachers will want to pair off in different ways during the working sessions. Organisation is easier if there is a maximum of 40 teachers with one leader to each group of 8. Many centres limit the number to 24.

A three-day course normally includes:

Sessions 1 and 2. Patterns in Statistics.

Sessions 3, 4 and 5. Patterns in Measurement: Planning the Programme.

6, 7 and 8. Patterns in Number.

9 and 10. Patterns in Shapes.

11. Discussion in groups: infant, junior, secondary.

12. In the Classroom, Films. Display and discussion of children's work.

Patterns in Statistics

1. In sessions 1 and 2, teachers find their own statistics and enter these on a sheet. Here is a selection of topics:
(Give measures to the nearest whole unit unless otherwise directed.) Sex has to be included in every question.

1. Number of children in the family in which you grew up (include yourself). Boys...... Girls...... Your position in family...... Sex.......

2. Your car registration number........... Make of car.......................... Colour of car...........

3. Waist measure........cm
   Neck measure........cm
   Girth ratio $\frac{\text{Waist}}{\text{Neck}}$ ....(to one decimal place).

4. Time taken to walk 20 paces......seconds
   Distance travelled in 20 paces......metres (to nearest $\frac{1}{10}$ metre). One pace is heel to heel or toe to toe of your normal stride.

5. Area of left footprint........cm^2
   Perimeter of left footprint........cm
   Make the 'string perimeter' of your foot into a square and find the area.
   Area of square........cm^2. Are the two areas the same?

The information for each of the five questions has to be transferred to five different sheets, question by question.

The sheets, when complete, should be distributed to the five groups: question 1 to group 1, question 2 to group 2, and so on.

Each group then receives 40 sets of information for one question.

The groups are then asked to communicate the results in as wide a variety of ways as possible. Teachers are asked to keep classroom needs in mind so that the representations show a progression from infant to secondary stages. Infant and lower junior teachers may want to use the results from one group only. They will want to emphasise vocabulary and to use real materials such as string, beads, etc.

Possible ways of representation are:

(1) Tabular form (the information from each table can be arranged in order from smallest to largest. Measures corresponding to each individual should then be linked).
(2) Diagrams.
(3) Pictorial and block graphs. (Number of people is normally represented on the vertical axis.)
(4) Three-dimensional graphs (when there are three variables to be represented, e.g. waist, neck, number of people.)
(5) These graphs are called scattergrams.

Teachers are asked to draw attention to interesting features of their representations by means of appropriate questions. For example:

1. On a graph showing neck and waist measures on two axes at right angles mark the vertical line which shows the greatest range in individual measures. What have the people on this line in common? How are they different?

2. On representations of individual families from one table:

   What do you notice about the families? How many families have (a) more boys than girls? (b) girls only? (c) equal numbers of boys and girls?

When the communication is complete, group tutors are asked to discuss the progression of the assigned topic from infant to secondary stages. How might the topic be developed further?

Patterns in Measurement: Planning the Programme

Each group chooses a topic from the following:

a. length
b. capacity and volume
c. weight (mass and force)
d. area
e. time and rate.

Session 3 will be spent on practical work on the topic selected. The questions are chosen to illustrate important mathematical ideas which should be kept in mind in subsequent sessions when the chosen topic is planned to cover the age range 5 to 16 years. The questions provided are starting-points and are not meant to limit investigations in any way. Each pair of teachers will work two or three problems so that all phases are covered. The group leader is then asked to lead a discussion on the investigations completed during the session.

Sessions 4 and 5 will be spent on planning the topic. It is suggested that during these planning sessions one or two members of each group should keep notes of the discussion which should include: (1) Stages of development; and (2) Starting points at each stage, consisting of good challenging questions and experiences.

One way of recording these questions is suggested in the plan shown. Each group will be concerned with one topic only from section 2. Another way of recording questions and experiences is by means of a flow chart.

The greatest value of these sessions is in the discussion. The order of development should be flexible since children respond to questions in many different ways. Teachers usually find these planning sessions a valuable opportunity for exchanging ideas. Similar discussions between the staff of a school or between the staffs of more than one school, can help teachers to cover all topics included in the chart.

When planning of this kind takes place at a teachers' centre, teachers from infant, junior and secondary schools can plan the work as a team. The questions can then be tried out in the classroom and pupils' work can be brought back for discussion. The scheme can be modified where necessary, as a result of classroom experience. The inclusion of starting questions at different stages is a useful way of informing teachers new to a school of the aims, scope and method of (mathematics) teaching through the school.

NOTES ON STAGES IN LEARNING AND STARTING QUESTIONS AND EXPERIENCES

I. Comparison

1. Direct—using matching but no actual measuring

using (a) two strips or ribbons of different lengths
(b) two containers of different sizes
two stones of different sizes
(c) two stones of different weights
(d) two leaves of different sizes

SUGGESTED OPEN PLAN FOR MATHEMATICS IN PRIMARY AND MIDDLE SCHOOLS

Each blank rectangle could contain starting points in the form of challenging questions or experiences showing progression of ideas in the 5 to 16 age range. Each topic should be developed on a separate sheet and should be modified as a result of classroom experience.

Communication of discoveries made is of great importance. This should be done in a variety of ways: verbal, by diagram, numerical, in tabular form, by graphs of many types, by algebra.

	TOPICS			
CONCEPTS OR IDEAS	I. NUMBER Including fractions, decimals, positive and negative integers. Algebra.	II. MEASURES Including volume, mass and weight, density, area, length, time and rate, temperature.	III. SHAPES Beginning with 3D shapes, properties of 3D and 2D shapes, symmetry, congruence, enlargement and tiling. Change of position, of size, of shape.	IV. STATISTICS AND PROBABILITY
1. *Sorting and matching*.		Infants Lower juniors Upper juniors Lower secondary Upper secondary		
2. *Comparison* (by subtraction and division). Putting in order of size. Conservation. Greatest and least. *Operations* of addition, subtraction, multiplication and division.				
3. *Estimation* and *Approximation*, *Averages*.				
4. *Pattern: variables* (things which change) Limits Ratio Direct proportion Inverse proportion Squares Cubes Growth Generalisation				

(e) How can young children compare spans of time, e.g. time, taken to walk across the room, first slowly then quickly?

Discuss development of vocabulary—the language of inequality precedes the language of equality.

There are *two* methods of comparison in frequent use:

How much longer? How many times....? Which operations (+ − × ÷) do the activities (a) to (e) represent?

2. Using non-standard units

(a) Compare the length and breadth of this room using your normal pace. (How could you find your normal pace?)
Which non-standard units would it be sensible to use when comparing

(b) the capacities of two containers, the volumes of two stones;

(c) the weights of two stones;

d) the areas of two leaves (which shapes, other than squares, could you use for comparing areas?);

(e) the times of completing two identical journeys?

What questions would you ask children to help them to understand the need for standard units?

3. Using standard units

Which units of length, capacity, volume, weight, area, time, would you introduce first?

(a) Cut two lengths of string which you think are (i) 1 metre and (ii) 10 cm long. Check.
Find two lengths which are one metre long, one straight and one curved. Find two lengths just greater and two a little less than one metre long. Repeat with 10 centimetre lengths.

(b) Find three containers, of different shapes, which you think hold a litre. Check in two ways.

(c) Find two objects which weigh almost exactly a kilogramme.
Find or make objects which weigh 100 g, 10 g, 1 g.

(d) Cut out a square of edge 1 decimetre (10 cm).
Find a leaf which is nearly a square decimetre in area.
Cut out a square of edge 1 metre. Use this to find two surfaces, one flat and one curved, each of which is about 1 square metre in area.

(e) Make a small hole in a flat plastic container or tin. How long does this take to sink in water? Try to make a tin which will take one minute to sink.

In all measuring with standard units estimate before measuring. How near were you?

A knowledge of the approximate sizes (and weights) of some common objects like doors, bricks, tiles, paving stones, will help in estimation.

4. Using two standard units or 1 unit and a decimal fraction of the unit

It is helpful for children to make and graduate their own measuring equipment before using purchased equipment such as measuring jugs or cylinders, compression and extension scales, area grids which normally use two standard units.

e.g. (a) a 2 metre height scale marked in centimetres and decimetres or a 10 metre string marked at 10 centimetre intervals can be prepared by the children themselves.

(b) clear containers of various sizes can be graduated first in 'egg cups' or marbles, then in appropriate standard units such as 100 ml, 50 ml, 10 ml depending on the capacities to be measured. Medicine bottles of various capacities and medicine spoons will be found very useful. Volumes (e.g. of pebbles and stones) should be measured in cubic centimetres so that clear containers should also be graduated in these units. Adults and children need to discover the equivalence of a litre and a cubic decimetre. Open cuboids of convenient volume e.g. 2 cm by 2 cm by 2·5 cm can be cut from graph paper. These can be made waterproof by dipping in melted candle-grease. (Children cannot do this for themselves.)

(c) It is particularly important to give children preliminary experiences with springs (extension and compression), elastic and a homemade see-saw if they are to understand the working of the variety of balance and other scales used for weighing.

e.g. (1) They can graduate a vertical scale to use with a plastic container suspended from elastic bands for weighing pebbles or heavier objects. This could be graduated first in 'marbles', then in 10 g, 20 g units according to requirements.

A compression scale (e.g. a metal spring from a hair roller) is harder to graduate.

(2) Make a homemade see-saw from a metre stick (ungraduated face uppermost) balanced over a wedge of wood shaped as in the figure and 5 cm in depth (for stability).

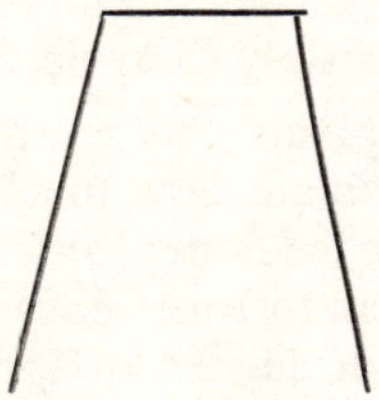

Use identical cubes, 50 g or 100 g weights as "children". What relations can you discover

i. When you leave the wedge in place but change the weight of the child on one side of the see-saw?

ii. When you move the wedge but have children of different weights on either side e.g. 100 g and 200 g at each end of the see-saw?

(3) How soon would you introduce the unit of force?

Force is measured in newtons. Children can find their pulling force using extension scales. They can find their "squeeze" using bathroom scales graduated in newtons instead of kilogrammes. They can find the approximate equivalent in newtons of the force of gravity exerted on a kilogramme mass by hanging this on extension scales calibrated in newtons.

At the top of the junior stage some children will be measuring forces. From viewing moon explorations on television, children are aware that objects weigh less when outside the earth's gravitational field:

The *farther* we are from the centre of the earth the *weaker* the earth's pull is. Many children will know that our weight (the result of the pull of gravity) would be slightly more at the flattened poles than at the equator. Many also know that the gravitational pull of the moon is far less than that of the earth. At the same time children are also prepared to accept that astronauts do not disappear when in space! When we use a compression scale to weigh ourselves, we are finding the gravitational pull (a force) and should give our answer in newtons. The unit of weight (a force) is a newton. The unit of mass is a kilogramme. There is a simple approximate numerical relation between these two units.

Historically, the kilogramme has been used as if it were a unit of force. When we are balancing "masses" it does not matter whether we use kilogrammes or newtons because *at any one place* mass is proportional to weight. However, as soon as children begin to measure force (top junior or lower secondary) it is better to use the correct units and vocabulary.

(4) How soon would you express measures in one unit, using decimal fractions? Outline an introduction to decimals using money and the measures.

How soon would you expect children to obtain a variety of equivalents for the units: metre, litre, cubic decimetre, kilogramme, square metre?

II. Putting in order of size

Use string, water, balance scales, plain paper—but no standard measures.

(a) Find three containers of different shapes which you think are of the same capacity.
Find out whether you were right.
Arrange the containers in order from smallest to largest.
Could you compare the contents in any other way?
Could you compare the containers in any other way?
How are they alike? How are they different?

(b) Find three medium large stones which you think are equal in size.
Compare the "sizes" of the stones in as many ways as you can. Put them in order from smallest to largest.
Were the stones equal in size in any of the ways you tried?

III. Equality and conservation

(a) Find someone in the room with the same waist measure as yours.
Has he the same weight? height? shape?

(b) Find someone of the same weight as you. Is he the same height? shape?

(c) Find two containers of different shapes which hold the same volume of water when filled to the brim.

(d) (i) Find two leaves of different shapes which have the same area.
Have they the same perimeter?

(ii) Find one half of sheets of paper (by a single fold) in as many ways as you can. What is the same about these half sheets?

(e) Suspend a pendulum carefully and find out whether it beats regularly.

Piaget and others have found that children require a great deal of experience before they grasp the idea of conservation of length, weight, volume, area. For example, when two cubes identical in size but of very different weights are put in two identical jars of water, will the water rise by the same or by different amounts?

IV. Approximation

All measuring is an approximation. We can never be "absolutely accurate" when measuring. Children (and adults) discover through experience, that they need to choose the measuring tool which is most suitable to answer a given question. They should be encouraged to approximate sensibly to avoid complicated calculations.

(a) Measure this room (i) for the caretaker to estimate how much polish will be required for the floor; (ii) for the architect to make a 1 cm to 1 metre scale drawing. Comment on your degrees of approximation.

(b) Measure the volume of (i) a pebble; (ii) a large stone using as many as possible of the nest of graduated beakers. Which gives the closest approximation?

(c) Weigh (i) a pebble; (ii) a large stone on every set of compression scales you can find. Which gives the best approximation? (Be careful not to overstrain fragile scales intended to weigh light objects.)

(d) In what units would you measure (i) the area of your hand; (ii) your total skin area? Study the physiological tables to compare the degree of accuracy given. Is this realistic?

(e) Find two ways of timing a pendulum. Which gives a more accurate result?

V. Averages

When pupils find an average they should understand the purpose. For example, it is important to know that the average height of 15 year olds has increased by 5 cm during the past 20 years—but it is difficult to justify finding the average height of the pupils in a class.
It is often useful to take the average of a variety of experimental readings.

(a) Find the length of your normal pace. Try taking a different number of paces each time e.g. distance covered in 5, 10, 20, 50 paces. Compare the answers. Which do you think is the most reliable answer? How long did you take to get into your stride?

(b) Find the approximate mass of a litre of water. Try this on several scales and find the average.

(c) Find the time taken to walk 25 metres. Repeat this five times in all. What is your average time to cover this distance?
Would this give you a reliable estimate of your time to cover 100 metres? 1 kilometre? Check this.

VI. Fractions

(Material for each group: balance scales, 8 identical clear glasses or jam jars, 2 lengths of ribbon or string, 1 jug of water, 1 cup of beans, 1 cup of cubes, a lump of plasticine, several sheets of paper.)

1. Find (i) one half, (ii) one quarter, (iii) three quarters — of everything on the table.
   Could you have done these experiments in other ways?

2. Using Cuisenaire or Colour Factor find as many equivalents to one half, one quarter and three quarters as you can.
   Using equivalent fractions, or paper folding, find (i) $3\frac{1}{4} - 1\frac{1}{2}$
   (ii) $4\frac{1}{4} - 1\frac{3}{4} - \frac{1}{8}$
   Will fractions more complicated than these be encountered at the primary stage?

3. Find (i) the thickness of a sheet of paper; (ii) the weight of a single drawing pin using two different methods for each. Compare your results.

4. How would you introduce children to multiplication of fractions using area of rectangles?

5. Without using the rule for division of fractions find
   (i) How many $1\frac{1}{2}$cm lengths can be cut from 7cm?
   from 13cm?
   from $13\frac{1}{2}$cm?
   from $13\frac{1}{4}$cm?
   (ii) Use the rule on the first example. How can you reconcile the two answers?
   (iii) At the secondary stage the 'rule' can be discovered once pupils are familiar with division as the inverse of multiplication.

$3 \times \square = 1$

$\frac{1}{4} \times \square = 1$

$\frac{2}{3} \times \square = \frac{1}{2}$

The multiplicative inverse of 3 is .... or the reciprocal of 3 is .... the reciprocal of $\frac{1}{4}$ is ....

and

$3 \times \frac{1}{3} = \square \qquad \frac{2}{3} \times \frac{3}{2} = \square$

$3 \div 3 = \square \qquad \frac{2}{3} \div \frac{2}{3} = \square$

$\div\ 3$ is equivalent to $\times\ \frac{1}{3}$, $\div\ \frac{2}{3}$ is equivalent to $\times\ \frac{3}{2}$

VII. Scale (and ratio)

(a) Cut your height and reach in string or paper. (Use a different colour for each.) Using string or paper strips make 'models' of yourself with arms outstretched:
(i) full size (ii) half size (iii) quarter size.
If you could make three-dimensional models of yourself what do you think your weight and your foot area would be in each case?

(b) Use an AA map to find the distance between your home town or city and another city. Use two methods and compare the answers. Compare the areas of your home county and that of another county. How do the corresponding perimeters compare?

(c) In metric units the equator is about 40,000 kilometres in length. Use this fact to help you to find the global distances between London and Singapore, Hong Kong, Sydney, Peking, Moscow, San Francisco. Can you find any major cities (i) 5,000 km (ii) 10,000 km from London?
Make a ready reckoner graph to help you to determine global distances quickly from the 'string' distances.

(d) Make a careful estimate, without actual measurement, of the number of small cylinders required to fill a large cylinder. Experiment to find how near your estimate was.

(e) Compare (i) 2 balls (ii) 2 discs of different sizes in as many ways as you can. Discuss your results. (iii) How many marbles would occupy the same volume as the small ball? Estimate then check.
For a more detailed approach, see Patterns in Shapes, pp. 142–3.

VIII. Idea of a variable

Mathematics is concerned with likenesses and differences. This is true of the various aspects of measurement too.

Some 10 year olds were comparing the size of their feet. One boy put a piece of string around his foot and cut a length equal to the perimeter. He made this into a square and found the area of the square. Would this give him the area of his foot?

Try this experiment with your own foot. Is the area of the square the same as (approximately equal to) the area of your foot?

When the perimeter of a shape is fixed does the area enclosed remain the same or does it vary? Try making any shapes you like.

Patterns (or relations)

1. Suppose the perimeter of your foot is 20 units. (See Patterns in Statistics, No. 5, p. 131.)
   (a) Make a table showing the width and length of the set of rectangles of perimeter 20 units with edges a whole number of units.

	Width	Length	Area
Put the widths in order. Can you find a pattern?			

   Cut out all these rectangles using (2 cm) squared graph paper.
   Enter the area in each rectangle.
   Arrange them in order of width.
   What do you find?
   What else is in order?
   What do you notice about the areas?
   What do you find when you push the rectangles together so that they overlap?
   What is the pattern?
   Which are the smallest, largest rectangles?

   (b) What is the pattern of the areas?
   Represent your results in any way which interests you.
   Find the algebraic relation between (i) width and length (ii) width and area.
   Draw the graphs and comment on these.

2. Suppose you fix the area of a shape would its perimeter be the same for all shapes? Experiment to see:

   Take a small number of identical squares, make any shapes with these (no overlap —squares to touch one another in at least one point).
   Does the perimeter change?

   When you work to a pattern is there a pattern of perimeters?

3. Make a table showing the width and length of the set of rectangles of area 36 squares with edges a whole number of units.
   Put the widths in order
   Can you find a pattern?

   Cut all the rectangles using (2 cm) squared paper.
   Arrange these in order of width.
   What do you find?

   What do you find when you push the rectangles together so that they overlap?
   Is there a pattern?

   Draw graphs showing the relation between
   (1) the width and length
   (2) the width and perimeter.
   What do the graphs tell you?

   Find the algebraic relation between
   (1) the width and length
   (2) the width and perimeter.

4. Extend both (1) and (2) to three dimensions and investigate the problems.
5. Investigate areas of triangles with fixed perimeter.
6. Discuss the variables of a set of cylinders. (i) Investigate by fixing one variable at a time. (ii) Make two identical sheets of paper into two different hollow cylinders. How are the two cylinders alike? How are they different?
7. (i) Make a set of cones. What are the variables?
   Investigate by fixing one variable at a time.
   (ii) Make a set of cones from identical circles and investigate the variables and the relationships between the variables.
8. Make a rain gauge using a tin about 10 cm in diameter with a funnel to fit. Graduate a bottle of much smaller cross section for use with the rain gauge.
9. Make a pendulum and experiment to find out in how many ways you can change its beat.
   Identify the variables. Do graphs tell you anything more?
10. Identify the variables when you let a truck or marble run down a ramp from rest.

Patterns in Number

In session 5, operations are studied using environmental materials. See Chapter 3, pp. 22–4.

(a) This session is normally introduced by means of the following activity: Each group requires a large sample of butter beans (or small shells). As a group, count the total number of objects on the table, organise the collection so that the total number of objects can be seen at a glance. Assume that adults cannot recognise more than five objects at a glance, unless the collection is patterned. You should have at least 200 beans. Compare your arrangement with that of other groups. Each member takes a sample from the pile, and divides the sample by 2. Use 10 different samples, replacing the former sample each time, and record each time whether you have a remainder or not.

Group leaders are asked to collect the totals from their groups, to check and to enter results on the blackboard.

R 0	R 1
✓	✓
	✓
	✓

etc.

Repeat, this time dividing 10 different samples by 3 each time.
Record results.
Repeat, dividing each of the different samples by 4.

Leaders collect, check and enter totals.

R 0	R 1	R 2
	✓	
	✓	
✓		✓

etc.

With a large number of samples, what are the chances of getting a remainder when dividing by 2? .... by 3? ... by 4? ....
How near were the experimental results?
With what age of children might this prove useful?

(b) Number knowledge.
What should we aim at? How should we record each child's progress?

In order to summarise number facts, teachers are asked to complete addition and multiplication tables for the numbers 1 to 10 (taken in pairs). For an outline, see Chapter 3, pp. 11(ii) and 24.

Each pair is then asked to throw two dice (e.g. for 5 minutes), adding and recording the score on each pair at each throw:

The total scores for every pair on the course are then obtained and entered for all possible scores 2, 3, 4, 5, 6, 7, 8, 9, 10, 11, 12.

From the addition table, teachers are then asked to mark off the section containing the numbers 1 to 6 and to record how many times each number occurs in this table.
e.g. 7 occurs 6 times out of the total of 36 entries, so that in a large sample, we might expect a total of 7 to turn up about $\frac{6}{36}$ or $\frac{1}{6}$ of the total number of throws. The experimental results are then compared with the theoretical results for each number. The addition and multiplication tables are then studied to determine the minimum number of facts children need to know.

Chapter 3, p. 11 and 24, Chapter 4, pp. 28–30.

In session 6 our written number system is studied.

Practical activities include work with Dienes's multibase arithmetic blocks, with an abacus and discs to fit and with a collection of beans or shells.

Chapter 4, pp. 31–34.

In session 7, ways of helping children to devise their own methods for written calculations in the four operations are discussed.

Chapter 4, pp. 28, 34–36.

The multiplication square affords many opportunities for the discovery of mathematical relationships as the next assignment shows.

Using square centimetre paper make a table square for the numbers 1 to 24 (see below).

With a pencil shade in all squares containing 24.

Could you draw a curve through these?

Can you explain why this happens?

What relation does this represent?

What other patterns can you find?

24
⋮
20 ....
19 ....
18 ....
17 ....
16 ....
15 ....
14 ....
13 ....
12 ....
11 ....
10 ....
9 ....
8 ....
7 ....
6 ....
5 10 ....
4 8 ....
3 6 9 12 15 ....
2 4 6 8 10 ....
1 2 3 4 5 6 7 8 9 10 11 12 24

It is interesting to extend this to three dimensions using centimetre squares of balsa wood (e.g. 1 mm or 2 mm thick) cardboard of uniform thickness or interlocking cubes. For example, on the bottom row, beginning at the left hand side, place 1 square on 1, 2 squares (one on top of the other) on 2, 3 squares on 3 and so on. The resulting shape resembles that used in the modern construction of the roofs of some school halls, churches and other buildings.

Properties of the number system

The set of natural numbers or counting numbers

1, 2, 3, 4, ⟶

This set of numbers can be generated by addition

1, 1+1, 1+1+1, 1+1+1+1 ⟶

What do you notice when we add, subtract, multiply and divide two natural numbers? Try with 8 and 4, 6 and 2, 7 and 3:

8+4=.... 8−4=.... 8×4=.... 8÷4=....
6+2=.... 6−2=.... 6×2=.... 6÷2=....
7+3=.... 7−3=.... 7×3=.... 7÷3=....

For which of these operations will the answers ALWAYS be natural numbers?

Addition.... Subtraction....
Multiplication.... Division ....

Extensions of the number system

Subtraction. You may find it helpful to use a number line for examples such as:

7−5=2

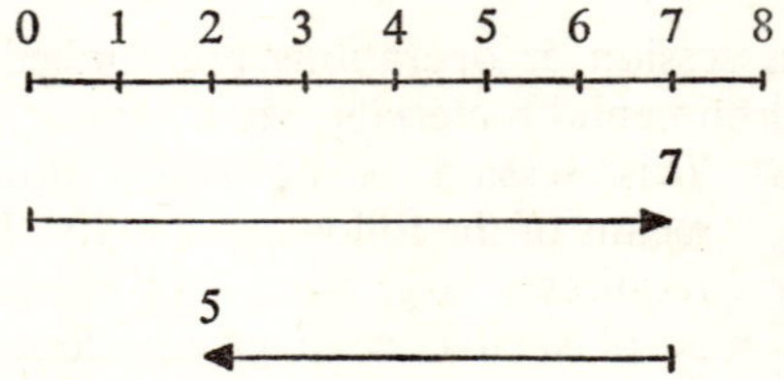

5 −7=?

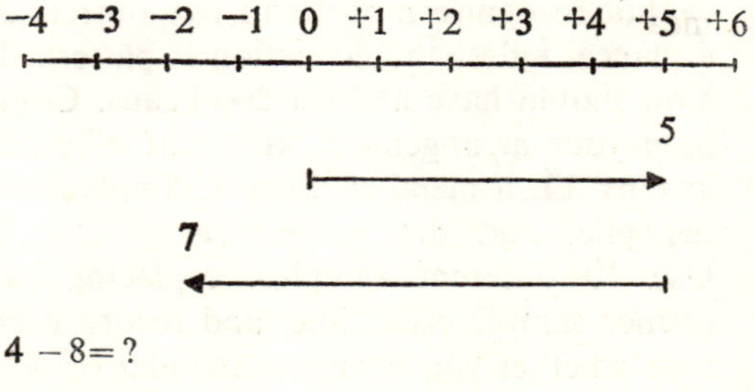

4 −8=?

Using the lower extended number line we find that $5-7=-2$

We have extended our system of natural numbers (or positive integers) to include the negative integers.

It is helpful to mark points on the number line with raised signs, e.g. $^{+}5$, $^{-}2$. Can you see why?

Division

$8 \div 4 = 2$ (that number which multiplied by 4 gives 8)

$4 \div 8 = \frac{1}{2}$ (that number which multiplied by 8 gives 4—there are 8 halves in 4)

$6 \div 2 = 3$

$2 \div 6 = \frac{1}{3}$

$7 \div 3 = \frac{7}{3}$

$3 \div 7 = \frac{7}{3}$

We have now extended the number system to include the fractions (ratio of two integers or rational numbers). Fractions can be assigned position on the number line.

Patterns in Shapes

SORTING, MATCHING, SHAPE RECOGNITION, CLASSIFICATION

Each teacher is asked to bring a container.

1. Working in pairs:

   How are your containers alike?

   How are they different?

   Working as a group of eight, draw on a sheet of paper a large square, a large rectangle and a large circle.

   Sort your containers into these three sets.

   Do any containers not belong to any of these sets?

   How can young children sort out all the cubes, giving a reason?

   How do they test for squares?

2. Working as a group of four, place your collection on a sheet of paper and sort the containers in different ways.

   Use coloured loops of string to help you and describe each region of the paper as you add each loop.

3. (i) Working as a group of four, use containers to make a model such as a child might make. Use adhesive as necessary. Paint the model to make it attractive. Describe the shapes used.

   (ii) If children first cover the model with newspaper (which they cut to fit and paste on the model) what do they learn about shapes and area?

   (iii) Make a rough sketch of the ground plan you see when looking down on the model from above. List the vocabulary you would introduce.

4. Children often need to find the centre of a tin lid to act as a wheel.

   How could they do this?

5. Cut a cuboid container so that you obtain its net.

   What equivalencies do you discover?

   Use squared paper to cut out the net of a closed cube. Find several ways of doing this.

   Are the perimeters of your net always the same?

COMPARISON

1. Working as a group of four arrange the containers in order of size in as many ways as you can. How might these situations arise in the classroom?

2. Using any two (or more) of the containers devise questions which would necessitate the use of each of the four operations ($+ - \times \div$) in turn. Can you devise situations which would arise naturally in the environment?

3. Are any two containers of different shapes but of the same capacity? the same weight? the same area?

APPROXIMATION, AVERAGES

1. Devise a practical method of finding

   (i) the average capacity, (ii) the average height, of the 4 containers. Can you think of a practical use for either of these averages?

I. Properties of Shapes—Congruence—Symmetry

1. Without using a ruler find the centres of a rectangular sheet of paper, a circular filter paper, a regular triangle, an irregular triangle. Try to find the centre of any geometrical shapes, regular or irregular, which interest you.

   Comment on your findings.

2. Take several identical sheets of paper. Fold each in half by a single fold, using a different method each time. Show that you are right (i) by folding, (ii) by cutting.

   What is common to all the folds?

   How many different ways are there of folding a rectangular piece of paper in half?

   Which mathematical ideas will this experience help children to understand?

3. Cut a rectangular sheet of paper in half along the diagonal.

   What do you have to do to show that the two pieces are identical?

   Using both pieces make as many shapes as you can with adjacent edges matching. What properties do you discover about angles, edges, diagonals and areas of the shapes you make?

4. Cut a sheet of paper in four along the two diagonals.

   How are the four pieces you have cut the same?

   How are they different?

5. Fold separate sheets of paper:

   (i) in half by a single fold

   (ii) in quarters by two folds

   (iii) in four longways like a concertina.

   Experiment with (i) and (ii) using a single straight cut across the fold(s) each time and describe the different geometrical shapes you obtain. Make a list of your discoveries, including the number of times you can fit the shape back into the hole in the paper.

   In (iii) cut through the layers to make a pattern.

   Discuss the repeating patterns you have made in these experiments.

   The three ways of making a repeating pattern are:

   (i) by reflection about an axis, as in a mirror

   (ii) by rotation, as in letters N and S

   (iii) by shifting or translation.

6. Use stiff card in two colours to cut out

   (i) a set of 12 identical regular triangles

   (ii) a set of 12 identical scalene triangles (all edges different lengths).

   Use each set to make a tiling pattern, adjacent edges matching. What angle properties can you discover?

   (iii) Use two of the scalene triangles to make all the shapes you can, adjacent edges matching. What do you discover?

II. Enlargement and Reduction—Scale—Mathematical Similarity

Of all topics concerned with shape this occurs most frequently and is very important.

Normally problems which involve enlargement arise in aspects of the curriculum other than mathematics—particularly in biology, physics and engineering, geography. The mathematical background is important if solutions to the problems which arise are to be found. Once such a problem has arisen, the topic of scale needs to be pursued in mathematics until pupils have a thorough understanding of the principles.

Examples of questions which have been asked are:

1. Why does a mouse eat for most of the day whereas a human adult eats only three or four times a day? Some ten-year-olds asked this question as a result of their records of the average daily food weight/body weight ratio of classroom pets: mice and guinea pigs. They extended their study to human babies, ten-year-old children and adults. It was the teacher's suggestion that the children should study the enlargement of 3D mathematical shapes. See pp. 63-66.

2. In 1962, when we had a very severe winter, mothers were warned not to take babies out of doors. Why was this?

3. Why has a baby who is burnt or scalded less chance of survival than an adult?

4. Why do large animals such as elephants have feet out of proportion to their length when compared with smaller animals such as the hippopotamus?

5. Engineers cannot make a scale model of a bridge, to test its strength, in the same material as the proposed bridge. Why?

Activities

1. Take a large handful of identical unit squares.
   (i) Without counting these make the largest square you can.
   (ii) Develop strategies which enable you to build patterns of squares of increasing size. What pattern is formed by the number of squares added each time?
   How many different strategies can you devise?
   (iii) Make a set of squares of edges 1, 2, 3, → 6 units
   Fill in the table:

Length of edges (units)	0	1	2	3	4	5	6
Perimeter (units)							
Area (square units)							

What happens to the perimeter when you double the edge?

What do you notice about
(i) the number patterns?
(ii) representation of these patterns by block graphs?

2. (i) Take a double handful of cubes. Without counting these make the largest cube you can. Develop strategies which enable you to build cubes of increasing size. What pattern is formed by the number of cubes added each time?
   (ii) Make a set of cubes of edges 1, 2, 3, 4 units
   Fill in the table:

Length of edges (units)	0	1	2	3	4	5	6		n−1	n	n+1
Area of base											
Skin area											
Volume											
Skin area/volume											

(i) What do you notice about the number patterns?

Represent the patterns in any way and comment on these. What happens (a) to the base area; (b) to the volume (and therefore to the weight), when the edge is doubled? (Does this explain the elephant's overlarge feet?)

(ii) What happens to the $\frac{\text{skin area}}{\text{volume}}$ rate when the edge is doubled? trebled? What relation is this?

What is the graph of the edge, $\frac{\text{skin area}}{\text{volume}}$ rate?

Compare the rates at edge 2 and edge 6. Does this explain why a baby of length 2 ft is more vulnerable in extremely cold weather than a man of height 6 ft?

3. Logiblocks. Find all the relations you can between the small shapes and the corresponding large shapes.

What have the pairs in common?

How can you check the perimeter and area relations for the circular discs?

4. Enlarge the "2" Cuisenaire or Colour Factor rod, making a sequence as for cubes.

When is the skin area numerically the same as the volume?

Repeat using the 3, 4 . . . rods. Generalise.

5. Which of the following shapes are *always* mathematically similar?

cubes, cuboids, cylinders, spheres, cones, pyramids.

If in doubt, experiment to find out. Under what circumstances would those shapes which are not similar fulfil this condition? Which two-dimensional shapes are always similar?

6. Fold a sheet of paper in half. Is the new rectangle mathematically similar to (the same shape as) the original? Fold in half again. Is this rectangle similar to the first? Repeat again and again, stating each time whether the new rectangle is similar to the original sheet of paper.

Complete the table, and make a graph of the results. What kind of relation is this?

Number of folded rectangles	Area as fraction of original rectangle
1	1
2	.
4	.
8	.
.	.
.	.

How far can you continue this?

7. Continue the following sequence in both directions:

$\longleftarrow$ 2 4 8 16 $\longrightarrow$

Is there an upper limit? a lower limit?

What connection has this sequence with the former question?

Where else have you met this sequence?

8. Make the largest square you can from a rectangular sheet of paper, by folding only. Cut off the spare piece. Press the fold firmly.

What shape have you now? Describe it in detail.

Fold in half again. What is the new shape?

Can you give a mathematical reason for your answer?

As you continue to fold, what is the sequence of the areas of the triangles you make (as a fraction of the original square)?

What will happen ultimately?

Unfold the paper and cut the original square along the diagonal. Using the two triangles make a triangle of the same shape. Join with a partner to see if you can make a similar triangle using the four triangular pieces.

How far can you continue this?

Colour the folds (or the unit triangles) on one piece and see what area and length relations you can discover.

9. Take a large square of plain paper and find the midpoints of the edges by folding. Join consecutive midpoints by folding (or by straight lines). Continue this process for the second square.

What patterns can you find from the sequence of edge lengths and areas of consecutive squares? Continue as far as you can. Why did you have to stop?

Can you reverse the process to obtain successively larger squares?

Are all squares mathematically similar?

Colour to make the patterns visible and attractive.

BRIEF SUMMARY OF MATHEMATICAL BACKGROUND TO THIS APPENDIX

I. Transformation
(Change of position and shape)

1. Congruence and symmetry—repeating patterns. Study these from scraps of textiles to find varieties. Use a mirror (and two hinged mirrors) to help you.
2. Mathematical similarity (enlargement) e.g. sequence of cubes and squares, volume and area relations: cube and square numbers.

II. Limits

Many examples in this section can be used to focus attention on the idea of a mathematical limit. Graphs will help.

e.g.

1. Rectangles of area 36 square centimetres: 1 by 36, 2 by 18, etc. $\frac{1}{2}$ by ? $\frac{1}{4}$ by ? $\frac{1}{10}$ by ? Children sometimes point out that the rectangles will become narrower than tracing paper but will never disappear.
2. Apply the idea of a limit to the area contained in a perimeter of 20 units, areas of sets of triangles with perimeter 24 units, sets of regular polygons with perimeter 20 units and an increasing number of edges.
3. Vanishing squares. See above.

4. Number sequences e.g. Extend these sequences in both directions:

←— 2 4 8 16 32 —→
←— 10 100 1000 10 000 —→

Is there a lower limit? An upper limit?

III. Proportion

1. DIRECT e.g. Length of edges of squares

0 1 2 3 4 —→ n

Perimeter of squares

0 4 8 12 16 —→ 4n

$P = 4n$

Do you recognise the graph?

All multiplication tables are examples of direct proportion also.

Ready reckoner —tables
—graphs

e.g. petrol gauges at garages
train fares
(Contrast bulk buying)
Algebraic relationship $y = 4x$, etc.

or $\frac{y}{x} = 4$, etc.

2. INVERSE e.g. width/length relation of the set of rectangles with area 36 cm^2

W	1	2	3	4
L	36	18	12	9, etc.

Do you recognise the relation? $xy = 36$.

Do you recognise the graph?

Other examples: Paper folding: number of thicknesses, area; Skin/Area/Volume and edge relation (cubes); Regular polygons; number of edges, centre angle. See also operation table for multiplication.

Appendix 4 SORTING, CLASSIFICATION AND SETS

Sets are best introduced, in the first instance as 'families'. (For example, the set of creatures with eight legs, the set of creatures able to live on land or in the water.)

The idea of a set is fundamental in mathematics and some teachers think its early introduction can be helpful. It is therefore included here so that teachers may decide for themselves whether the idea of a set would be of value to their children or not. Here are examples given to teachers on follow-up mathematics courses.

Work with a partner for questions 1 to 4.

1. Arrange 4 objects from your pocket or handbag on a sheet of paper (in order to define your 'universal' set).

   Use a loop of string to divide these objects into 2 subsets. Describe these. Could you divide the 4 objects into 2 subsets in a different way?

2. Use identical plastic squares (edges about 2·5 cm) each with one of the numerals 0, 1, 2 → 9. Place these on a sheet of paper and sort the numerals in as many ways as you can. Use loops of coloured string to enclose each sub-set (e.g. the sub-set of even numbers. There is no need to enclose the sub-set of odd numbers in another loop. Where does 0 belong?). What can you say about the set of multiples of 4? As your sorting becomes more complex, describe each region of your paper carefully.

   Extend your set to include the numbers 0, 1 to 16 inclusive.

3. What can you say about the numbers in this set? (Fig. 1).

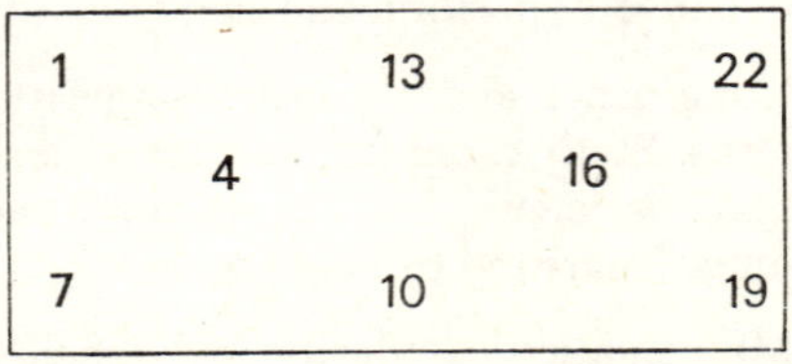

Fig. 1

Divide these numbers into 2 sub-sets in several ways.

Illustrate your answers in more than one way, e.g. (Fig. 2).

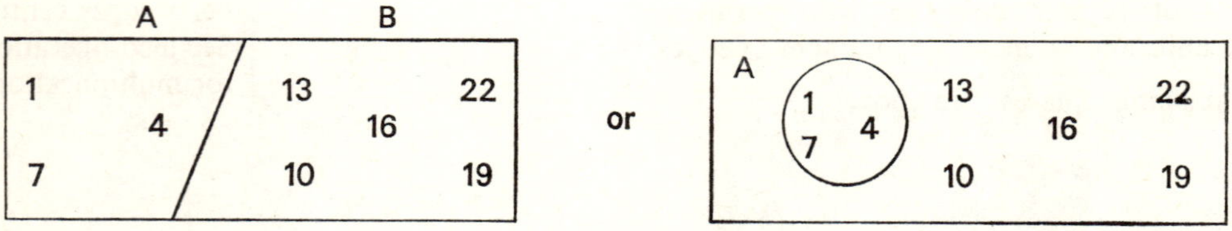

Fig. 2

Set A is . . .

Set B is . . .

4. Find 4 sorts of 'sameness' each of which allows you to separate these numbers into two sets.

Can you use different sorts of 'sameness' at the same time?

Describe each sub-set carefully.

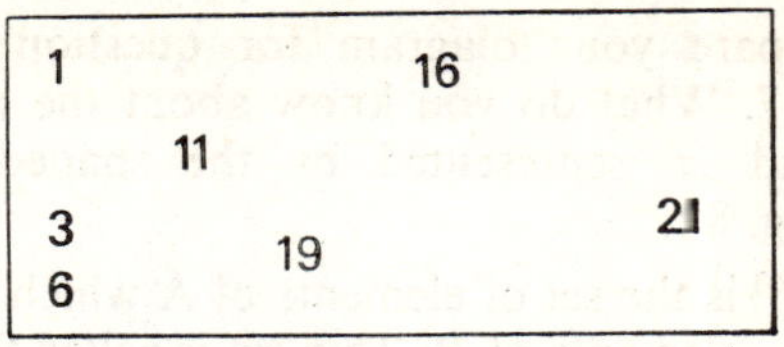

Fig. 3

5. What have the numbers in each loop in common?

What is the same about the numbers in the overlap?

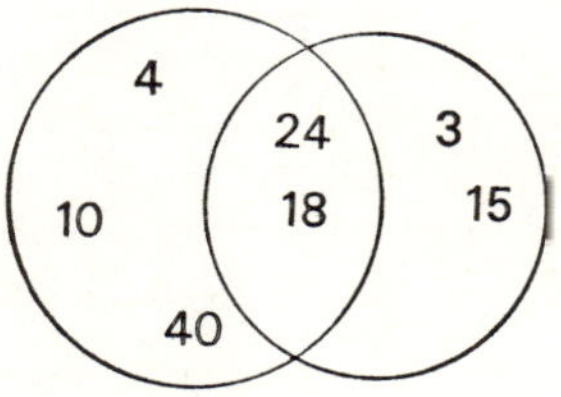

Fig. 4

6. In this diagram the 'universal' set (often called E from "ensemble", French for set) is the set of people at this course.

M is the set of men.

G is the set of people wearing glasses.

What does the shaded region represent?

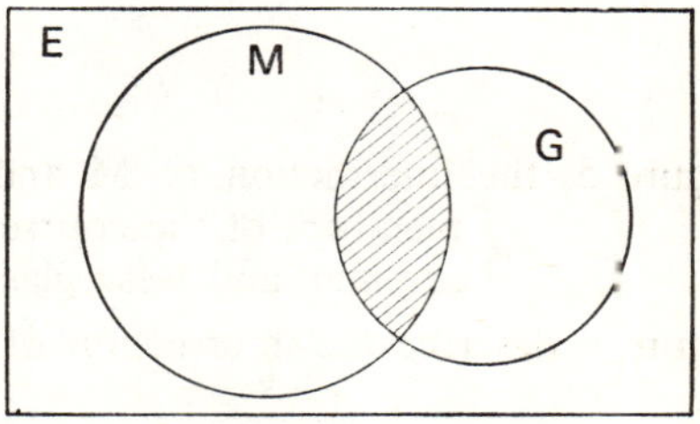

Fig. 5

7. Draw a diagram to show the universal set of whole numbers less than 17, the sub-set A of the multiples of 4 and the sub-set B of the squares of the whole numbers.

8. In the diagram:

E = (members of this course)

C = (cigarette smokers)

P = (pipe smokers)

What does the shaded region represent?

Which part of the diagram represents the non-smokers?

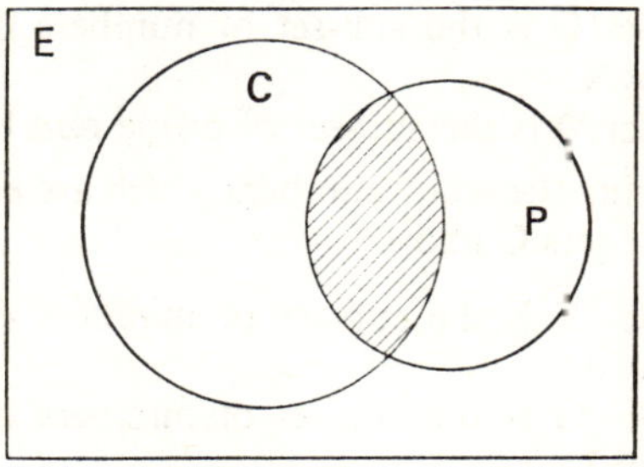

Fig. 6

Compare your diagram for question 7 with Fig. 7. What do you know about the numbers 4 and 16 represented by the shaded region in Fig. 8?

{4,16} is the set of elements of A which are also elements of B. This set is called the intersection of A and B since its elements belong to A *and* B.

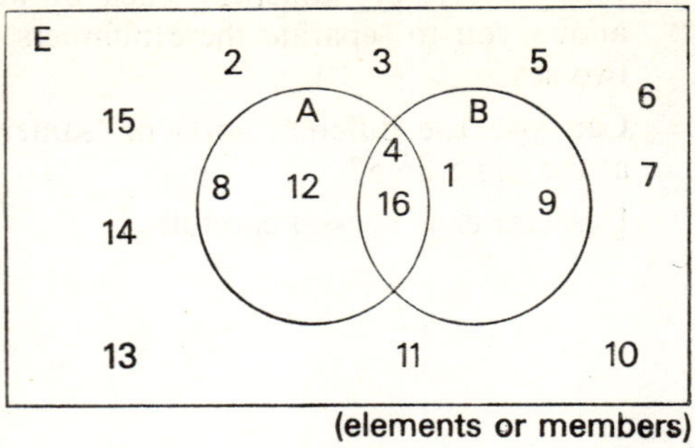

Fig. 7

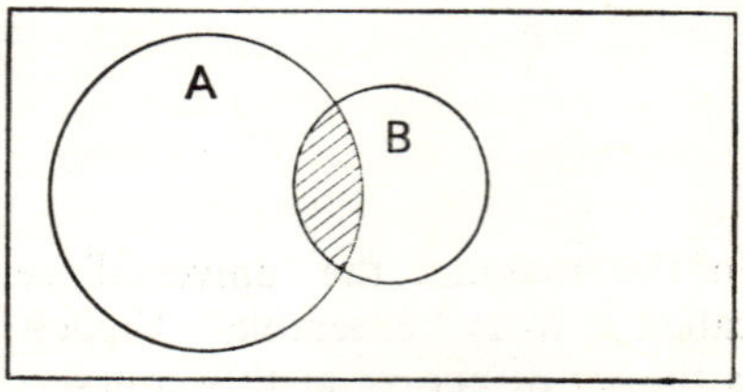

Fig. 8

In Figure 5, the intersection of M and G = {members of the course who are men and wear glasses}

In Figure 6 describe the intersection of sets C and P.

In many textbooks you will find this written $C \cap P$ (belonging to C *and* P).

The universal set is the set of whole numbers 20 to 40 inclusive in questions 9 to 11.

9. Set A is the sub-set of even numbers
   Set B is the sub-set of square numbers

   Find the set of numbers which are elements of set A and of set B.

10. Set C is the sub-set of numbers divisible by 4
    Set D is the sub-set of prime numbers.

    Find the set of numbers which are elements of sets C and D.

11. Set F is the sub-set of numbers divisible by 5
    Set G is the sub-set of numbers divisible by 3

    Find the intersection of F and G.

12. On a graph sketch the set F of points satisfying $x = 3$ and the set G of points satisfying $y = 4$. Find the intersection of set F and set G.

13. On a graph sketch the set A of points satisfying $x = 4$ and the set B of points satisfying $y = x + 2$. Find the intersection of set A and set B.

14. If set C is the set of points satisfying $y = 2x - 3$ and set D is the set of points satisfying $y = 3 - 2x$ find the intersection of set C and set D.

15. If set F is the set of points satisfying $y = x^2$ and set G is the set of points satisfying $y = x(10 - x)$ find the intersection of set F and set G.
Illustrate.

SUMMARY

Shade in the regions, if any, that represent the intersections of:

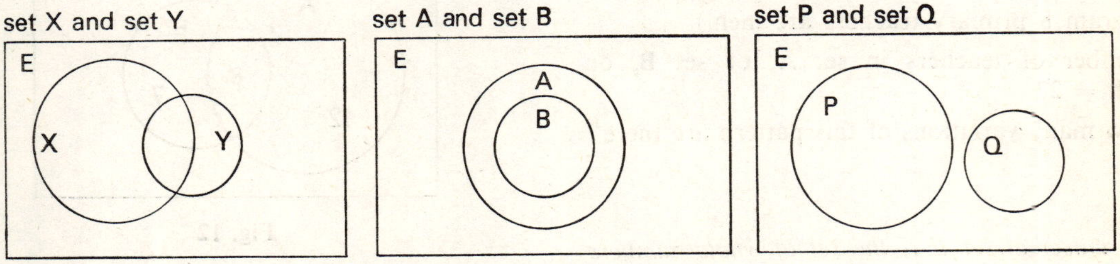

Fig. 9

THE UNION OF SETS

At a teachers' course (universal set E) 15 of the teachers work in primary schools and 20 teachers are men.

Set A is the set of 20 men. Set B is the set of 15 primary teachers.

How many teachers are there altogether? Can we be sure?

How many possibilities are there altogether?

The solution of this problem involves the second way of combining sets: the *union* of sets.

(1)

The 15 primary teachers are all women.

(Set A and set B are disjoint sets.)
Number of teachers in set A or set B = 35.

(cf. the addition of 2 disjoint sets with 20 and 15 elements respectively)

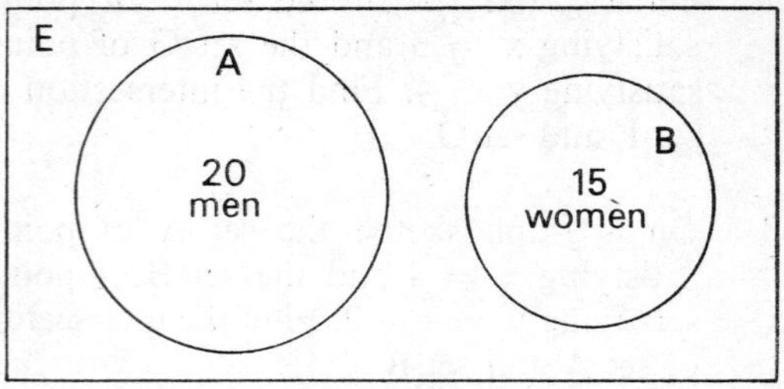

Fig. 10

(2)

The 15 primary teachers are all men.

B is a sub-set of A

Number of teachers = 20

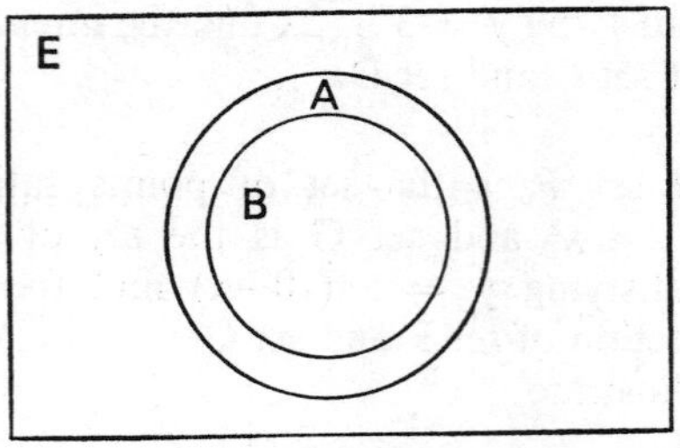

Fig. 11

(3)

Some of the primary teachers are men. (In the diagram 8 primary teachers are men.)

Number of teachers in set A, or set B, or both = 27

How many variations of this pattern are there?

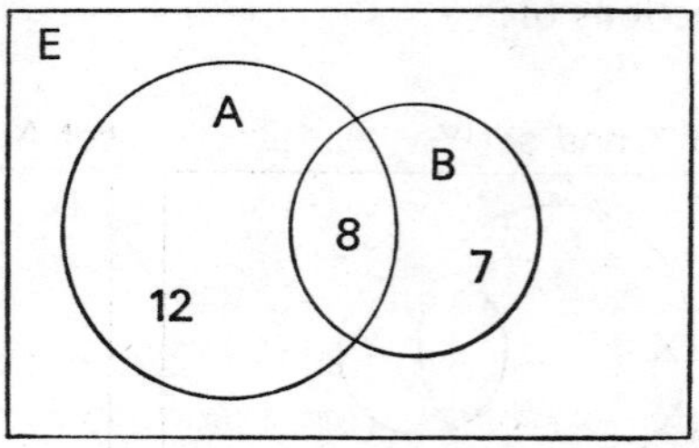

Fig. 12

The universal set E is the set of whole numbers 1 to 100 inclusive in examples 16 to 19. (Use a *100* square for this.)

16. A is the sub-set of even whole numbers less than 20
B is the sub-set of square whole numbers less than 20
Set of numbers in set A or in set B or in both = ...
Set of numbers in set A *and* set B = ...

17. C is the sub-set of whole numbers less than 30 divisible by 5
D is the sub-set of whole numbers less than 30 divisible by 3
Set of numbers in set C or in set D or in both = ...
Set of numbers in set C *and* in set D = ...

18. F is the sub-set of even whole numbers between 90 and 100
G is the sub-set of odd whole numbers between 90 and 100

Set of numbers in set F or in set G or in both =

Set of numbers in set F *and* in set G =

19. M_2 is the sub-set of even numbers
M_4 is the sub-set of multiples of 4

$M_2 \cup M_4 =$ (i.e. find the set of numbers which belong to M_2 or to M_4 or to both)

20. Find the other interesting relationships concerning the union and intersection of sub-sets M_2, M_3 (multiples of 3), M_4, M_6 etc.

PUNCHED CARDS

21. You will need a group of at least 10 people for this.

Give each person a card punched with 6 holes (Fig. 13).

Clip the righthand top corner so that all cards can be collected facing the same way.

Decide on 6 pieces of information you wish to collect from each member of the group.

If you possess the first characteristic, cut away the part above the hole so that the card will drop out when a knitting needle is pushed through (Fig. 14).

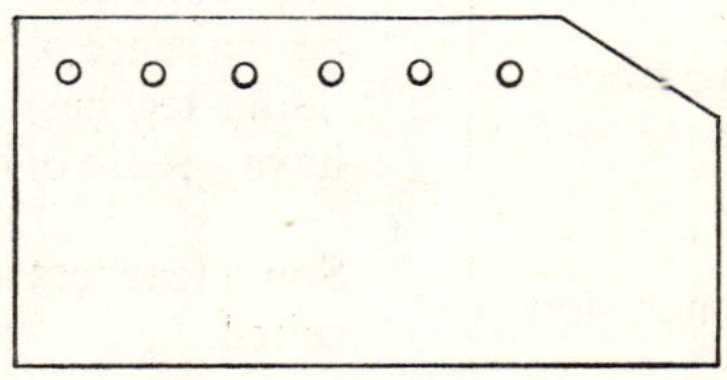

Fig. 13

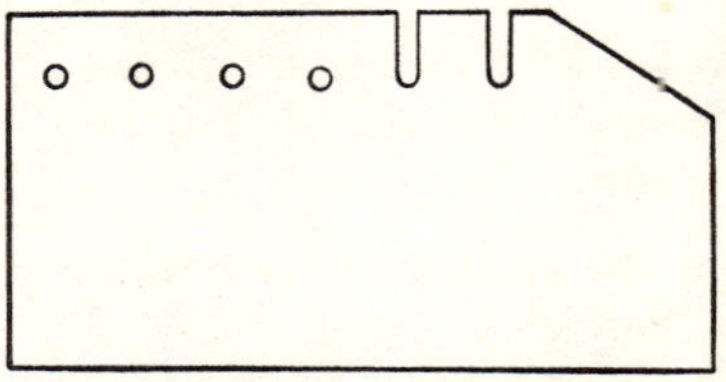

Fig. 14

Suggestions for information:

1. Married or single
2. Male or female
3. Non-smoker
4. Is over 25 years old
5. Is under 160 cm in height
6. Is wearing brown shoes.

Figure 14 represents a married man who smokes, is under 25, over 160 cm in height and is not wearing brown shoes!

Make up your own list of information and use a knitting needle to sort out the sub-set you require e.g. a single woman, non-smoker, etc.
Information collected by insurance companies (such as causes of fire) is often kept on a punched card system which can be sorted out by machine.

22. Would you believe a market investigator who reported that of 1,000 people 816 like sweets, 723 ice cream, 645 cake while 562 like both sweets and ice cream, 463 like sweets and cake, 470 like ice cream and cake while only 310 like all? A diagram may help!

23. Use diagrams to test the validity of the following arguments:

Hypothesis
1. No conceited people have a sense of humour
2. Some teachers do not have a sense of humour

Conclusion
Some teachers are conceited.

24. Hypothesis
1. All murders are immoral acts.
2. Some murders are justifiable.

Conclusion
Some immoral acts are justifiable.

ATTRIBUTE BLOCKS (or logical blocks)

Other sets of shapes could be used for sorting into sub-sets and for operations on these sub-sets. It is not essential to purchase Attribute blocks.

1. How many different variables (attributes) are there?
2. Find 2 blocks with
   a. *one* thing the same
   b. 2 samenesses and 2 differences
   c. 3 samenesses and 1 difference
   d. no one of the 4 attributes in common.
3. Use coloured loops of string to sort out a random collection of the blocks (placed on a sheet of paper). Describe each region of your paper carefully.
   At what stage would you introduce the ideas in this appendix to children? See Appendix 1 for further reading on this subject.

Appendix 5 DYNAMIC GEOMETRY OR THE GEOMETRY OF TRANSFORMATIONS

Symmetry

1. Experiment with boxes of various shapes with fitting lids and find out in how many ways you can replace the lids. Can you discover anything about the symmetries of the different shapes from your experiments?
2. Which capital letters, geometrical and other shapes can be cut from a piece of paper; (a) folded in two; (b) folded in four. In how many ways can you put the geometrical shapes back into their holes?
   Experiment using parallel folds of paper.
3. (a) Draw two intersecting lines. Use one mirror to see if you can get regular geometrical shapes by reflecting the two lines.
   (b) Make a kaleidoscope using *two mirrors*. What happens as the angle changes? Can you discover a relationship? Experiment using a single object—e.g. a pin with coloured head, and a line segment with an end on each mirror.
4. Fold over a corner of a piece of tracing paper. Draw and trace (or map) a shape. What do you discover about distances and angles?
   Movement in a plane without distortion can be brought about in three ways:
   (a) by reflection in an axis in the plane.
   (b) by rotation about an axis at right angles to the plane. Rotational symmetry is familiar in natural forms (e.g. flowers, snowflakes) and in man-made forms. This is sometimes called S symmetry. The angle of rotation is usually quite easily seen. If not, the basic shape can be traced and then rotated about a pin through the centre of symmetry until the basic shape coincides with the repetitions of this shape in turn.
   Investigate the symmetrical properties of an equilateral triangle, a rhombus, a parallelogram, a five-pointed star, a hexagon and the letters of the alphabet. Which shapes occur most frequently in nature?
   (c) by translation or movement sideways, upwards or both. Translation results in the familiar repeating patterns of wallpapers and textiles. What is the distance between each pattern? Is this the same in all wallpaper patterns?

The different types of transformation can be performed one after the other in a variety of ways. The interested reader may like to try the following transformation on a square.

A square is chosen here because it is the most familiar and the simplest of all geometrical shapes; probably this is the first plane shape which children recognise. The reader will find this section easier to follow if he cuts out a square and performs the prescribed operations on it, following the steps one by one. The angles at the vertices of the square are labelled 1, 2, 3, 4, in order; the same figures appear at each vertex on the front and back surface of the square. (Milk straws can be used for axes of symmetry, fixed between two identical squares of gummed paper.)

A square has, in all, five axes of symmetry as shown in Fig. 5.1. Four of these are in the

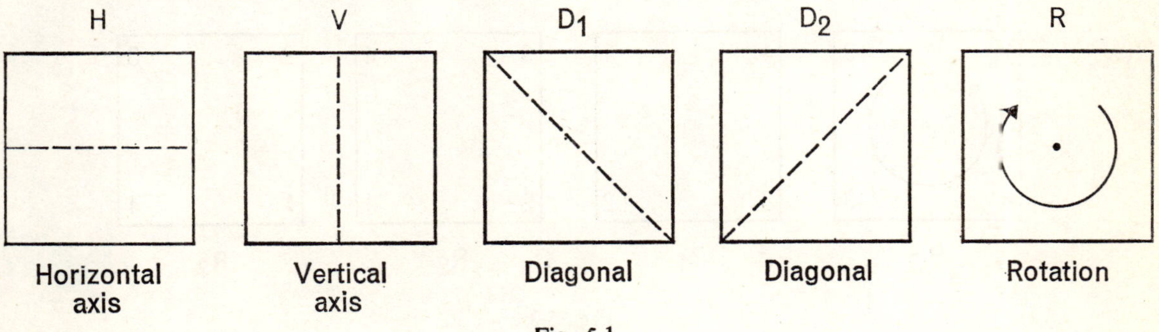

Fig. 5.1

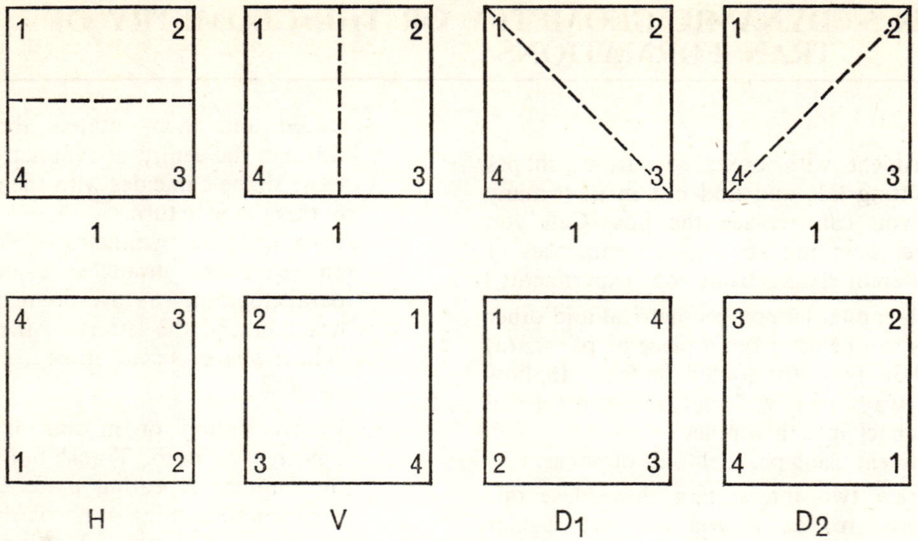

Fig. 5.2

plane of the square (shown by dotted lines), the fifth is perpendicular to the plane of the square through its centre.

1. Reflection, in this instance, is most easily obtained by rotation about the axis so that, in the subsequent position, the square has its underside uppermost. To check that the same result is obtained by reflection in the plane of the square, set up a double mirror along each axis in turn and examine the reflection on each side. In the first line of Figure 5.2 the square is in the original position (1) before reflection has taken place about the axis marked; the figures in the second line show the positions of the square after rotation about the various axes has taken place.

2. Rotation about the axis through the centre O through 1, 2, 3 right angles produces the figures shown which we have called R_0 (no rotation), R_1 (rotation through 1 right angle), R_2 (2 right angles), R_3 (3 right angles) (Fig. 5.3).

We include the following examples of operations on sets not only because of the symmetries revealed but as an illustration of the unity of different branches of mathematics.

1 We are going to find the effect of combining 2 of the sets of 4 rotations (R_0, R_1, R_2, R_3) performing these one after the other and entering the results in a table. Try this for yourself before you look at the table (Fig. 5.4). You may find it easier to discover a pattern in your table if you use a colour code instead of symbols and stick small squares of gummed coloured paper on your table.

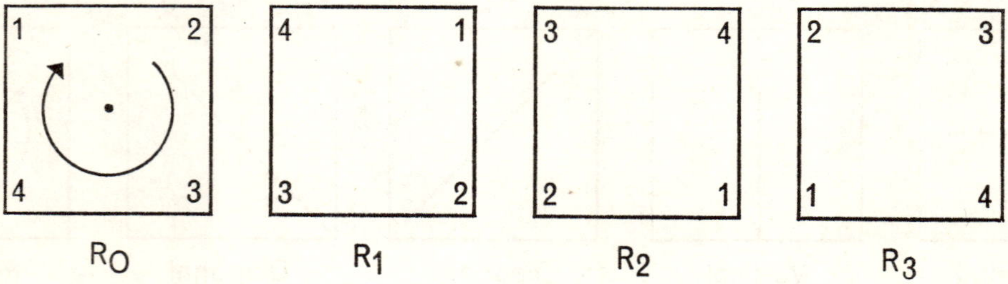

Fig. 5.3

Operations	*Code* 1	*Code* 2
No rotation	R_0	Red
rotation 90°	R_1	Yellow
rotation 180°	R_2	Blue
rotation 270°	R_3	Green

(This table can be extended to include the other types of transformation. Codes: H, V, D_1, D_2).

2 Next we are going to find the effect of combining two numbers of the set {0, 1, 2, 3}. Let the operation be 'Add two numbers of the set' and let us work in modulus 4 so that when the sum is 4 or more we divide by 4 and enter the remainder in the table (Fig. 5.5).

e.g. $3 + 2 = 5$
$5 \div 4$ gives remainder 1

Again if you use the original colour code you can compare the colour patterns of the two tables.
What do you notice about the patterns of the two tables?

3 Those who can brave an unfamiliar symbol (or who are familiar with the symbol) may like to make a table of operations for the set: (1, i, − 1, − i). This time the operation is multiplication. All you need to know is a definition of i^2.
$i^2 = -1$, therefore $-i^2 = ?$
Compare this third table with the other two using a colour code if preferred. Why is it that operations in geometry, arithmetic and algebra can lead to the same table? Modulus arithmetic is sometimes called clock arithmetic (Fig. 5.6). This may help you to discover why the first two tables resemble each other.

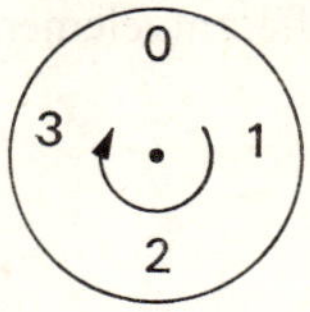

Fig. 5.6

Those with a knowledge of complex numbers in algebra will know why the third table resembles the other two.

These tables have the same structure. Test the truth of the following statements about the three 'sets' of four symbols on which you have been operating.

1 Any two of the set combine to form a third which is also a member of the set, e.g. R_1 then R_2 gives R_3; R_2 then R_1 gives ?

2 There is a neutral member (R_0, no rotation in 1, which leaves the position unchanged).

3 Each member has a unique inverse which combined with it gives the neutral member, e.g., R_1 is the inverse of R_3. R_2 is the inverse of ?

4 The associative law holds:

(R_1 then R_2) then R_3 = (R_3) then R_3 = R_2.
R_1 then (R_2 then R_3) = R_1 then (R_1) = R_2.
etc.

Second operation

First operation		R_0	R_1	R_2	R_3
	R_0	R_0	R_1	R_2	R_3
	R_1	R_1	R_2	R_3	R_0
	R_2	R_2	R_3	R_0	R_1
	R_3	R_3	R_0	R_1	R_2

Fig. 5.4

Second operation

First operation	+	0	1	2	3
	0	0	1	2	3
	1	1	2	3	0
	2	2	3	0	1
	3	3	0	1	2

Fig. 5.5

These four statements are the conditions that a set should form a *group*. The groups we have considered are also isomorphic because they have the same form (or pattern) despite their apparently different elements. If you extend your table to include the set (R_0, R_1, R_2, R_3, V, H, D_1, D_2) of transformations on the square test your results to see whether this set satisfies the conditions for a group.

Appendix 6 EQUALITIES AND INEQUALITIES

Children learn the language of inequality before they learn the language of equality e.g. more than taller than, shorter than, heavier than, lighter than, faster than, before as many as, as tall as, as heavy as or the same weight as.

The language of sets can be conveniently applied to graphical relationships. For example:

X=4 is a straight line containing the set A of points for which X=4. Y=3 is a straight line containing the set B of points for which Y=3. $A \cap B$ is the point where these straight lines intersect i.e. (4,3). Inequalities can also be represented graphically. For example,

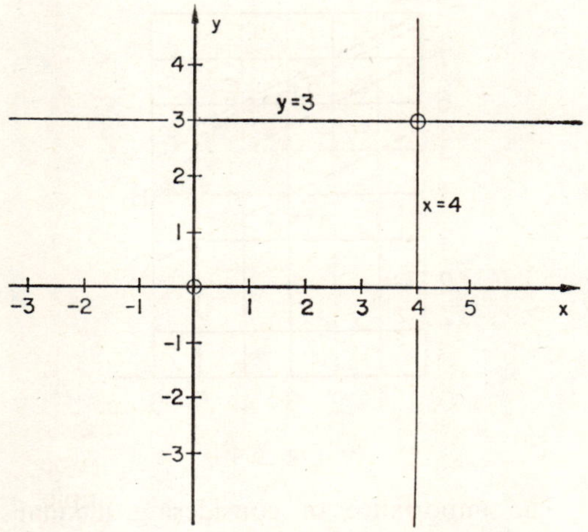

Fig. 6.1

$x + y = 10$ is a straight line containing the set of ordered pairs (x, y) such that $y = 10 - x$ (or the set of ordered pairs $(x, 10 - x)$).

$x + y < 10$ is the shaded area in Fig. 6.2 containing the set of ordered pairs (x, y) for which $y < 10 - x$.

(Why are points (x, y) called ordered pairs?)

These methods are sometimes used to give advice to industrial firms as the following example shows.

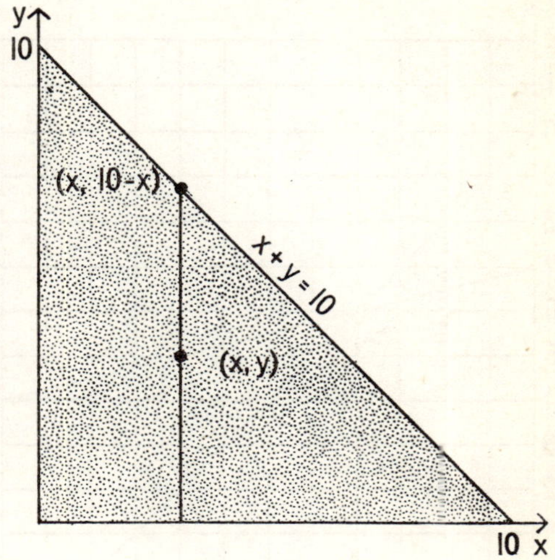

Fig. 6.2

Industrial problems are sometimes very complex and, once the conditions have been expressed algebraically, the problem is solved by computer. The method involves making one of the quantities as *large* as possible (e g. profit).

Problems appropriate (to linear programming) are those involving a large number of very simple conditions.

EXAMPLE

A firm manufactures two products marketed as: Baby Powder (P) and Blackboard Chalk (C).

(1) The total production capacity is 10 tons a day of both products together. The firm is under contract to make (2) at least 3 tons of Baby Powder every day and (3) at least 4 tons of Blackboard Chalk every day. (4) Each ton of Baby Powder requires 20 machine hours in production (for example 20 machines for one hour or 10 machines for two hours and so on). Each ton of Blackboard Chalk requires 80 machine hours in production. The number of men and machines available is such that not more than 560 machine hours can be worked each day. (5) The whole of the firm's output

can be sold. The profit on each ton of Baby Powder sold is £5 and the profit on each ton of Blackboard Chalk sold is £10.

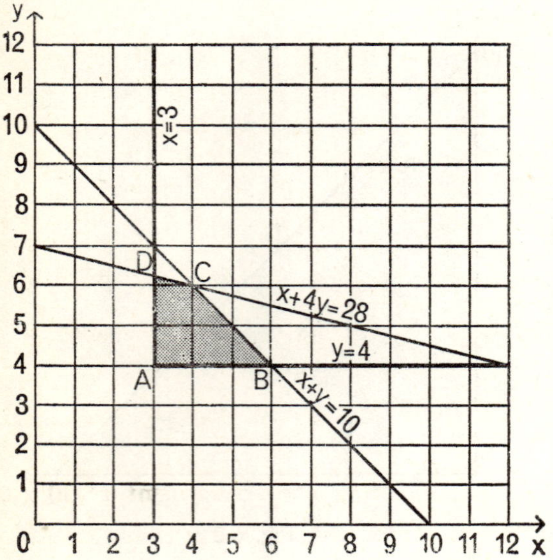

Fig. 6.3

Find how many tons of Baby Powder and how many tons of Blackboard Chalk the firm should make every day to obtain the greatest profit.

Each condition is expressed in algebraic terms. Let x be the number of tons of P and y the number of tons of C made each day. The conditions (1) to (5) are expressed:

(1) $x + y \leqq 10$ ($\leqq$ less than or equal to)
(2) $x \geqq 3$ ($\geqq$ greater than or equal to)
(3) $y \geqq 4$
(4) $20x + 80y \leqq 560$ or $x + 4y \leqq 28$
(5) Profit $= 5x + 10y$.

Each of these conditions is entered on the graph. Normally it is easier to shade the areas excluded by each condition in turn. Try this for yourself. In Fig. 6.3 the quadrilateral remaining, ABCD, has been shaded instead.

At A (3,4) the profit in £ is
$5 \times 3 + 10 \times 4 = 55$.
At B (6,4) the profit is £70.
C is the point of intersection of lines
$x + y = 10$ and $x + 4y = 28$, i.e. where
$10 - y = 28 - 4y$ which gives $y = 6$, $x = 4$.
At C (4, 6) the profit is £80.

D is the point of intersection of $x + 4y = 28$ and $x = 3$ so that D is (3, $6\frac{1}{4}$); the profit at D is £$77\frac{1}{2}$.

As a series of values is given to the profit, a series of parallel lines $5x + 10y = 55$, $5x + 10y = 70$, $5x + 10y = 80$, $5x + 10y = 77\frac{1}{2}$, is obtained. From Fig. 6.4 it will be evident that the maximum profit will be the extreme position of the line complying with the given set of conditions as the line moves across the quadrilateral from A to C. This position will be reached when the line passes through C; the profit earned at C has been found to be £80.

In general the set of conditions in a problem such as the one considered is far more lengthy than this. The solution is then most easily obtained by means of a computer.

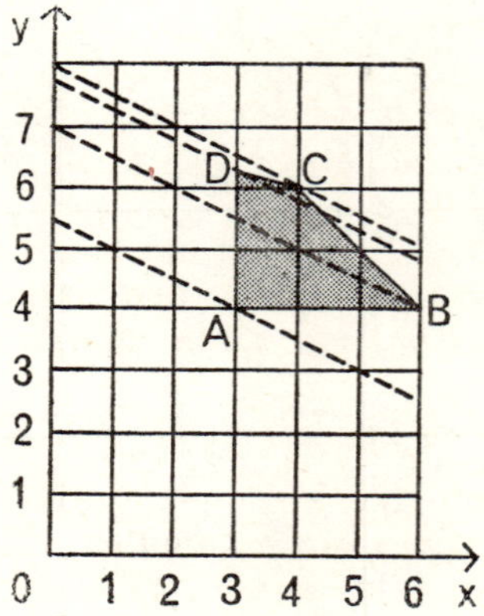

Fig. 6.4

The importance of considering inequalities as well as equalities is at once apparent from this example. The set of points (often called ordered pairs) which belong to a given relationship are of importance, but so also are the vast number of points which do not obey this relationship. In the preceding example, one of the conditions was that x should be greater than or equal to 3 so that, not only do the points on the line $x = 3$ conform to this condition but so also do all those points for which x is greater than 3. In other words the field of points in which x is less than 3 is cut out. Some teachers may well like to discuss such conditions with children and question them to discover how much meaning such inequalities can have for them.

Appendix 7 DEVELOPMENT OF REPRESENTATION, INCLUDING GRAPHS

Mathematics is an abstract subject. We use many different kinds of materials from the environment to help children

1. to discover patterns and relations
2. to communicate their discoveries, and
3. to generalise from their results.

Representation is only the beginning—interpretation and further applications should follow.

Graphs are one of many methods of communication. These should develop naturally out of a situation and should be used to record and represent information at every stage of mathematical development. In the early stages discussion is more important than the drawing of graphs. Later, observation, comment, questions and writing will develop as a result of graphical representation.

Activities of sorting and matching, comparison and ordering, estimation and approximation, pattern recognition are important at all stages.

1. Count or Block Graphs

Block graphs are always representations of a count of one kind or another. They are a complex form of abstract representation and there are several experiences which children require before they are ready for this degree of abstraction.

Stages in development

Stage A. No framework or base line

1. Direct recording with *real* objects—unequal units.

2. Pictures drawn, cut out and placed in appropriate sets—unequal units.

3. Use of counters, beads, etc. to represent each child—equal units.

4. Mapping, e.g. children's names linked to favourite fruits (*later* leading to tabular form: FAVOURITE FRUIT/NAME

Stage B. Base line emphasised

5. Natural baseboard. Traffic or bird count using cubes piled one on top of another.

6. By discussion need for identical units and for units to be touching emerges. Children given identical pieces of paper for drawings.

Frameworks drawn on squared paper with horizontal axis prepared by children after discussion with teacher. The *spaces* below each set (column) are labelled.
Vertical axis is neither drawn nor labelled.
Squares can be counted as necessary

Stage C. Introduction to block graphs

7. When the count is a large one (middle or upper junior stage) it is convenient to label the vertical axis.

Lines and not spaces should be labelled. Why?

As before, spaces on the horizontal axis should be labelled.

At this stage a continuous strip or block can be used to represent the count or frequency.

Activities for teachers

1. Each member of the group takes a square to represent the results of enquiries such as: colour of dress or tie you are wearing, colour of shoes, the daily paper you take, shoe sizes, birthday months.

How do the last two enquiries differ from the others?

2. Collect information from 40 teachers about the newspapers they read. Represent this on a block graph with papers in order of popularity. Use continuous strips or blocks. Give the graph a title and label the axes.

3. Collect the "head" measure in cm (round forehead) of 40 adults of the same sex. Arrange your results in order and make a frequency graph.
More information is sometimes obtained from a large sample by "grouping" the measures. Arrange your results in order but this time assign the measures to groups of 2 cm intervals:

Circumference of head (cm)	*Frequency tally* (number of people with this head measure)
60,61	1
62,63	111
64,65	1 etc.

Make a frequency graph. What effect has the grouping had on your graph?

4. Collect a sample of 50 measures e.g. mass in kg, volume in litres, height in cm. Make frequency graphs using grouping with different intervals e.g. for mass try 5 kg, 10 kg intervals. Comment on your results.

2. Graphs Which Make Themselves—all of continuous quantities and not count graphs.

Activities for children or adults

1. Draw the shadow of (i) a vertical post, (ii) a brick, at half hourly intervals during the day from early morning until evening. Comment on your results.

2. To a set of identical elastic bands suspended from a set of equally spaced nails arranged in a horizontal line fasten identical metal washers: one washer on the first band, two on the second and so on. Comment on your results.

3. Strip graph. Cut strips (each in a different colour) to represent the actual lengths of your waist, neck and wrist. In your group of 4, is the order the same for each measure?

What difficulties might children have in arranging the strips in order of length?

4. Strip graph. Match the diameters and circumferences of a set of circular tin lids with thin ribbon or string. Mark the diameters directly along the horizontal axis.

Corresponding "string" circumferences can then be placed "vertically" at the appropriate points of the horizontal axis. What do you notice?

Should you include the zero value or origin?

Should the ends of the ribbons or strings be joined?

Have intermediate points any meaning?

5. Scale. Cut your height and reach (arms out-stretched) in string. Make half and quarter scale models of yourself with arms out-stretched.

3. Point Graphs Leading to Graphs of Relations

Stage 1—Graphs showing a single relation between successive members of a set of numbers.

1. 2 → 5 → 8 → 11 → represents the relation?
2. 8 → 4 → 2 → 1 → represents the relation?

Represent 1. and 2. in other ways.

3. Here is part of a graph (2, 3, 6, 9, 10) showing the relation IS A FACTOR OF

Complete the graph

What does 2 imply?

Other relations represented:

Complete the graph

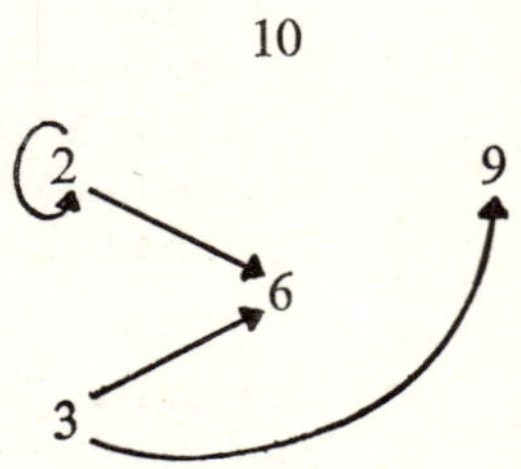

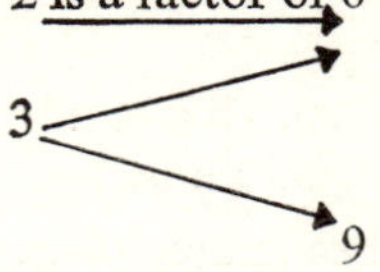

4. Complete this graph of (2, 3, 6, 9, 10) for IS A MULTIPLE OF

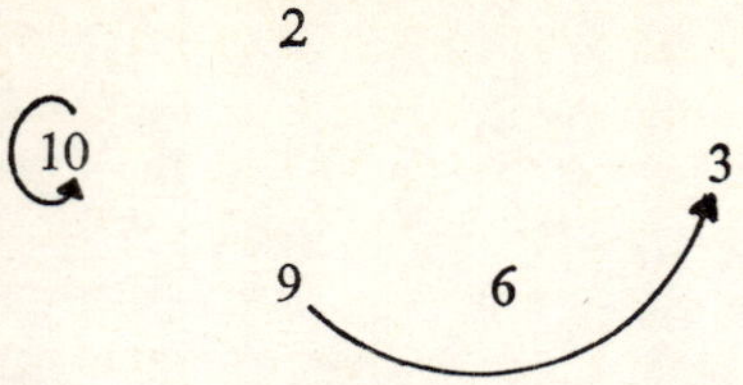

5. Draw graphs of (1, 4, 9, 16, 25, 36) for
   1. is the square of
   2. is the square root of
   3. is a factor of
   4. is a multiple of

6. Fill in numbers which fit exactly the following graphs:

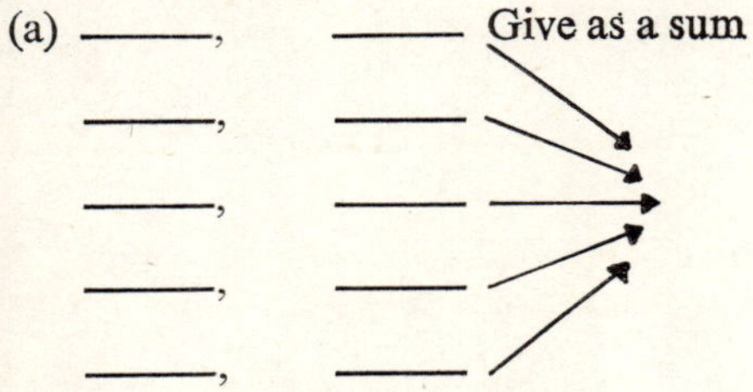

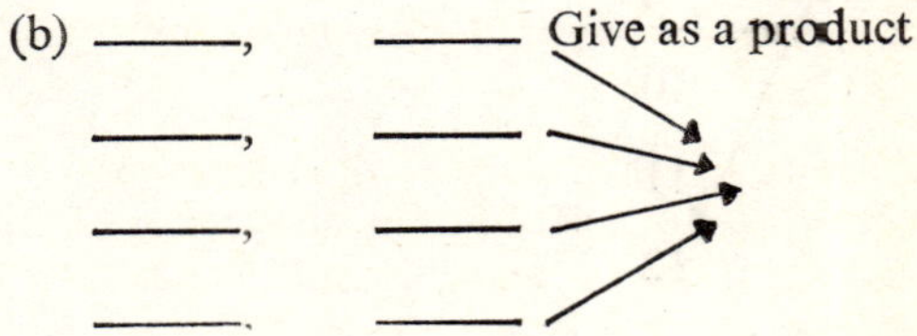

Is there more than one set of numbers to fit each graph?

Stage 2—Graphs showing correspondences between two sets of numbers (or correspondences between a set of ordered pairs of numbers)

1. a set of natural numbers

a second set of natural numbers
What is the relation represented?

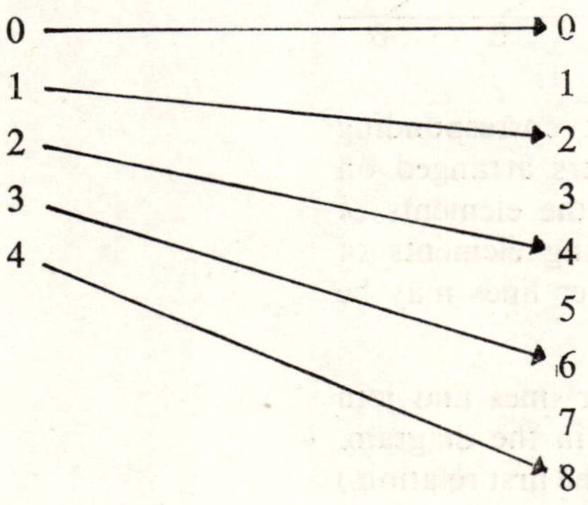

2. Find the relations represented in these graphs

a. 1st set 2nd set b. 1st set 2nd set

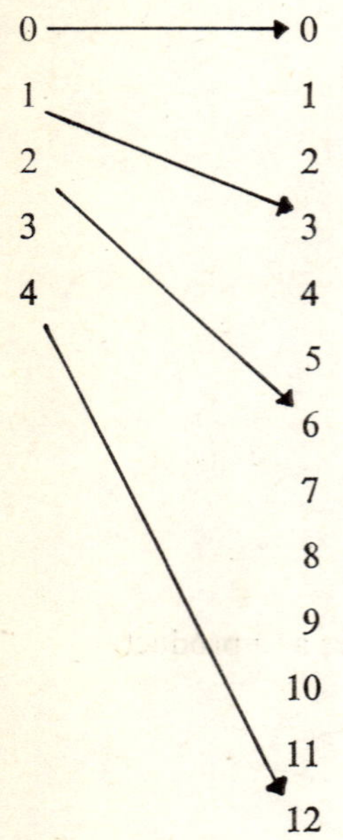

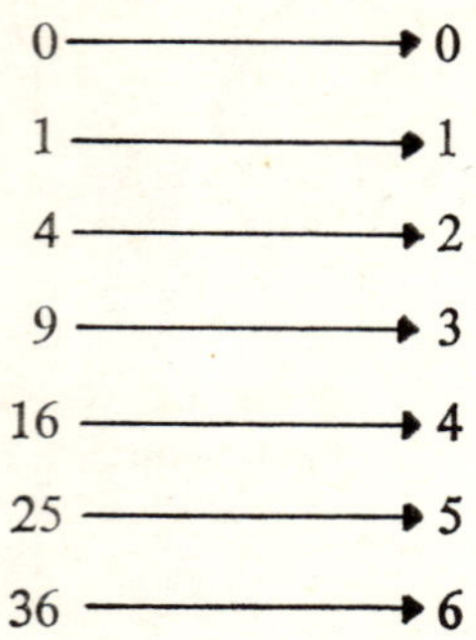

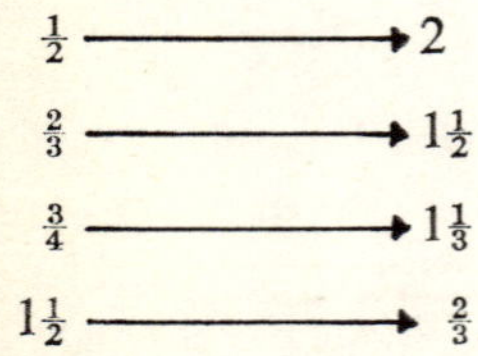

Stage 3—Representation on 2 number lines.

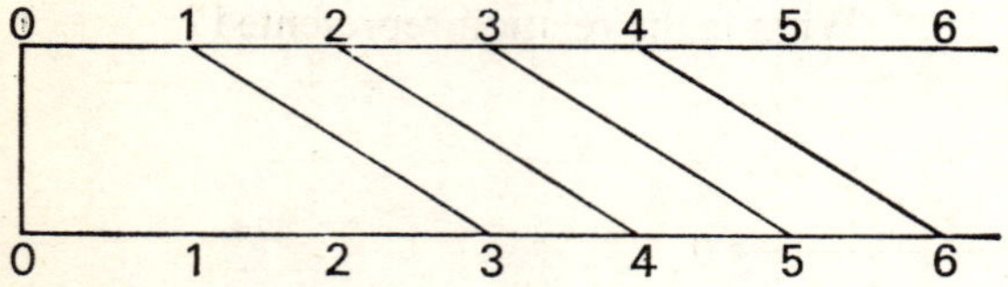

It is often convenient to link corresponding elements of two sets of numbers arranged on two number lines (or to map the elements of one set on to the corresponding elements of the second set). The two number lines may be parallel or intersecting.

1. Use two parallel number lines and join corresponding points as in the diagram. (The diagram illustrates the first relation.)

Find and continue each relation (in both directions)

1 → 3	1 → 2	1 → 12	1 → −1	1 → 1	1 → 7
2 → 4	2 → 4	2 → 6	2 → 0	2 → 4	2 → 6
3 → 5	3 → 6	3 → 4	3 → 1	3 → 9	3 → 5
4 → 6	4 → 8	4 → 3	4 → 2	4 → 16	4 → 4

You will find it convenient to use squared paper (cm or 2 cm squares) for the parallel number lines. In each case what do you notice about the lines joining corresponding points? Experiment and justify your suggestions.

2. Repeat (or use other interesting relations) on two *intersecting* number lines. Comment on your results.

Stage 4—Location of points on a lattice or grid made by two number lines intersecting at right angles (e.g. location of treasure on a map drawn on a grid with compass points marked). See km grid on Ordnance Survey maps.

1. Use two axes at right angles on squared paper. Plot ordered pairs showing
   (1) multiplication tables e.g. (1, 2) (2, 4) (3, 6) etc.
   (2) natural numbers and their squares
   (3) natural numbers whose product is 12
   (4) a set of consecutive natural numbers and corresponding numbers 2 more than each.

   Compare this method of representation with the (birthday month, date) and (reach, height) scattergrams in statistics. In plotting ordered pairs it is important to remember that the first number is always represented on the normal horizontal number line and the second number on the "vertical" number line.

On the same axes plot the (edge, perimeter) ordered pairs for the sequence of squares. What do you notice about this sequence of points?

What do you notice about the points in each sequence?

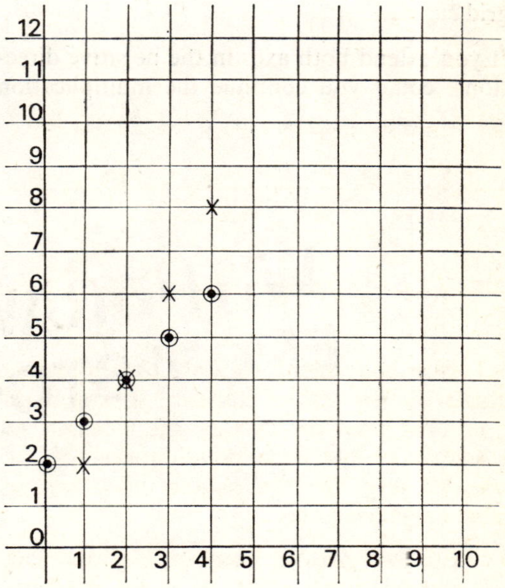

Edge	Perimeter
1	4
2	8
3	12
4	16
↓	↓

(1, 4) (2, 8) (3, 12) (4, 16)

Do you recognise these ordered pairs?

Could you describe this sequence in any other way?

Could you fit in a pair *before* (1, 4)?

Would you be justified in joining these? You can justify this only if you can give a meaning to intermediate points, e.g.

> The perimeter of a square with edge $1\frac{1}{2}''$ is $6''$. The edge of a square with perimeter $9''$ is $2\frac{1}{4}''$. In fact a meaning could be given to every point on the line joining these points.

Plot also the 5 times table, the 3 times and the one times tables.

What do you notice about the multiplication 1, 2, 3, 4 . . . 10?

Plot the 1 times table. Which multiplication tables would come in the lower part of the grid?

If you extend both axes in the negative directions, could you continue the multiplication tables? What meaning could you give to these? (A ten-year-old asked if all multiplication tables end at zero. Do they? What does the graph show?)

Express each of the following relations in words, as ordered pairs, and by a graph. In each example discuss whether you could use a continuous line or not. In which could you extend the graph to include negative integers? You may want to use different scales on the two axes. How would you introduce the idea of scale to children? What effect does a change of scale on one axis have on your graph? Experiment and see.

1. From a sequence of squares, length of edge and area of square.
2. From a sequence of cubes, length of edge and volume of cube.
3. Width and length of rectangles of area 36 square units.
4. Width and length of rectangles of perimeter 20 units.
5. Width and area of rectangles with perimeter 20 units.
6. From a sequence of regular polygons, starting with an equilateral triangle, number of edges and angle at centre.
7. Diameter and circumference of discs.
8. Diameter and area of discs.
9. Diameter and volume of balls.

Printed in England for Her Majesty's Stationery Office by McCorquodale Printers Limited Dd. 503801 K320 6/72.